1815, Waterloo

1815, Waterloo
An account of Napoleon's last campaign

Henry Houssaye

1815, Waterloo
An account of
Napoleon's last campaign
by Henry Houssaye

First published under the titles
1815, Waterloo

Leonaur is an imprint
of Oakpast Ltd

Copyright in this form © 2009 Oakpast Ltd

ISBN: 978-1-84677-930-5 (hardcover)
ISBN: 978-1-84677-929-9 (softcover)

http://www.leonaur.com

Publisher's Notes

In the interests of authenticity, the spellings, grammar and place names used have been retained from the original editions.

The opinions of the authors represent a view of events in which he was a participant related from his own perspective, as such the text is relevant as an historical document.

The views expressed in this book are not necessarily those of the publisher.

Contents

The Last Army of the Empire	7
The Plans of Campaign	55
First Combats	66
The Morning of June 16th	80
Battle of Ligny	93
The Battle of Quatre-Bras	113
The Retreat of the Prussian Army	130
The Retreat of the English Army	148
Blucher and Grouchy	164
The Battle of Waterloo - Morning	174
The Battle of Waterloo - From Half-past Eleven to Three O'Clock	191
The Battle of Waterloo - From Three O'Clock until Seven	205
The Battle of Waterloo - From Seven to Nine O'clock	224
The Rout	241
The Combats of Wavre and the Retreat of Grouchy.	257
The Campaign of 1815	274

Book 1
Entrance into Campaign
Chapter 1
The Last Army of the Empire

1

On his return from the isle of Elba the Emperor found no more than 200,000 men under the flags. If he had felt himself to be all-powerful as formerly, he would have had recourse for doubling the Army, to an extraordinary levy of the classes of 1806 to 1814, to the recall of the class of 1815, and to the anticipated call of the class of 1816. But, having hardly resumed the throne, he hesitated before so unpopular a measure as the reestablishment of the conscription, which had been abolished by Louis XVIII. He had then for sole resources the return into the ranks of the soldiers on limited and unlimited leave and the recall of numerous deserters carried on the muster-rolls as "absent without permission."

The men on six months' furlough amounted to 32,800, the deserters to 85,000. Almost all of the men on six months' furlough could be counted on to rejoin their colours; already three or four thousand had arrived at the depôts, in conformity with the royal ordinance of March 9th. But among the 85,000 men "absent without permission" it was necessary to admit that there would be a great number who would not rejoin their regiments and also a great many who would be entitled to receive definite discharges, either on account of infirmities, or as supports of their families. Marshal Davoût, Minister of War, estimated that the recall of soldiers of every category would give scarcely 59,000 men.

The decree calling out the reserves, which had been prepared on March 28th, was not made public until April 9th. This delay was attributable to reasons of a political nature. The Emperor, who at that time was attempting by all possible means to enter in negotiations with the powers for the maintenance of peace, feared that the putting of the army on a war footing would belie his pacific protestations. Towards the French population, who so ardently desired peace, he felt constrained to show the same consideration. The West was in agitation, the Midi was in arms; in the rest of France the Royalists were labouring to destroy the popularity of the Emperor by predicting war.

This was not the moment to alarm, to dissatisfy all the country by calling out the reserves. Moreover, Napoleon still preserved a ray of hope that there would not be a rupture with Europe. This illusory hope diminishing from hour to hour, he decided to publish the decree in the *Moniteur* of April 9th. As he foresaw, this decree struck a blow at public opinion. In a few days the *rente* fell eight *francs*. Sadness and discouragement prevailed throughout the land. The peasants, generally very happy at no longer having to endure the vexations of the country nobility or to fear the re-establishment of privileges and the *replevin* of the property of the *émigré's*, felt their sentiments for the Emperor growing weaker at the thought that his return was about to bring, if not a second invasion, at least an interminable war.

By reason of the time necessary for the transmission and the posting of orders and legal delays, the mustering-in of the men began only on April 25th. Public opinion was so opposed to the idea of war that among the men recalled, though all of them were old soldiers of Napoleon, a great many presented themselves only in order to show cause why they should be exempted or discharged from further service. It is true that, though a great number of these men had deserted in 1814 in order to avoid wearing the white cockade, a great number had left their corps because they were weary of war. During the last year they had resumed work in the fields and workshops, and a great many of them had married; hence they were still less disposed to take up arms again.

In the departments in which the Royalist spirit predominated, and in which those who had been recalled to arms felt themselves supported by the population, the meetings of the Board of Examiners were tumultuous. The men cried: "We will not set out. Long live the King!" Fearing an insurrection in the West, the Emperor authorized many prefects of that region to apply the decree with great circumspection, and even to suspend its execution. In spite of everything, the levy gave 17,000 men more than Davoût, who was little inclined to illusions, had presumed. In the first days of June 52,446 men had been incorporated and 23,448 were *en route* to rejoin their regiments.

The voluntary enlistments, which had been so rare during the Campaign of France, amounted to nearly 15,000 men. A Royal ordinance of December 31, 1814, granted to each enrolled volunteer a bounty of fifty *francs*. The Emperor suppressed this bounty. "This method," said he, "is not in accord with the sentiments manifested by the French in the defence of their independence." In order to increase the enlistments, the Emperor thought of causing to be read by officers of the Guard calls to arms, accompanied by the beating of drums, upon the public places, around the workshops, and in the villages. But, Davoût having represented to him that "this would cause useless disorder," he abandoned this expedient of the recruiting sergeants of the eighteenth century.

Reduced to a few vessels in condition to take the sea, without crews (two-thirds of the sailors had been sent home on furlough), and without supplies, the fleets could only be employed in some cruises in the Mediterranean. With the available men in the ports and the naval reserves the Emperor hoped to constitute fifty or sixty battalions of sailors. It was only with great difficulty that twenty were formed, and by the middle of June only one had been put *en route*; it formed the garrison of Calais. The three regiments of the artillery of the Marine, of a real effective of 5,284 men under the Restoration, were raised to nearly 6,000 by the organization of a new battalion. Six battalions remained in the ports, whose defence they assured; two were detached to Paris, one went to Lyons, and another fought in Brittany in the mobile column of General Bigarré.

Of the three foreign regiments which existed under Louis XVIII., the Emperor preserved the second (Isenberg) and the third (Irish), presenting together 875 bayonets; the first (*La Tour d'Auvergne*), which had remained faithful to the Duke of Angoulême during the short campaign in the Midi, was disbanded. The Emperor would have liked to have kept the four Swiss regiments, but the opposition manifested by the officers to taking the tricolour cockade necessitated the disbanding of these troops.

Napoleon busied himself with organizing five new foreign regiments: one of Poles, quickly raised to 800 men, thanks to the soldiers of the ex-legion of the Vistula, who, although disbanded in 1814, had not yet returned to Poland; one of Swiss, into which entered 502 men of the four regiments suppressed on April 2nd; one of Italians, one of Germans, and one of Dutch-Belgians. These three last were to be formed with deserters from the armies of Frimont, Blücher, and the Prince of Orange. At the beginning of June the Dutch-Belgian regiment counted 378 bayonets. Finally there were raised in the Gironde a battalion of Negroes and a few companies of Spanish refugees.

The country being threatened, the laws and decrees of 1791, 1792, 1805, and 1813, which had not been abrogated, gave the Emperor the right to increase the Army by means of mobilized National Guards. Some days after his return to the Tuileries he occupied himself, with Davoût and Carnot, in reorganizing the National Guard. There were at that time in all France nearly 200,000 National Guards, aged from twenty to sixty years, and Carnot estimated that this number could be raised to 2,500,000. A decree, rendered on April 10th, prescribed that all citizens liable to service in the National Guard should be inscribed upon the muster-rolls in order to be formed into battalions. The Emperor did not think of organizing such a multitude, but he counted on taking therefrom a great number of mobilized battalions, composed solely of men from twenty to forty years old. He remembered that at Fère-Champenoise in 1814 the National Guards had fought like old soldiers. By new decrees the Emperor ordered the mobilization of 326 battalions of 720 men each, which were to be directed immediately upon the frontier places and the entrenched camps. This was putting again in force the decree of the Legislative Assembly of July 11, 1792, with this attenuation., that in the war battalions the providing of substitutes was fixed at the small sum of 120 *francs*.

In a score of departments, notably in Aisne, Ain, Ardèche, Ardennes, Aube, Côte-d'Or, Isère, Jura, Marne, Meurthe, Meuse, Mont-Blanc, Haut-Rhin, Bas-Rhin, Rhône, Haute-Saône, Saône-et-Loire, Seine-et-Marne, Seine-et-Oise, Vosges, and Yonne, the levy was effected very easily, the battalions soon received their full complement of men, and the mobilized National Guards quitted family and fireside with cries of "Long live the Emperor!" and with the enthusiasm of 1791. Those of the Guards who were able to do so purchased their own arms and uniforms. But the same patriotism and the same goodwill did not animate the whole of France. In half of the country, in spite of the Guards and mobile columns, hardly one-fourth of the fixed contingents could be raised. By the end of May Orne had furnished 107 Guards out of 2,160 demanded, Pas-de-Calais 437 out of 7,440, and Gers 98 out of 1,440. At Amiens this proclamation was circulated:

"Who has recalled Bonaparte? The Army. Well, let it defend him. His enemies are our friends. We will not arm to defend a man whom hell has vomited forth."

In Vendée and Brittany, where an insurrection was feared, the National Guards were not called out; but when civil war began, some thousands of citizens took up arms spontaneously and seconded the troops against the Royalist bands without, however, leaving their department.

Out of the 234,720 National Guards called into service by the decrees from April 10th to May 15th, nearly 150,000 were by June 15th assembled in the fortresses or on the march for them. A third of the officers for the battalions were named from the officers on half-pay and for the other two-thirds from the civil element. The Emperor had not wished to leave the selection of the officers to election. He named them from civil lists, prepared in each department by a committee composed of a prefect, a councillor-general, two generals, and a superior officer. Almost all of the National Guards not only appeared resigned to do their duty, but determined to do it willingly. They drilled their best, yielded docilely to discipline, and entered the cities with branches of lilac in the muzzles of their guns, singing the "*Marseillaise*," and terminating each couplet with cries of "Long live the Nation! Long live the Emperor!"

If there sometimes arose complaints, it was from those who were yet neither armed nor clothed and who demanded guns, overcoats, and shoes. Mortier, Jourdan, Leclerc des Essarts,. Rouyer, Lanusse, Berckheim, and all the general officers who commanded mobilized National Guards or passed them in review, praised the good spirit and fine attitude of these improvised soldiers. Gérard wrote Vandamme, June 5th: "The ten battalions of National Guards of the reserve of Nancy are superb. In three weeks there will be no difference between them and the troops of the Line."

If the war lasted any length of time, the men from twenty to forty years of age, forming the first ban of the National Guard, could be counted on to give at least 150,000 more men, for a great number of refractory men from the departments of the Centre and Midi would end by submitting to the law; thanks to the pacification of Vendée, which was near and certain, the decrees relating to the mobilization of the National Guards could be applied in the departments of the West; and, finally, there would be an opportunity to decree new levies in the patriotic departments of the East. For the second ban of the militia, its organization was not pressed, save at Paris and Lyons. When the lack of time and arms prevented the forming of the mobilized battalions, it was not the hour to increase the sedentary battalions, which, by reason of the pacific services which they were to render, were already sufficiently numerous.

In the mass of citizens aged from forty to sixty years there were, however, a great many men who could be used advantageously in the defence of the fortresses. They were the old officers, subalterns, and soldiers retired after a minimum service of twenty-four years. Since the month of April many retired officers had requested permission to re-enter the Army; but there were so many officers on half-pay that all of them could not be utilized. With the retired officers and soldiers Davoût thought of forming battalions of veterans for the fortresses. "They will set an example for the National Guards," wrote he to the Emperor, "and will inspire them with the military spirit."

Napoleon did not fail to adopt this proposition. On May 18th he rendered a decree inviting all retired soldiers to resume service temporarily, in order to be organized into battalions and batteries for the fortresses. The retired soldiers, who numbered 94,000, but of whom hardly half appeared eligible for service, hastened to present themselves at the mustering-places. With the most robust there were formed fifty-six battalions and twenty-five companies of artillery, of a total strength of nearly 25,000 men.

At Paris the sedentary National Guard was raised to 36,518 men. The workmen of the *faubourgs* had demanded spontaneously to cooperate in the defence of the city, and from these workmen twenty-four battalions of Federate Sharpshooters were formed. These 18,000 sharpshooters, commanded by officers on half-pay, were destined to occupy the advance posts and the works of the first line. At Lyons there were by June 12th 4,000 sedentary National Guards, and Mouton-Duvernet was busy forming fifteen battalions of Federate Sharpshooters. In Aisne and Ardennes and in all the departments of the East the levies *en masse* could be counted on in case the country was invaded. Composed of foresters, *gendarmes*, custom-house officers, sedentary National Guards, and in general of all the able-bodied citizens, the levies *en masse* were to assemble at the sound of the tocsin upon the order of the military authorities in order to occupy the mountains and defiles.

With the 150,000 mobilized National Guards, the 25,000 retired soldiers, the 26,000 Federates of Paris, Lyons, Toulouse, and Nancy, the urban and rural National Guards, the free corps and the levies en masse, it seemed that the fortresses, the large cities, the defiles, and the bridge-heads would be sufficiently provided with defenders. But in spite of voluntary enlistments and of the return of two-thirds of the men on furlough, the active army was still too weak. After much hesitation, the Emperor decided to call out the class of 1815. The conscription had been abolished by Article XII. of the Royal Charter; and this article having been interpreted as having a retroactive effect for the conscripts of 1815, though a *sénatus- consulte* of October 9, 1813, had called them under the flags, it was to be feared that the recall of these conscripts would be regarded as an abuse of power. Davoût himself, ordinarily so resolute, represented to the Emperor that it would not be prudent to pronounce the unpleasant word "conscription."

"It would be better," said he, "to change the name of the thing, and declare that all young men having entered into their twentieth year since the 1st of January last will make a part of the National Guard and will be directed upon the depôts of the Army, with the promise of being discharged after the end of the war." The Council of State, to which the projected decree relating to the conscription of 1815 was submitted in the meeting of May 23rd, refused to give its adherence to the measure, "the levying of men being within the jurisdiction of the legislative power."

To await the meeting of the Chambers! But would the enemy await until they met before entering France? Now, the conscription of 18 15 would furnish 120,000 soldiers, of whom 20,000 had fought during the last campaign. The Emperor removed the scruples of the Council of State by proposing to assimilate the conscription of 1815 with the soldiers on leave of absence. To recall them a decree would be no longer necessary; a simple administrative measure would suffice. The Council of State enunciated a favourable opinion, and in the first days of June Davoût was able to issue instructions for the levy of the class of 1815. The country had then decided that, since war was inevitable, it was necessary to make the best of it.

The departure of the conscripts was effected without the resistance and rebellions which had been occasioned in so many of the departments by the recall of the soldiers on furlough and in a less degree by the mobilization of the National Guards. On June 11th—that is to say, one week after the decree had been made public—46,419 conscripts had assembled, ready to set out, in the *chefs-lieux* of the departments. In Alsace, Lorraine, Champagne, Franche-Comté, Burgundy, and even in many provinces of the Centre, an extreme goodwill was reported. The prefect of Seine-et-Oise wrote:

"The conscripts of 1815 have assembled in three days with an astonishing facility." The prefect of Mont-Blanc remarked that his department had furnished more combatants than at any time of the Revolution. Aisne, which from April 1st to June 12th had given 18,200 volunteers, recalled soldiers, conscripts, mobilized National Guards, irregular sharpshooters, and retired soldiers—among whom were to be seen some old men of seventy-three years—merited these words from Napoleon: "In this department (Aisne) there will be found as many men as there will be guns with which to arm them."

2

A great many guns, munitions, provisions, horses, uniforms, and shoes were necessary, and there were very few. Almost all of the material had to be improvised. If the artillery possessed 13,947 pieces of ordnance, it was in need of horses, harness, and 600,000 projectiles. In the infantry and cavalry regiments, both with greatly reduced effectives, the armament was complete; but to arm the recalled soldiers, the unlisted volunteers, the naval reserves, the mobilized National Guards, the Federate Sharpshooters, and the conscripts of 1815, who, according to the expectation of everyone, would amount towards the middle of September to more than 500,000 men, there were in the arsenals and magazines but 195,000 muskets, of which 74,000 were in need of repairs.

"The safety of the country," wrote Napoleon, "depends upon the quantity of guns with which we shall be able to arm ourselves." The imperial factories, to which all the gunsmiths, exempted from the different conscriptions since the year 8. (1799), were recalled by decree, received an order for 235,000 muskets and musketoons and 15,000 pairs of pistols. The bayonets were made in the cutleries of Langres and Moulins. Ten thousand fowling-pieces and 4,000 blunderbusses were distributed among the peasants of Alsace; Lorraine, Champagne, and Burgundy.

For repairing the unserviceable guns, one had recourse to private industry. Workshops were established in the principal cities, in which were employed all the gunsmiths, locksmiths, cabinet-makers, and braziers; in Paris there were six of these shops, which employed 2,000 workmen. The Government also attempted to purchase some guns in England, and a few thousand were brought from Belgium and the Rhenish provinces, concealed in coal barges. Others were brought in by the peasants, a reward of 12 *francs* being offered for each gun restored; and others still were requisitioned from the merchants and shipowners, who had been notified by means of placards to furnish a list of all the arms in their possession.

In spite of the activity displayed and all the means employed, the men arrived at the depôts faster than the arms entered into the arsenals. The factories and shops could furnish but 20,000 new and almost the same number of repaired guns per month. In the first days of June hardly half of the mobilized National Guards had received muskets. As for the short swords for the infantry, the making of which had been suspended, for it was first necessary to make bayonets, it was decided that, even in the Line, only the companies of grenadiers should be provided with them. *Cuirasses* were lacking.

"Cause the men to rejoin anyhow," wrote Napoleon; "*cuirasses* are not indispensable for making war." Everywhere the making of cartridges was pressed in such fashion as to raise the supply to 100 cartridges per man; 50 in the cartridge-box and 50 in the *caissons* of the park. At Vincennes 12,000,000 were manufactured in two months. On June 1st the reserve supply of the Army of the North amounted to 5,500,000 cartridges, and the soldiers of all the regiments in the first line had, with a few exceptions, their complement of 50 cartridges.

Not only the Government of the Restoration had done nothing to restore the magazines of clothing emptied by the gigantic armaments of 1812 and 1813, but it had not even provided for the maintenance of the troops who had remained under the flags. From May, 1814, to February, 1815, the War Department had allotted to the service of clothing but 4,000,000 of *francs*, of which sum 1,000,000 alone had been paid. The uniforms were in rags. In more than twenty regiments the men were in need of shoes; and in the crack corps, such as the Royal Chasseurs, some of the men had neither boots nor shirts.

In the 14th Light the men had worn for two years, in winter as well as in summer, linen trousers. To the 27th of the Line there were due 30,000 *francs* for the clothing of the prisoners repatriated prior to January 1, 1815. These men made the campaign in police caps. The Emperor was forced to raise to 30,000,000 the credits for the service of clothing, and the Administration of War estimated that it would be necessary to increase them to 51,000,000 in the course of the year. Some shops established in Paris furnished 1,250 coats per day. Work was pursued actively in the depôts, to which the manufacturers were invited to advance supplies, the cities guaranteeing the payment. As blue cloth was not to be had in sufficient quantities, some overcoats were made from cloth of different colours.

On March 20th the cavalry possessed only 27,864 horses, the artillery and auxiliary services 7,765. Of these 35,629 horses, 5,000 had been, as a measure of economy, loaned to the farmers;

these horses were ordered to be returned in haste to the corps. The departments were struck with a requisition of 8,000 horses against reimbursement, whilst at the central depôt of remounting at Versailles the horses presented voluntarily by the breeders and farmers were purchased. The horses of the military household of the King and of the Royal Volunteers were distributed in the Guard. The depôts of each corps were authorized to make direct purchases.

Finally the Emperor had the excellent idea of taking half of the horses of the *gendarmerie*. Each *gendarme* received an indemnity of 600 *francs*; he was to remount himself under fifteen days, which was easy for him to do by reason of his situation in the country. Thanks to this expedient, 4,250 vigorous and trained horses were immediately distributed between the *cuirassiers* and dragoons. The requisition in the departments gave more horses than had been expected; but at the great depôt of Versailles the remounting proceeded very slowly. From the past services of General Préval, it seems that he should have been selected to resume the command of this depôt, where he had performed such prodigies in 1814.

Rightly or wrongly, he was suspected of being a Royalist. The Emperor sent or rather exiled him to the depôt of Beauvais, and appointed to Versailles General Bourcier. The latter was a formalist, a slave of regulations, stopping at trifles. He refused the horses over eight years old and those that were lacking a half-inch of the height required by the regulations. In the midst of war, during the single month of March, Préval had collected more than 7,000 horses; in two months of peace Bourcier had been able to find but 2,579! In spite of this disappointment, there was on the day when the Army took the field a fine body of horses. The cavalry counted 40,000 with the armies and in the depôts; the artillery, including the train and equipages, 16,500.

Threatened by the whole of Europe, Napoleon knew that he would be unable to prevent the invasion on all points of the territory. Perhaps he would be reduced, as in the preceding year, to commence operations only on this side of the Oise, the

Aisne, and the Marne. Even upon the most favourable hypothesis, his next campaign must be at the same time offensive and defensive. The putting in a state of defence of the fortresses was therefore no less necessary nor less urgent than the reorganization of the Army. On March 27th the Emperor gave orders for this work, which was not undertaken until April 15th. It had been necessary to await the reports on the state of the fortresses, the instructions of the Committee of Engineers, the opening of credits, and the establishment of workshops.

At Metz, 700 workmen were employed; at Rocroi, 500; at Toul, 700; at Landrecies, 400; at Dunkirk, 1,000; at Huningue, 500; at Grenoble, 400; at Cherbourg, 500; at Bayonne, 400; at Bordeaux, 200; at Perpignan, 150; and upon the entrenched camp of Maubeuge, 1,000. On the 15th the defiles of the Vosges and the passages of Argonne were provided with redoubts, abattis, and blinds; everything was prepared to inundate the departments of the North; and in more than eighty towns the works were either completely terminated or in a way to be promptly finished. Besides, in almost all of the fortresses, there existed no breaches in the ramparts. It had been only necessary to raise the talus of the counterscarp, prepare the platforms for the barbettes, repair the embrasures, the *banquettes*, the glacis, and to establish accessory and a few outworks.

Lyons and Paris needed works of far greater importance. At Lyons 4,000 workmen were engaged. The old wall of Fourvières, as well as that which extended from the Rhône to the Saône, was restored; some bridge-heads were erected at La Guillotière and Brotteaux and some redoubts at Pierre-Scise, Saint-Jean, and Croix-Rousse. Fearful, doubtless, of alienating from him the Parisians by showing them the peril with which they were threatened. Napoleon, urgent as appeared to him the necessity of fortifying Paris, gave his first orders in this regard only on May 1st.

This was much time lost, all the more as the Emperor desired a vast system of fortifications with continuous lines, horn and crown-works, redoubts and forts crossing their fire. Generals Haxo and Rogniat laid out these fortifications. It was only towards the middle of May that the works began to be actively pressed. Fifteen hundred, 2,000, and then 4,000 workmen were employed upon these works, without counting numerous detachments of volunteers from the Guard, the Line, the National Guard, and the Federates. When Napoleon set out for the army, the entrenchments and the works on the right bank, which had been undertaken first, as being destined to cover the most probable points of attack, were partly finished, but those on the left bank were hardly begun.

The works upon the fortifications, the arming and provisioning of the fortresses, were actively pushed. The arsenals of Metz, Douai, Lille, Grenoble, and Toulouse, furnished cannon and powder for the fortified towns in which the material of artillery was insufficient. Foundries were established for the casting of projectiles. The Marine sent from Toulon to Lyons by way of Aries and the Rhône 100 twenty-four-, twelve-, and six-pounders, and from Brest and Cherbourg to Paris 300 pieces of ordnance by way of Havre and the Seine. The armament of Paris comprised, moreover, 300 field pieces, 100 of which were distributed into movable batteries.

"We must place guns wherever we can," wrote the Emperor, "for one fights with cannon-shots like one fights with blows of the fist."

In order to gain time, Davoût at first charged the commanders of army corps to occupy themselves, in conjunction with the prefects and *ordonnateurs*, with the victualing of the fortresses. But it was to be feared that by this system, which moreover gave rather good results, the requisitions would be neglected. There existed an agreement concluded between the Government of Louis XVIII. and the contractor, Doumèrc. This agreement was maintained. But Doumèrc, a brother of the cavalry general, was only the proxy of Ouvrard, who failed to fulfil his obligations. There were complaints everywhere; it became necessary to encroach upon the reserve supplies in order to nourish the men and horsey. Ouvrard was accused of using in speculations upon the Bourse the money advanced by the Treasury. Davoût authorized the prefects to purchase what was necessary, regardless of the price, for the account of the contractor. The general application of this measure would have ruined Ouvrard. He proposed through Doumèrc a new contract, which was entered into on May 24th with Davoût and Daru; according to the terms of this contract the victualing of the fortresses was to be completed within thirty days by means of an anticipated payment of 4,000,000 *francs*. By the middle of June the places of the first and second lines were, with a few exceptions, provisioned for four months on an average, and the convoys in the rear of the Army of the North carried a supply of provisions for eight days.

In order to push a successful conclusion this immense armament, more time and money would have been necessary. The royal budget of war of 1815, which was to be presented to the Chambers during the April session, amounted to 298,000,000 *francs*, of which 25,000,000 were for the unitary household, the Swiss regiments, and the pensions of the *emigrés* and Vendéans. The Emperor was quick to see that, in spite of the saving to be realized under these heads, the military budget must be increased by 100,000,000. Still, the estimate was modest. If the war had lasted any length of time, the expenses would have greatly exceeded these expectations. Napoleon was not in favour of loans, because, according to his saying, "he did not wish to spend income in advance," and also because he did not believe in credit. In 1815 he did not desire to increase the imposts, for fear of rendering himself unpopular.

Far from seeking resources in new taxes, he suppressed the tax on drinks, the home tax, and, in communes of less than 4,000 inhabitants, the tax on liquids. This reform, which history has passed over in silence, in the midst of such great events, had nevertheless some influence upon public opinion. The Bourbons, who had solemnly promised the suppression of the *droits réunis*, had taken great care to change nothing, and Napoleon, who had promised nothing, abolished those imposts which were regarded as the most vexatious and the most intolerable. Among the peasants, the small stock-holders, and in the already influential class of grog-sellers and wine-brokers, this reduction rallied more men to the imperial cause than were driven away by the Additional Act, especially attacked by the wits of the salons and the political professors.

The Emperor found an unhoped-for resource in a coin reserve of 50,000,000, which existed in the Treasury on March 20th. The Minister of Finance, Baron Louis, had employed a part of this fund in stock-jobbing: he had not felt at liberty to carry the remainder to Ghent. The imperial Government profited by the time at which the revolution had taken place. On March 20th the tax-payers had as yet paid very little of the imposts which had become due. There was, in fact, a continual flow of money into the chests of the receivers during the months of April and May, for generally these contributions were paid without difficulty. Nevertheless, the ordinary receipts and the available money being insufficient to meet all the expenses, Gaudin, upon an order from the Emperor, negotiated a loan of 3,600,000 *francs* from the Sinking Fund, and deposited as collateral checks to the same amount, redeemable out of the national funds. This transaction, managed with the cooperation of Ouvrard, produced, clear of all discount, 40,000,000 in cash.

The expenses of arming, equipping, and clothing the mobilized National Guards, expenses estimated at 24,000,000, did not figure in the budget of war. They were charged to the departments, which were to provide for them out of the tax on substitutes, which had been fixed at 120 *francs*, and by the setting aside of one-tenth of the communal revenues and the proceeds arising from the sale of one-fourth of the forest reserves. There was allotted, moreover, to the expenses of the National Guards the entire sum arising from the patriotic gifts, and a reserve fund of 6,000,000 to be taken from the Sinking Fund.

Thanks to these resources and to these expedients, France was put on a war footing. But in how many fortresses was the work interrupted for the lack of money! How many soldiers carried equipments that were unfit for service! And how many National Guards, already brigaded, awaited, useless and dissatisfied, for their arms to be given them! In May they had received their pay only after great delay and many difficulties. On June 12th there were for the entire Army of the North but one thousand pairs of shoes in reserve; the gratuity promised the soldiers on taking the field had not been paid them, and, at the time when the pay amounted to 5,000,000 per month, the military chests contained only 670,000 *francs*.

The extraordinary resources (coin reserve left by Baron Louis and the product arising from the alienation of 3,600,000 *francs* of the Government funds) were exhausted, and the regular receipts began to fall off. Though the Emperor and his councils were opposed to exceptional measures, it became necessary to resign themselves to them, for the expenses foreseen by Davoût for the month of July alone amounted to 72,000,000. In the budget presented to the Chambers on June 19th there figured a national loan of 150,000,000, guaranteed by the forests of the State. All the tax-payers were to subscribe an amount equal to the sum of their realty and personal taxes. It was a forced loan.

3

The Emperor did not even await the commencement of the mobilization in order to organize the army corps. Thanks to the concentration of the troops under Paris ordered by Louis XVIII., to the numerous regiments which had rejoined the Battalion of the Isle of Elba since Grenoble, and finally to the strong garrisons of the frontier towns of the North and East, Napoleon, immediately after his return to the Tuileries, found that he had in a manner under his hand a great part of the available forces of the Army. In order to be ready for every emergency, he hastened, on March 26th, to order the formation of eight army corps, called corps of observation.

The 1st Corps was to assemble at Lille; the 2nd at Valenciennes; the 3rd at Mézières; the 4th at Thionville; the 5th at Strasbourg; the 6th at Chambéry; the 7th at the foot of the Pyrenees;

and the 8th, or reserve corps, at Paris. Temporarily, the regiments entering into the composition of these army corps would be of two battalions. The skeletons of the 3rd battalions and the depôts would be concentrated in the military government of Paris and in the towns of the interior until the calling out of the reserves would permit of the forming of the 3rd, 4th, and 5th battalions, which would go immediately to rejoin the army. The mobilized National Guards would replace the troops of the line in the fortresses.

The light cavalry was distributed at the ratio of one division for each army corps. With the surplus of this cavalry and the dragoons, *cuirassiers*, and *carabineers*, there were formed eight divisions of reserve cavalry, to each of which was attached a battery of horse artillery.

On March 20th the Imperial Guard comprised only the two regiments of grenadiers and the two regiments of *chasseurs* of the Old Guard and four regiments of cavalry. The Emperor augmented the effectives of the cavalry regiments, created a Third and Fourth regiment of Grenadiers, a Third and Fourth regiment of Chasseurs (Middle Guard), eight regiments of *voltigeurs* and eight of *tirailleurs* (Young Guard), and a Second regiment of Horse *Chasseurs*. He re-established the two regiments of horse and foot artillery of the Old Guard, as well as the regiment of the train, the squadron of picked *gendarmes,* the battalion of marines, and the company of sappers.

The Young Guard was organized with the enrolled volunteers and the recalled soldiers having formerly belonged to this corps, and in which each man received a *sou* as extra pay. The men of the Elba battalion were incorporated with the Old Guard. For the Middle Guard, the artillery and cavalry, it was necessary to recruit them from the *gendarmerie* and the line. The *gendarmerie* gave 500 men. Each regiment of the Line was to furnish thirty of its best men, large and strongly constituted; a minimum service of four years in the infantry and of eight years in the cavalry was required.

When, at the end of May, the recalled soldiers, the mobilized

National Guards, and the volunteers had increased the army, the Emperor made a new distribution of his forces. The I St Corps (under Drouet d'Erlon), the 2nd Corps (under Reille), the 3rd Corps (under Vandamme), the Army of the Moselle, called thenceforth the 4th Corps (under Gérard), and the 8th Corps (become the 6th, under Lobau), the Cavalry Reserve (under Grouchy), and the Imperial Guard, formed the Army of the North, 124,139 men strong, and commanded by the Emperor in person. The 5th Corps became the Army of the Rhine (23,097 men, of whom 3,000 were mobilized National Guards, under Rapp); and the 6th Corps became the Army of the Alps (23,617 men, of whom 13,000 were mobilized National Guards, under Suchet).

The 7th Corps was divided into two fractions—one fraction took the name of Corps of the Western Pyrenees (6,280 men, of whom 3,000 were mobilized National Guards, under Clausel); the other, that of Corps of the Eastern Pyrenees (7,633 men, of whom 3,300 were mobilized National Guards, under Decaen). The Emperor created finally three new army corps: the Army of the West (nearly 10,000 men, under Lamarque), whose duty it was to repress the Vendéan insurrection; the Corps of the Var (5,544 men, under Brune), and the Corps of Jura (8,420 men, of whom 5,500 were mobilized National Guards, under Lecourbe), both destined to second the army of Suchet in the defence of the Alps.

Four divisions of picked National Guards, of a total strength of 17,466 men, camped under Avèsnes, Sainte-Menihould, Colmar, and Nancy; 90,000 mobilized National Guards and 25,000 retired soldiers were assembled in the fortresses and in the depôts; 11,233 cannoneers of the line and 6,000 cannoneers of the Marine assured in the fortified towns, in conjunction with 2,071 veteran and 6,000 sedentary cannoneers, the service of the artillery; 13,934 soldiers of all arms were *en route* by detachments to join the active armies; finally, 59,559 available and non-available men were in the depôts of the line and 5,559 in the depôts of the Guard. There were, in addition to these, 4,700 men of the war battalions detached to the island of Elba and in the colonies; 8,162 men in the hospitals; 10,000 marine and 5,129 veteran fusiliers; 14,521 foot and horse *gendarmes*; finally, 12,000 custom-house officers organized militarily and 6,000 partisans. Thus the Emperor had raised the active army from 200,000 men to 284,000, and he had formed an auxiliary army of 222,000 men.

One month later these two armies would have been augmented, first, by 19,000 recalled soldiers, who had received their orders of route prior to June 10th, but had not yet reached the depôts; second, by some thousands of recalled soldiers who, on June 15th, had not arrived in the *chefs-lieux* of the departments; third, by 46,500 conscripts of 1815 who, at this same date, were assembled in the *chefs-lieux* of the departments; fourth, by 15,000 mobilized National Guards, put *en route* by the middle of June for the points of concentration.

Finally, from July 15th to September 25th, there would have been the 74,000 men forming the complement of the contingent of 1815 and the 84,000 men forming the complement of the levy of the mobilized National Guards. It would have been possible to mobilize even 60,000 or 70,000 more National Guards, in applying to the departments of the West, for which they had been deferred, the decrees calling the National Guards into active service, and in ordering a new levy in all the extent of France. When Napoleon said that by October 1st the Army would have numbered 800,000 men, he was not so far from the truth.

4

In execution of the decrees of Lyons, the officers who, having emigrated or quitted the service at the time of the Revolution, had been introduced into the army since April 1 1814, were struck from the muster-rolls. But, as many of these officers were provided with employment in the military household and in the staffs, this wholesale removal produced but few vacancies in the Line. The officers in line of promotion sufficed to complete the lists. The officers on half-pay were placed in the battalions, squadrons, and batteries of new formation, in the Young Guard, and in the Federate Sharpshooters. In the midst of May 2,500 officers of this category, to whom, moreover, the Emperor had given their entire pay pending employment, were still available; they were directed upon the frontier places to command the mobilized National Guards.

Certain of the devotion of the officers who lived in immediate contact with the troops. Napoleon had legitimate reasons for mistrusting many colonels and generals. Among the general officers, there were in 1814 some weakness and treason; in 1815, some hesitation and resistance. Numerous changes imposed themselves in the high military personnel. But it was rather the interest of the army than personal rancour or sympathy which dictated to the Emperor his exclusions and selections. Pitiless for the officers who had shown themselves during the Campaign of France incapable, as Augereau and Oudinot, or criminal, as Marmont and Souham, Napoleon knew how to forget the conduct of those who from the 1st to the 20th of March had attempted to change his triumphal return into a miserable failure.

Colonel Cunéo d'Ornano, who had imprisoned twenty-five grenadiers in the citadel of Antibes, was promoted general; General Miollis, who had led the garrison of Marseilles in pursuit of the little imperial column, was invested with the command of the place of Metz; Colonel Roussile, the tenacious defender of the gate of Grenoble, remained at the head of the 5th of the line; Colonel Dubalen, of the 6th, who had publicly given his resignation to Ney upon the place of arms of Lons-le-Saunier, was recalled to his regiment; General Marchand might have also returned into favour, but he refused, he said, "to figure upon the list of traitors."

A Republican under the Empire and converted under Louis XVIII. to constitutional monarchy, Foy had put himself, on March 24th, at the head of the Bonapartist movement at Nantes, only after having done everything to arrest it. He was none the less provided with a fine division in the Army of the North.

Many officers of the 10th of the line, promoted by the Duke of Angoulême during the campaign in the Midi, were confirmed in their new grade. Harispe and Heudelet, though seriously compromised by their manifestations in favour of the Bourbons, had, nevertheless, a command. The Emperor employed Rapp, Belliard, Ruty, Haxo, Kellermann the younger, and Gourgaud, just as if they had not served in the army assembled at Villejuif under the orders of the Duke of Berry.

"Would you have dared to fire on me?" said Napoleon to Rapp.

"Doubtless, sire; it was my duty."

And Napoleon gave him the Army of the Rhine.

The Emperor, however, removed or retired a hundred officers of every rank: Dupont, whose favour under Louis XVIII. had not effaced the dishonour of Baylen; Dessolles, who had so well seconded Talleyrand in April, 1814; Beurnonville, Donnadieu, and Bourdessoule, who had emigrated to Belgium; Maison, also an *émigré*, and who, solicited by the imperial Government to return to France, replied that he would return there only at the head of 500,000 bayonets; Curto, whose furious words against Napoleon had provoked a mutiny in the garrison of Thionville; Generals d'Aultanne, Monnier, Ernouf, Loverdo, Briche, and the colonels of the 10th of the Line and of the 14th Chasseurs, who had fought in the Midi under the Duke of Angoulême eight days after the imperial Government had been recognized by two-thirds of France.

Without remorse for his complicity with Marmont in the defection of Essonnes, Souham had hoped to preserve his command of Périgeux; removed, he presented himself at the Tuileries at a public audience in order to attempt to move the Emperor. "What do you still wish from me?" said Napoleon, turning his back on him. "You see that I no longer know you!"

At the request of Davoût and the corps commanders, many colonels, majors, captains, and lieutenants were, on account of their persistent hostility, struck from the lists. The disgrace of Colonels Moncey, Oudinot, and Zoppfell appears less explicable. Moncey had only sought to maintain the 3rd Hussars in obedience to the King, and that only up to the 13th of March; now Napoleon had shown himself indulgent to many analogous acts. Oudinot could be reproached only for bearing the name of his father, and Zoppfell for being a protégé of the Duke of Feltre. Denounced as a Royalist, Bugeaud was put on half-pay by Davoût in the course of April, but Suchet, Grouchy, Gérard, and Bertrand hastened to speak in favour of "the best colonel of the Army." Replaced at the head of the 14th of the Line, Bugeaud received, as a compensation for his momentary disgrace, the rank of commander in the Legion of Honour.

General de Bourmont was also unemployed for some time. From Lons-le-Saunier he had hastened to Paris to join Louis XVIII. The Emperor ordered his arrest at the request of Ney; but the latter was the first one to solicit Napoleon to give a command to this general. Gérard, who had had Bourmont under his orders during the campaigns of 1812 and 1814, demanded him as a general of division in his army corps. After having hesitated for a long time, the Emperor finally yielded. It was necessary for him to impose his will upon Davoût, who yielded only to a formal order.

"Gérard answers for Bourmont with his head," said the Emperor.

"Gérard is wrong," replied the Prince of Eckmühl; "I answer for no one. I only answer for myself."

Lenient, as we see, towards those who had wished to combat him, the Emperor did not lavish recompenses upon those who had first compromised themselves for him. If he promoted La Bédoyère, already proposed during the Campaign of France, and Mallet, commander of the Battalion of the Island of Elba, to be generals of brigade, if he promoted Simmer, who had brought him two regiments at Lyons, to be general of division, and if he named Brayer peer of France, Dessaix, Girard, Allix, Ameil, Mouton-Duvernet, Gilly, Piré, Proteau, and Chartran received no favours of any kind; they were employed in the armies only according to the strict rights of their rank.

Now, Dessaix had accepted the command of Lyons seven days before the Emperor's return to the Tuileries, Girard had commanded from Avallon the Imperial advance guard, Allix had proclaimed the Empire at Nevers, Ameil had been arrested at Auxerre as an emissary of Napoleon, Chartran was to pay with his life for his devotion to the imperial cause, and Mouton- Duvernet, Gilly, Piré, and Proteau had ardently and efficaciously seconded Grouchy in the campaign of the Midi against the Duke of Angoulême. General Porret de Morvan, who, for having led to Sens the foot *chasseurs* of the Old Guard, flattered himself that he would be selected to replace Curial as colonel of this corps, saw Curial disgraced, but the command of the *chasseurs* was given to Morand. Prince Jérôme, Imperial Highness though he was, was only invested with the command of a division of infantry.

Merlin, who had forced the Governor of Vincennes to capitulate, received the three stars, but Sebastiani, who had hastened the defection of the army of the Duke of Berry, was charged with a mission which he justly regarded as unworthy of his merit and services—namely, the organization of the National Guards in the 16th Military Division. Exelmans, who had been first to enter the Tuileries on March 20th, was given a corps of cavalry, but Kellermann, who had been employed in the Army of Villejuif, was also given the command of one. Lallemand the elder, one of the principal chiefs of the conspiracy of the North, was made lieutenant-general; but Lefebvre-Desnoëttes and Lallemand the younger were simply replaced at the head of the horse *chasseurs* and of the artillery of the Old Guard. After the fiasco of Compiègne, Colonel Marin had gone at full speed to rejoin Napoleon at Auxerre; he doubtless hoped to obtain the command of the horse artillery of the Guard, of which he had been major. It was Colonel Duchand, of the artillery of the Line, who was selected.

5

Of the twenty marshals of France, three—Berthier, Marmont, and Victor—had accompanied or rejoined Louis XVIII. in Belgium; the Emperor ordered their names to be struck from the list of marshals. Pérignon, who had foolishly compromised himself with Vitrolles at Toulouse, and Augereau, whose recent recantation could not redeem his pitiful conduct at the head of the Army of Lyons in 1814, were the object of the same measure.

Napoleon also desired to remove both Gouvion Saint-Cyr and old Kellermann; the first for having disregarded his orders after March 20th and for having caused the troops of the 22nd Military Division to resume the white cockade; and the second for having voted the Act of Deposition on April 1 1814. Madame Gouvion Saint-Cyr wrote a letter to Davoût which appeased the Emperor; the Marshal escaped with a forced sojourn in this *château* of Reverseaux. Napoleon also failed to carry out his first decision in regard to the Duke of Valmy. Serurier, who had also, as senator, voted the Act of Deposition, was maintained in his functions as Governor of the Invalides. The Emperor contented himself with not naming him to the Chamber of Peers, and the lesson was well merited.

Oudinot, like Gouvion Saint-Cyr, had refused, after March 20th, to obey the orders of Napoleon. He had not permitted the Empire to be proclaimed at Metz until the garrison and the revolted populace had forced him to do so. Relieved of his command, he used every effort to obtain his pardon. He addressed a letter to the Emperor, and supplicated Davoût, Suchet, and Jacqueminot to intercede for him.

"Go at once to the Emperor," he wrote to Suchet, "and tell him what you think of me; tell him that you did not forward your letter and that of Ney to me until the evening of the 27th. You will also tell him that never has Oudinot forgotten what he owes to Napoleon; and that if Oudinot has been guilty of any wrong, he will no sooner know it than he will expiate and repair it. I am in need of your intercession for my wife and children, who all share the misfortune which prostrates me."

The Emperor revoked the order exiling him to Lorraine and

consented to receive him at the Tuileries, but he left him without employment. Doubtless Napoleon would not have harboured any ill-will against the Marshal for his conduct at Metz; but he could not forget that the Duke of Reggio had, the preceding year, caused himself to be beaten at Bar-sur-Aube, on account of his faulty dispositions on the eve of the battle and by his fatal indecision during the combat.

Though Macdonald had shown himself to be a very zealous Royalist, and though he had done his utmost at Lyons and Villejuif to organize resistance, the Emperor was disposed to give him a command. But the Marshal, who had returned to Paris after having accompanied Louis XVIII. as far as the frontier, was firmly resolved not to serve under the new Government. It was in vain that General Maurice Mathieu, his old chief of staff in the Army of the Grisons, supplicated him to come to the Tuileries, where the Emperor awaited him; it was in vain that Davoût himself forced his door in order to determine him to accept a command; he remained inflexible. Being tired of war, the sole favour that he would deign to ask of the Emperor was permission to be allowed to live like a good *bourgeois* on his property of Courcelle, near Gien. Napoleon granted his request.

After having published a violent order of the day against Napoleon, Moncey had left Paris on March 20th. He wrote two days later to the Emperor that he intended to retire to the country. Napoleon had already replaced him as Inspector-General of *Gendarmerie* by Rovigo. But should he not have remembered what Moncey had done in 1814 at the head of the Parisian National Guard and restored this command to him? He contented himself with naming him a member of the Chamber of Peers, the same as Lefebvre, who had had no command during the Campaign of France and who had remained without employment under Louis XVIII. In justice to Lefebvre, we should state that he was sixty-seven years old, and the Emperor rightly wished to have young men in command of his army corps.

Masséna had seconded but feebly the Duke of Angoulême during the short campaign upon the banks of the Rhône, and immediately after the capitulation of La Pallud he had hastened to proclaim the Empire. On April 14th he addressed to Napoleon a report justifying his conduct, which closed as follows: "I cannot conceal from Your Majesty how desirous I am of seeing you again in order to assure you of my boundless devotion."

The Emperor wrote to the Prince of Essling a letter of congratulations, summoned him to Paris, and received him there with great marks of friendship; but, in spite of his half-promise, he preferred not to restore to him the government of the 9th Military Division. In order to contain the Royalists of Marseilles, it was necessary to have a man who had not commanded there in the name of Louis XVIII. The Emperor offered to Masséna, whose infirmities rendered him incapable of serving in the active armies, the government of the 4th and 5th Military Divisions, comprising the Moselle, the Meurthe, and the Vosges. The Marshal refused this post, and remained in Paris, where he showed himself very assiduous in attending the sittings of the Chamber of Peers.

Although Mortier, Governor of Lille, Suchet, Governor of Strasbourg, and Jourdan, Governor of Rouen, had remained faithful to the King during three or four days after March 20th, they had not compromised themselves like Oudinot and Gouvion Saint-Cyr. The Emperor could not feel towards them any resentment. He did not wish, however, to maintain them in the posts which they held from Louis XVIII. This was with him a principle. Charged at first with the inspection of the places of the Northeast, Mortier was selected to command the cavalry of the Guard and finally put at the head of the Young Guard. Suchet was invested with the command of the Army of the Alps; and Jourdan received the command of Besançon, a fortified town of the first line, where Davoût judged it necessary that there should be a marshal of France.

In disgrace since 1807 for having, it is said, closed too complacently his eyes upon the peculations of Bourrienne in the Hanseatic towns, Brune had demanded vainly, at the beginning of the Campaign of France, permission to resume service. During the Restoration he had also remained without employment. After the return of the Emperor, Brune again offered his sword. The administrative qualities, of which he had given proof in Belgium, the Gironde, Vendée, and Tuscany, designated him for the government of one of the provinces in which the troubles still existed. Sent to Marseilles as governor of the 9th Military Division, he was at the same time charged with the organization and the command of the army corps of the Var.

Marshal Ney, having arrived with his troops at Paris on March 23rd, was entrusted on the same day with a mission in the departments of the north and east. The patent object of this mission was to inspect the fortresses; the secret object, to judge of the state of minds, to furnish information regarding the officers and functionaries, and to propose, if necessary, some removals and substitutions. Ney performed this mission with zeal, but he had the bad taste to manifest against the Bourbons sentiments of an unheard-of violence. In the meetings of the officers he exhaled insults against the King and Princes. "It is a rotten family," said he. These words were not of a nature to pacify public opinion, which was generally hostile to him.

Among the Bonapartists, and even in the entourage of the Emperor, his conduct at Lons-le-Saunier was criticised. This malicious play upon words was repeated all over Paris: "*Il fallait être né* (Ney) *pour ça.*"—"One must be born for this!")—and his sudden change of sides did not free him from suspicion. "If Ney is employed in the field," wrote an anonymous person to the Emperor, "he should be given a staff upon which one can depend." There were no lack of men to recall to Napoleon the never-to-be-forgotten scene of Fontainebleau, and perhaps one had reported to him the words of Ney at the time of his recent passage through Dijon: "I had congratulated myself on having forced the Emperor to abdicate, and now I must serve him!"

In addition to all this, the Marshal, on returning from his tour of inspection, about April 15th, had been so utterly lacking in tact as to attempt to excuse himself to the Emperor for his words concerning the iron cage. "This speech is true," he said, "but it was because I had already made up my mind, and I did not think I could say anything better to conceal my projects."

Napoleon remained silent, but in his eyes the Marshal saw a flash of lightning.

Desperate, full of confusion and remorse, accusing every one and himself, Ney retired to his property of Coudreaux. For six weeks nothing was heard from him. It was said that he was in disgrace; it was even reported that he had been arrested. He returned to Paris for the ceremony of the Champ de Mai. Named peer of France on June 2nd, he went to the Elysée four days later to obtain the written order for the payment of a sum of 37,000 *francs* due him for back pay and the expenses of his tour.

"Here you are," said Napoleon to him; "I thought you had emigrated."

"Would that I had done so sooner!" bitterly replied the Marshal.

On June 11th he again returned to the Tuileries, but there was no question in these two interviews of a command for him in the Army of the North. Ney doubtless, who knew that Napoleon called him *la bête noire*, dared not solicit one. But on June 11th, at the moment of quitting Paris, the Emperor became doubtful as to the wisdom of his course. Could he condemn to a degrading repose the hero of so many battles? Could he, in the hour of peril, deprive both France and himself of such a soldier? He wrote to the Minister of War:

"Summon Marshal Ney; tell him that, if he wishes to be in the first battles, he must be by the 14th at Avèsnes, where will be my headquarters."

Napoleon, no doubt, believed that he, was acting in the interest of the Army or, what was identical, in his own interest. He acted also through commiseration. The tone of his note indicates it. It is not an order; it is only a notice, which leaves the Marshal free to do as he pleases. Let Ney come if he desires. But Ney could not but desire to be present in the first battles, should it be only in the hope of being killed. He set out from Paris on

June 12th and reached Avèsnes on the 13th, where he dined with the Emperor, but he received the command of the 1st and 2nd Army Corps only on the afternoon of the 15th—that is to say, after the operations had begun.

Since he had *"passe Roi,"* according to the expression in vogue in the Army, Murat figured no longer upon the list of marshals. Three weeks before Napoleon took the field, Joachim, who had fallen from the throne, had sought refuge in the environs of Toulon. Not even his soldier's sabre remained to him. He besought the Emperor to restore it to him. "I desire," he wrote, "to shed for you the last drop of my blood."

Napoleon refused his offer. He could not see his way clear to give a command in the French Army to a Frenchman who had fought against it one year before. Besides, he was angry with his brother-in-law for having commenced too soon, in spite of his instructions, the war against the Austrians; he was especially angry with him for having allowed himself to be defeated. Later, in his reveries at St. Helena, Napoleon regretted his decision in regard to this great cavalry leader.

"At Waterloo," he said, "Murat would have perhaps gained us the victory. What was necessary? To overthrow three or four English squares. Murat was precisely the man to do this."

Would Murat, who possessed the double gift of inspiring in his horsemen a furious *élan* and of terrifying the enemy, have succeeded in riding down the English? It is possible.

The memory of Grouchy is henceforth so intimately associated with the cursed remembrance of Waterloo that the fine services and brilliant actions of this valorous captain have been forgotten. If he had not the magnetic *élan* of Murat, he knew like him how to manoeuvre masses of cavalry. Second in command of the expedition to Ireland in the year 5. (1796), Governor of Madrid in 1808, colonel-general of the *chasseurs* and *chevau-legers* in 1809, and chief of the Sacred Squadron during the retreat from Russia, he had contributed to the victories of Hohenlinden, Eylau, Friedland, Wagram, and the Moskowa. After Vauchamps it is said the Emperor had thought of naming him marshal of France. In disgrace under Louis XVIII., Grouchy was sent to Lyons on March 31st to combat the Duke of Angoulême. Promoted marshal after this short and easy campaign, he was put at the head of the Army of the Alps, then recalled to Paris on May 8th. The Emperor intended to give him the four cavalry corps of the Army of the North. It was as commander-in-chief of the cavalry that Grouchy entered Belgium on June 15th; for his misfortune, he was on the next day to be charged with a still more important command.

6

The selection of a major-general seriously preoccupied Napoleon. By whom could he replace Berthier? The Prince of Wagram was neither a great captain, an organizer, nor a man of superior intellect; but he possessed extensive technical knowledge, and he had raised to the hundredth power the qualities of a good clerk. Indefatigable, conscientious, diligent, quick to grasp the most complicated orders, skilful in translating them in all their details with wonderful accuracy, precision, and clearness, and, finally, punctual in transmitting them at the right moment, he had been for Napoleon a perfect instrument.

With him as chief of staff, the Emperor was tranquil; the orders were always drawn up in such a manner that those who received them had no doubt or hesitation as to the manner in which they were to be executed. And these orders always reached their destination, even should Berthier be forced to cause each order to be carried, when he deemed it prudent, by eight officers, taking as many different routes. It was said that Berthier had grown feeble in mind and body. In 1814, however, his correspondence bears witness that his pen had lost nothing of its activity and luminous precision. The Emperor, who remembered the services of the Prince of Wagram during the last campaign, regretted him and despaired not of seeing him return to France.

"That brute of a Berthier!" said he to Rapp, "He will return. I will pardon him everything, but on condition that he will don his uniform of a Life Guardsman and appear before me."

Berthier, in fact, attempted to return to France, where he had left the Princess of Wagram with his son and his two daughters. Having remained a short time at Ghent, he went to the Château of Bamberg, a property of his uncle by marriage, the King of Bavaria. At the beginning of May he set out to gain by way of Basle the French frontier; he was unable to pass beyond Stockach, where he found the headquarters of the Prince of Hohenzollern. The Allies, no doubt, preferred to keep Berthier a half-prisoner in Bavaria than to know that he was in Napoleon's staff. He returned very sadly to Bamberg. In the afternoon of June 1st, as a regiment of Russian dragoons on the march for France was defiling in front of the *château*, Berthier was seen to quit suddenly the window on the first floor, from which he was watching the soldiers, to appear shortly afterwards at a window on the third floor and to fall upon the pavement. He was picked up dead, with his skull fractured.

For three weeks the Emperor had decided to take for major-general Marshal Soult, who, as it seems, had offered himself for this position.

Suspected by the friends of the King, hated by the Bonapartists as well as by the Liberals, and execrated by the entire body of officers, Soult had retired to Villeneuve-l'Etang. This retreat being near Paris, he came to the Tuileries on March 26th. It is hardly probable that this visit was made in order to remind the Emperor that he had spoken of him as a madman and adventurer in his last order of the day. At the end of this interview, of which nothing has become public, Soult exchanged many letters with Davoût, who manifested some friendliness towards him. But, in spite of Davoût's steps in his behalf, the Emperor was some time in reaching a decision.

"I desire," wrote Soult, on April 11th, to the Minister of War, "that your Excellency will have the kindness to reply to my letter written to you a few days since, in order that I may be in position to conform to the decision of His Majesty in my regard."

Some days later Soult, who had sent his oath in writing, was invited to come to renew it solemnly before the Emperor.

Thenceforth the Duke of Dalmatia could regard himself as being restored to favour. On May 9th he was named major-general. Soult was as superior to Berthier as a man of mind and action is to a good clerk. But he had never discharged the duties of a chief of staff in an army corps; he had had no experience in this office, and was lacking in the qualities of application and exactness, which are so essential to the proper discharge of its duties. Bailly de Monthyon, who, regarded as Berthier's right arm, had been chief of the General Staff from 1812 to 1814, and who, in 1813, during the absence of the major-general, had twice discharged the duties of this office; Drouot, aide-major-general of the Imperial Guard; Belliard, Murat's chief of staff from 1805 to 1808 and aide-major-general during the campaigns of Saxony and France; Reille and Drouet d'Erlon, both old chiefs of staff of Lannes; Bertrand,, for so long an aide-de-camp of the Emperor, and so accustomed as grand marshal to receiving and transmitting his orders; Gérard, ex-chief of staff of Bernadotte; Ruty, chief of staff in 1813 of the artillery of the Grand Army; and so many other generals of division, would have been perhaps more capable of replacing the Prince of Wagram.

But for hierarchical reasons, or etiquette, the Emperor desired to have a marshal of France for major-general. Now, none of the marshals, save Davoût and Suchet, appeared more capable: of discharging the duties of this office than Soult. At the moment when France was in the midst of a military organization, on the eve of a war which threatened to embrace in its theatre of operations La Vendée, the northern frontier, the Alps, and the Pyrenees, and at a time when a political crisis might arise, it was of the utmost necessity that Davoût should be left in the ministry of war and in the command of Paris.

But there was Marshal Suchet, ex-chief of staff of Joubert and Masséna. It seems that, at least from the standpoint of moral effect, the Emperor would have been well inspired in preferring him to Soult, for Suchet could have awakened no suspicion nor provoked any mistrust. Soult would have replaced, without disadvantage, the Duke of Albuféra in the command of the Army of the Alps, and this post, being less in evidence, would have attracted less attention upon him. Thus would have been avoided that great scandal, that the first man in the army, after the Emperor and the Minister of War, should be, of all the general officers, he who had rendered himself most odious to the army under the royal Government.

Soult having addressed an order to Vandamme before his nomination had been rendered official, the haughty general wrote to Davoût the following ironical letter:

"I have received a letter from the Duke of Dalmatia, in which he announces himself as major-general. I think it best to forward it to your Excellency before answering it. As the Duke of Ragusa could give me the same notice, I shall regard it as null and void until I am informed of this nomination by your Excellency or by an imperial decree."

7

Before occupying himself with the marshals the Emperor had selected for the principal commands the generals who were desirous of obtaining the marshal's baton, and whom he had already promoted in his mind. He expected to find among these men "having their road to make," as he said, more ardour and devotion than among his old comrades loaded down with glory and honours. He gave the 1st Army Corps to Drouet d'Erlon, a general of division since 1805, a combatant of Jena and Friedland, and one of the best lieutenants of Masséna and Soult in the Spanish wars. Reille, a veteran of the Italian campaigns, a general of division since 1807, commanding a division of the Guard at Wagram, and entrusted at the end of 1812 with the chief command of the Army of Portugal, had the 2nd Corps.

Gérard, colonel at Austerlitz, brigadier-general at Jena, general of division at the Moskowa, one of the heroes, with Ney, of the retreat from Russia, and the sole officer of his rank who had commanded an army corps during the campaign of France, received the 4th Corps. The 5th Corps (later Army of the Rhine) was entrusted to Rapp, the man of twenty-two wounds, the heroic defender of Dantzig, a general of division since 1807, and an *aide-de-camp* of Napoleon for twelve years. Mouton, Count de Lobau, one of the most skilful officers of the army in the art of manoeuvring troops and a general division since 1807, had the command of the 6th Corps, in formation at Paris. Charles Lebrun, a son of the Duke of Plaissance, and a valiant cavalry general, was placed temporarily at the head of the 3rd Corps. The Emperor intended to replace him, at the proper time, "with a more skilful general."

About the middle of April he gave this army corps to Vandamme. Napoleon did not love this rude soldier, bad bed-fellow that he was; but the superior military qualities of Vandamme and his seniority of rank (he had been named general of division in 1799, when only twenty-two years old), designated him among all others for a command. He exercised it, at least so long as left to himself, with an incomparable conscientiousness, firmness, and zeal—careful of all the details pertaining to the organization, the clothing, and the instruction of the troops; prompt in proceeding against those who wished to persuade the soldiery to desert and the alarmists; ardent in inflaming the minds of the soldiers, the mobilized National Guards, and the inhabitants of Ardennes and the Meuse. Vandamme merited this praise from Davoût: "You have communicated all your fire to the country where you command."

Sent to Bordeaux to cause the Imperial Government to be recognized in that city, Clausel, who had particularly distinguished himself in Italy and Spain, remained in that city as governor of the 11th Military Division. He received, moreover, the command of the Corps of the Western Pyrenees. General Decaen, a veteran of the campaigns of the Rhine and La Vendée, and for six years Governor of the isles of France and Bourbon, had sincerely wished to preserve Bordeaux for the King; but, like the Duchess of Angoulême, he had been compelled to yield to the force of events. He returned to Paris, from whence he set out for Toulouse at the end of May.

The Emperor had confided to him the command of the 8th

and 10th Military Divisions and the Corps of the Eastern Pyrenees. Decaen would have preferred a corps or a division in the Army of the North to this post, at the same time political and military. On account of his conduct at Bordeaux, he was about to find himself at Toulouse under the alternative of awakening the suspicions of the Emperor, if he showed little zeal, or of rendering himself doubly odious to the Royalists, if he acted with the rigorous firmness demanded by the circumstances. Decaen took this last course, as he should have done, and caused himself to be execrated throughout all Languedoc.

Struck from the list of officers in 1804 for having manifested openly his indignation at the trial of his comrade Moreau, Lecourbe had been restored to his rank by Louis XVIII. At Lons-le-Saunier he had attempted to prevent the defection of Marshal Ney, and, upon the report of the latter, Napoleon had ordered his arrest. But he came to the Tuileries to protest his devotion. Happy to attach to his cause this tried officer, who passed for a Republican and whose name had remained dear to the veterans of the armies of the Sambre-et-Meuse, of the Rhine, and of Helvetia, the Emperor gave him the command of the Corps of the Jura.

Lamarque had, on March 20th, installed himself in the command of Paris. Replaced two days later by General Hullin, who had occupied this post from 1807 to 1814, he received the command of a division in Reille's corps; then he was sent to La Vendée as general-in-chief of the Army of the West. He had formerly combated the bands of Abruzzes and the guerrillas of the sierras of Aragon. His experience in partisan warfare caused him to be selected to command against the Vendéans.

General Durosnel, ex-*aide-de-camp* of the Emperor, was second in command of the Parisian National Guard, Napoleon being nominally commander-in-chief. Durosnel had greatly distinguished himself in the cavalry; but, whilst Moncey, Ornano, Hullin, d'Hériot, and Lespinasse had found themselves in Paris during the campaign of 1814, he, having been made prisoner at Dresden, had not returned to France until after peace had been declared. Thus, being ignorant of what the National Guard had done, and especially of what it might have done, he found himself badly prepared for commanding it. With a little zeal and energy he might have made up for his lack of experience; but he permitted himself to be circumvented by his staff, which numbered a great many secret Royalists and deluded Liberals.

Far from breathing the spirit of patriotism and abnegation in all the National Guard, he was not long in contracting the sentiments of egotistic prudence which guided the *élite* of this militia. Charged with the revision of its *personnel*, he carried out this work in a half-hearted manner, as if he only wished to appear to give satisfaction to the Emperor. It was, indeed, necessary for him to strike from the lists some officers at the same time too compromised and too well known, like Decazes and Rémusat; but he maintained upon the lists such men as Major Billing, an intimate friend of Comte, editor of the *Censeur*, and Colonel Aclocque, who prohibited the band from playing "Let us watch over the safety of the Empire," under pretence that it was "an incendiary air." Some very warm partisans of the Emperor were removed, notably Major Beck, the only one of the superior officers of the 6th Legion who had fought at the Buttes-Chaumont in 1814; Captain Albert, who had made the trip to the isle of Elba; and Captain Olivier, who had equipped at his own expense half of his company.

Moreover, Durosnel set everything at work to prevent the creation of the Federate Sharpshooters, then to delay their organization. "To arm such men," he said, "would create uneasiness and dissatisfaction in the National Guard." Now, commanded exclusively by officers on half-pay, and having for commander General Darricau, who had gained all his grades at the siege of Toulon, in Egypt, in the Grand Army, and in Spain, and who, contrary to Durosnel, had faith and ardour, the Federate Sharpshooters would have contributed efficaciously towards the defence of Paris. As Carnot and Davoût said, the creation of these battalions of workmen could impress unfavourably only the hostile and pusillanimous spirits.

The promotions in the army were made by the Emperor *motu proprio*, or upon the proposal of Davoût; sometimes even the Minister of War promoted the officers to the posts without referring the nominations to the Emperor. Davoût was no more infallible than Napoleon. There were some awkward selections—nay, some pitiful ones. Berckheim and Millet, who had never served but in the cavalry; and Molitor, a general of division since 1802, who, on account of his great military qualities, should have been employed in the active armies, were called to command some National Guards; whilst Marcognet, a poor officer, and Donzelot, who had lost the habit of war during the seven years that he was Governor of Corfu, were both given a division in the 1st Corps of the Army of the North.

A few days after having been relieved of his command, the colonel of the 14th Chasseurs, one of the most faithful officers of the Duke of Angoulême during the campaign of the Midi, was proposed for a regiment of mobilized National Guards. Another colonel, whose cowardice under fire had led to his retirement, was also proposed for a regiment of the Line. Finally, General Moreau, the pusillanimous commander of Soissons in 1814, who had avoided a capital condemnation only thanks to the fall of Napoleon, was selected to command a brigade in active service. The Emperor was justified in saying: "It seems to me that, among the general officers, there are a great many young men more skilful than those proposed to me."

Overtasked and absorbed by the gravest cares, the Emperor often ratified the nominations of Davoût without examining them. He then visited his displeasure upon this minister, who, as it appears, was disliked at the Tuileries on account of his stiffness and severity in the service. So there was no lack of individuals in the imperial entourage to incriminate all his acts that were susceptible of criticism. In order to have one guarantee more for the military *personnel*, the Emperor charged his *aide-de-camp* Flahault with revising the nominations proposed by the Minister of War.

"Collect," he wrote to Flahault, "all the information possible upon the generals and officers, for, if I make some bad selections, it is you whom I shall hold responsible."

Very brave and an excellent staff officer, Flahault had shown himself as brilliant a cavalier at Friedland and the Moskowa as skilful diplomat at Neumark and Lusigny. None the less, his truly extraordinary advancement was attributed to favour. In fact, though he had never commanded more than a squadron, he had been named, at twenty-eight years of age (in 1813), general of division. So young a lieutenant-general should have, perhaps, declined this mission—very delicate with a man like Davoût. At all events, without displaying less zeal, he might have discharged it in a more discreet manner. Each day he installed himself for many hours in the War Office, overturning the documents, causing reports to be made directly to him, erasing of his own authority some names upon the lists, and even giving some orders directly opposed to those of Davoût. The selections were no better, for, in spite of his devotion and intelligence, the Emperor's *aide-de-camp* could judge no better than Davoût. The Prince of Eckmühl was deeply wounded by this inquisition, from which he was quickly delivered. He had an explanation with the Emperor, telling him that, if it were not an act of cowardice to abandon his post under such circumstances, he would not remain one hour in the ministry.

Among the officers provided with commands, there were some men incapable, worn out before their time, or of doubtful devotion; but the high personnel of the last Imperial Army formed, nevertheless, an admirable whole. We may even say that, unless in revolutions or in wars analogous to those which succeeded each other from 1789 to 1814, never will the French Army possess such chiefs. Independently of their innate military qualities, they possessed this advantage—experience, and this virtue—youth. All had made war for more than twenty years, and none were fifty years old.

Napoleon was forty-six; Davoût, forty-five; Soult, forty-six; Ney, forty-six; Grouchy, forty-nine; Drouet d'Erlon, forty-nine; Lobau, forty-five; Lamarque, forty-five; Kellermann, forty-five;

Reille, forty-four; Vandamme, forty-four; Rapp, forty-three; Clausel, forty- three; Suchet, forty-three; Pajol, forty -three; Gérard, forty- two; Drouot, forty-one; and Excelmans, forty-one—this for the commanders of the army and cavalry corps. Among the generals of division, many—Allix, Piré, Flahault, Berckheim, and Teste—were less than forty. The youngest of the generals of brigade was La Bédoyère; he was twenty-nine.

8

Among these men who had so often led the French to victory, their faith in success, unfortunately, did not equal their physical vigour and military talents. They were too well informed regarding the formidable armaments of Europe and the feeble resources of France, both in soldiers and *matériel*, not to see that, unless favoured by Fortune, which, however, was always possible in war, the Emperor would be unable to fight long with his small army against the masses of the coalition. On June 10th, in passing through La Fère, General Ruty, commander-in-chief of the artillery, said to Colonel Pion des Loches: "Bonaparte is irretrievably lost. The King will soon return. What will become of us? Miserable army that would not fire a shot three months since!"

In a reunion of officers, on the eve of the passage of the Sambre, another general uttered words so discouraging that, in contempt of all discipline, Major de Négrier severely criticised them: "It is not for you," he cried, "to make such reflections. The wine is drawn, and you should drink it, and not attempt to demoralize us."

Confidence was lacking, even in the general officers who had been led by their sentiments or by the force of circumstances to declare themselves first for Napoleon, and who, compromised as they were, should have had so great a interest in strengthening the *morale* of their comrades. But they were all the more uneasy, as they felt their heads would be one of the prizes of this lost game.

Variance reigned in the staffs. The generals who, without

being very fervent Royalists, would have demanded nothing better, however, than to finish tranquilly their career under the Bourbons, were vexed with the accomplices of March 20th for having thrown the country into an adventure and provoked a frightful war. These last suspected the others, and denounced them as officers without energy, lukewarm patriots, and timid Royalists. Finally, more ardent than ever were the competition, rivalry, and jealousy for commands.

As sparing of recompenses as the Emperor had been in regard to his true partisans, the other generals feared none the less that, after the first battle, there would be advancement only for the former. And, on the other hand, those who had rallied to the Emperor from the first hour were astonished to see still in the Imperial Army men like Soult, Durutte, Bruny, Bourmont, and Dumonceau. General Piré protested against the insufficiency of the indemnity for taking the field.

"It is the lack of attention to private interests," said he, "that often leads to the loss of the general cause."

General Maurice Mathieu asked to be retired in order not to become the subordinate of Clausel, his junior in rank. Duhesme, who had at first been attached to the 3rd Corps, was given a command in the Young Guard.

"He cannot," wrote Davoût, "be placed under the orders of Vandamme."

General Bonnet accused General Ornano of having spoken disparagingly of him to the Emperor, challenged him, and lodged a ball in his chest. Vandamme, who had a corps of 18,000 men, complained to the Minister of War that some generals younger than he were given more important commands. Gressot wrote to Soult that the generals of the Army of the Rhine were unanimous in regretting being under the orders of Rapp, "a man of complete nullity." If it had not been on the very day of taking the field, more than one general would have refused to serve under the Prince of the Moskowa, and Vandamme, and even Gérard, passed with displeasure under the command of Grouchy.

An officer of the Emperor's staff wrote to Davoût: "All regard themselves as crusaders, engaged in the same venture, but without any obligation towards one another."

As to the comradeship and solidarity existing among the generals of 1815, we have these fine words of Cambronne before the Council of War: "I refused the rank of lieutenant-general because there were so many jealous persons. You saw the effects of this at Waterloo; we had a renowned captain. Well, even he was unable to put everything in order. One would have said that my nomination was an injustice; that I was too young. I would have been placed in an embarrassing position, and I was unwilling to run the risk of compromising the safety of the Army."

Contrary to the staffs, the soldiers and almost all of the regimental officers were full of ardour and confidence. Whilst the generals saw things as they were in reality, the soldiers recommenced the dream of glory which the invasion had interrupted, but which they could not believe ended. Had not the Emperor, whose return had been predicted for a year by the barrack refrains and the marching songs, returned to his own? In the eyes of the soldiers Napoleon was invincible.

If he had been conquered in 1812, it had been by the snow; in 1814, it was by treason. This faith, so suitable for strengthening the *morale* of the army, and which the Emperor, moreover, had always attempted to inspire, had, unfortunately, for counterpart the suspicion of everything that was not Napoleon. One may be conquered only by treason, but the soldiers suspected treason, everywhere. "Do not employ the marshals during the campaign," one wrote to the Emperor. The quarters of the corps commanders, the Tuileries, and the War Department were flooded with complaints and denunciations of the officers who, during the other reign, had manifested sentiments in favour of the Bourbons and the Orleanists, or who were only members of noble families.

At the advance posts of the Army of the Rhine a sentinel fired upon an individual who was seeking to reach the German bank by swimming. The report spread among the troops that a note had been found upon the dead body announcing that there was a plot to blow up the powder magazine at Strasbourg. The commandant of Condé, Colonel Taubin, excused himself for certain delays in the provisioning of the fortress by saying that "his orders were not obeyed"; and driven mad by the harsh reply of the assistant chief of staff of the 1st Corps, that "an officer who could not command obedience was unworthy to command," he blew out his brains. The garrison believed that he had killed himself to avoid being sent before a council of war as an accomplice of a conspiracy.

The minds of the soldiers being thus troubled by the fear of treason, we can imagine what an emotion was caused in the 1st Army Corps by the distribution of false cartridges. The fact was, indeed, very grave, for the ordnance department of Lille had delivered not wooden cartridges, used in drilling, but ball cartridges, containing bran in place of powder. Drouet d'Erlon had the colonel in charge of the ordnance department shadowed.

"For a long time," said he, in a report to Davoût, "I have had some suspicions regarding his opinions." Davoût ordered an investigation, which, like all investigations, ended in nothing. It was impossible to ascertain how, why, or since when these strange cartridges came to be placed in the magazine.

The bonds of discipline, which even in the armies of Austerlitz and Wagram were not near so strong as one imagines, became still further relaxed from the effects of this almost universal suspicion, as well as from the events that had occurred during the past year. Soldiers are not quick to obey chiefs whom they believe capable of *ragusades* (this was the word in vogue), and to respect generals and colonels who, after having caused them to march against their Emperor three months before, henceforth manifested the most ardent Bonapartism. Only the officers who, during the period extending from March 5th to the 20th, had by their words or acts encouraged or provoked the men to desert to the Emperor, preserved their authority.

And not always was this the case. Six officers of the 1st *Cuirassiers*, having been advanced a grade by the Emperor for having won over their regiment, were installed in their new grades, according to the regulations, before the assembled regiment. The *cuirassiers* received them with murmurs and hisses. "We have done as much as you," they cried, "and we have received neither advancement nor other recompense." In more than one regiment it was hoped that all the officers would be replaced by the subalterns; in more than one address from the regiments to the Emperor the soldiers demanded the removal of their colonel.

"We demand," wrote the dragoons of the 12th Regiment, "the removal of our colonel, whose ardour for Your Majesty is not abreast with our sentiments."

"We are persuaded," wrote the officers, subalterns, and soldiers of the 75th of the Line, "that the intention of Your Majesty is not to maintain a traitor at the head of a French regiment."

There was still another reason for this spirit of indiscipline. Deceived by appearances, as were almost every one at that time, the soldiers imagined that they alone had brought about the revolution which had brought back the Emperor to the Tuileries; consequently they believed that no one but them had a right to cry, "Long live the Emperor!" Had not Davoût declared that the abandonment of their regiments by the soldiers during the late events should be considered only as a proof of devotion for the Emperor? and had not the sage Drouot himself decided to reinstate in the *cadres* of the Old Guard the subalterns cashiered in 1814 for having deserted "from grief at the departure of His Majesty?" What an example for an army!

On March 20th the dragoons of the Guard arrived from Tours; they learned upon the quays that the Emperor was holding a review. A year had passed since they had last seen their idol. They hurried their officers along with them, filed through the gate of the Louvre, and debouched at a rapid trot, all covered with mud, and horses reeking with sweat, upon the Place du Carrousel, vociferating, "Long live the Emperor!" Some days later, at an inspection with open ranks, some dragoons gave the signal. Suddenly the first rank wheeled about, and the two ranks raised their sabres and crossed them above the head of the Emperor. He laughingly bowed his head, and finished the inspection under a vault of steel. Fanaticism for Napoleon may excuse this lack of discipline and these caprices contrary to the regulations. But there were graver faults.

The troops of Grouchy, on the march from Pont-Saint-Esprit to Marseilles, after the capitulation of La Pallud, were guilty of the greatest excesses at Orgon, under pretence that the preceding year, when the exiled Napoleon had passed through this town, the inhabitants had wished to hang him. At Aire (Pas-de-Calais) the 105th of the Line, *en route* for the frontier, commenced to demolish a new house whose façade was decorated with *fleurs de lys*. In order to calm the soldiers, the commandant of the place was compelled to imprison the unfortunate owner.

At Aix some cannoneers, offended at seeing some young Royalists walking about with enormous white roses pinned to the lapels of their coats, dispersed them with sabre-blows. At Saint-Germain the sharpshooters of the Young Guard mutinied and refused to enter their barracks because there was no tricolour flag over the entrance. In the theatres the soldiers maltreated the spectators who did not applaud the "Marseillaise." In the cafés they beat the men who refused to cry, "Long live the Emperor!" Having entered Belgium, they pillaged as hard as they could.

"The Army," wrote General Radet, commander of the *gendarmerie*, to Soult on June 17th, "is infected with the spirit of marauding and pillage. The Guard itself sets an example. Some magazines of flour have been pillaged and horses at picket stolen. All night the homes of the Belgians, who have given every- thing willingly and have cared for our wounded, have been sacked. The soldiers do not recognize the authority of the *gendarmerie*. I herewith tender my resignation as provost-general of the Army."

Some of the regiments refused the sea-biscuits. Friant complained that the grenadiers of the Guard carried women with them. A *voltigeur* of the 96th deserted in arms to visit his parents. He returned at the end of eight days, and his colonel only inflicted upon him a slight disciplinary punishment. Two hundred and ninety-two soldiers of the 39th and 59th of the Line declared that they would desert if they were not placed in the Guard. Some men of the train, who had followed the Emperor from Grenoble, had themselves incorporated with the 1st Hussars, and some hussars belonging to this regiment caused themselves to be placed in the Guard. General Barrois, commanding a division of the Young Guard in formation, received this singular request:

"*Monsieur le Comte*, we are 1,374 men of the 1st and 2nd of the Line and of the 1st Light who have always served with honour. We believe that it is our duty to inform you that we do not wish to remain longer in our regiments, although we have nothing to complain of. But, having served in the Guard, we wish to continue to do so. It would be imprudent to attempt to hinder us, as the course which we have taken is irrevocable. You can prevent the fault which we are about to commit by obtaining our reinstatement in the Guard. But we do not wish to wait longer than four days. Our colonels are informed of our intentions."

There existed a state of rivalry between the different regiments, which provoked brawls and duels. The Emperor was forced to order the suppression, in the five regiments of cavalry bearing the No. 1, of the white shoulder-knots, of which the other regiments were jealous. The soldiers belonging to the Battalion of the Isle of Elba having been lodged in the Hôtel des Cent-Suisses, Place du Carrousel, some enthusiastic persons substituted for the inscription above the main entrance that of "*Quartier des Braves.*" The other braves of the Army, though they were all Bonapartists, looked upon this as an insult. The *grognards* were joked by their comrades of the line and even of the Old Guard. Many sabre-blows were exchanged. It became necessary to efface the inscription.

But if the Army was enervated by indiscipline, it was animated by impatience to fight, resolution to conquer, idolatry for the Emperor, and hatred of the foreigner. A spy wrote from Paris to Wellington about the middle of May:

To give a just idea of the enthusiasm of the Army, I need only to draw a parallel between the epochs of '92 and the present year. Still the balance will be in favour of Buonaparte, for today it is no longer enthusiasm; it is frenzy. The cause of the soldiers, who have nothing to hope for after the fall of their chief, is inseparable from his. So I cannot conceal from your Excellency that, whatever the Bourbonists may say, the fight will be bloody and bitterly contested.

"The troops," relates General Hulot, "were exalted to the highest degree; their ardour was a species of fanaticism."

"The moment chosen for taking the field," writes General Foy, on June 15th, in his daily notes, "is well timed. The troops experience not patriotism, not enthusiasm, but a veritable rage for the Emperor and against his enemies."

It was in all sincerity that a deserter and traitor, the Adjutant-Commandant Gordon, sent this information to Clarke:

The King, on his return, should disband the Army and create a new one. The soldiers are furious; their spirit is dreadful.

"The spirit of the soldiers is dreadful"—that is to say, all the soldiers demanded to be passed in review by the Emperor. They received the new eagles with enthusiastic acclamations and threatening oaths. They replied to the cries of "Long live the Army!" by cries of "Long live the Emperor!" They put for prizes small tricolour flags in the muzzles of their muskets. They swore, with sabres crossed above the flames of punch, to conquer or die.

They said, showing the bust of the Emperor: "He will be with us!" They raised at their expense a monument at the Gulf of Juan. They ordered medals struck commemorative of the Emperor's return. They abandoned one, two, and even five days' pay for the expenses of the war. They quitted their garrisons and traversed towns and villages crying, "Long live the Emperor!" and singing "*Le Père la Violette!*"' They tore the white flags in rags, which they put to the vilest uses. They arrested those who attempted to entice the soldiers to desert and beat them with the butts of their muskets. They tore the deserters from the hands of the gendarmes and degraded them without further trial. They wished to double the marches in order to be in the first battles. They declared they had no need of cartridges, since they would attack the enemy with the bayonet. They said "they cared not what became of them, provided the Emperor thrashed the Allies."

Sensitive, insolent, undisciplined; suspicious of its chiefs, troubled by the fear of treason, and thus accessible, perhaps, to panic, but inured to and loving war; a thirst for vengeance; capable of heroic efforts and furious transports, and more haughty, more exalted, and more ardent in fight than any other Republican or Imperial Army—such was the Army of 1815. Never had Napoleon had under his hand an instrument of war so redoubtable nor so fragile.

CHAPTER 2

The Plans of Campaign

1

On March 25, 1815, when, at Vienna, the sovereigns were busy hatching a seventh coalition against France, they had, to resist a sudden attack of Napoleon in Belgium, no more than 80,000 soldiers—30,000 Prussians, 14,000 Saxons, 23,000 Anglo-Hanoverians, and nearly 10,000 Dutch-Belgians. Furthermore, the Saxons were disposed to mutiny, and defections among the Dutch-Belgians were to be feared. The greater part of the latter had served under Napoleon; and in Brussels, in all the Walloon country, and particularly in the provinces of Namur and Liège, which were subjected to the harsh occupation of the Prussians, there was a French party.

Stationed from Treves and Coblentz as far as Courtray and Antwerp, over an extent of seventy leagues, the allied troops had, on March 15th, commenced some movements of concentration; but Napoleon would have none the less been able to cross the Belgian frontier with 50,000 men on April 1st, and three days later to enter Brussels without striking a blow. Wellington was at Vienna and Blücher at Berlin. The French would have met with no resistance, as the Prince of Orange and General Kleist, who commanded the Prussian Army in the Rhenish provinces, had decided to effect their concentration, in case of an attack, at Tirlemont (eleven leagues to the east of Brussels).

Would this easy success have sufficed, as the Emperor imagined, to raise Belgium? At all events, without imposing upon experienced soldiers, the occupation of Brussels would have produced a great effect in France and in foreign countries. The Prussian generals, the Prince of Orange, and even Wellington, feared this sudden attack.

"It is necessary to cover Brussels," wrote Müffling to the King of the Low Countries, "in order that this city may not become the focus of a revolution."

"It would be of the utmost importance for Bonaparte," wrote Wellington to Gneisenau, "to cause us to retrograde behind Brussels, to drive away the King of France, and to overturn the order of things which has been established by the King of the Low Countries. It would have a terrible effect upon public opinion." But this audacious blow, of which Napoleon had conceived the idea, and the execution of which he judged easy and certain, was abandoned by him as soon as conceived. He understood too well that a victory gained over only one-tenth of the forces of the coalition would be regarded by the Allies as a simple advance-guard affair, and that this victory, even should it result in the uprising of Belgium, would not end the war.

In passing the Sambre on April 1st he would have then compromised the future for an ephemeral success, for the ex-Royal Army, while being able to furnish immediately 50,000 excellent troops, was not in condition to undertake a campaign of some duration. Men, arms, horses, supplies—all were lacking. Now the Emperor could not at the same time direct the operations in Belgium and reorganize the Army. Moreover, in order to form an army of 50,000 men, it would have been necessary to take all the available men in the garrisons of the northern departments, whose population was so hostile to the Empire, and to employ the reserve of Paris, destined in case of necessity to act in the West, where the Vendéan chiefs were very active, and in the Midi, where Bordeaux, Toulouse, and Marseilles still recognized the authority of the Duke of Angoulême, who was preparing to march on Lyons.

If the military state of Prance prevented the captain from taking the field too quickly, the political situation prohibited the sovereign. Eight days after having re-ascended the throne. Napoleon could not abandon the government to fight unless circumstances imperiously demanded it. It was more urgent to reorganize the administration, to fill the treasury, and to pacify the country. For gaining the hearts of the French, all of whom so ardently desired peace, what an admirable expedient would have been the invasion of Belgium!

Would not the effect produced by the capture of Brussels have been counter-balanced by the fright occasioned by seeing Napoleon, hardly returned to France, putting on his seven-league boots to hasten to new conquests? The Emperor had still another reason—and it was better than the others—not to commence war before having exhausted all means of accommodation; like his people, though doubtless not for so long a time, he desired the maintenance of peace.

For more than one long month the Emperor persisted in believing peace possible. "If we have war . . . .," he wrote again on April 30th to Davoût, from whom he had nothing to conceal. Nevertheless, whatever might be the tenacity of his illusions, he none the less prepared to defend himself. He had called out the reserves, mobilized the National Guards, and given orders for the reorganization of the *matériel*. But it was only about the middle of May, when he had almost lost all hope of avoiding war, that he decided upon his plan of campaign.

2

The Allies had been at work upon their plan since the beginning of April. There were many plans proposed. Knesebeck seriously proposed to deceive Napoleon by delivering to him a false plan. He said: "We will lead the enemy to believe that we intend operating by way of Bâle; that he has nothing to fear from the English Army, which will be occupied with the siege of Dunkirk, or from the Prussian Army, which will remain on the defensive. We will thus attract Buonaparte between the Marne and the Upper Rhine against the Austrian, Bavarian, and Russian armies, whilst the English and Prussians advance without opposition towards Paris."

Schwarzenberg renewed the art of war by gravely declaring that the Allies should "neither divide themselves too much, for fear of weakening themselves, nor march in such large masses, for fear of not being able to subsist." He concluded by saying that it was necessary to march on Paris in three strong columns, "and to leave the details of the operations to the knowledge and experience of the commanders."

The plan of Gneisenau—a crushing and redoubtable plan—was based upon the enormous numerical superiority of the Allies. Gneisenau said: "Four great armies, of which the fourth—the Russian Army—will form the reserve, will enter France simultaneously and march straight on Paris. Regardless of what may happen to one of the three armies of the First Line—whether it is beaten or not—the two others will continue to advance, making some detachments upon their rear to observe the fortresses. The Russian or reserve army will be destined to repair the checks which may be suffered by one of the armies of the first line. For this, it will advance directly to the aid of the army that may be in retreat, or will manoeuvre on the flank of the enemy.

Supposing that Napoleon defeats one of the armies of the first line, the other two, continuing to advance, will gain ground and thus draw nearer Paris, whilst the army of reserve will assist the defeated army. If, in place of pursuing the beaten army, Napoleon directs himself on the flank of another army of the first line, the re- serve will unite with the latter, so that the battle will turn to the disadvantage of the enemy. Meanwhile, the third army will continue to advance, and the one which will have been defeated will rally and then resume the offensive."

Wellington's idea was to begin hostilities without awaiting the arrival of the Russian Army, and even before the three armies had finished their concentration. He wrote on April 10th:

"It is sufficient to direct between the Sambre and the Meuse 60,000 Anglo-Dutch, 60,000 Prussians, and 140,000 Austro-Bavarians, in order to find ourselves in France with forces superior to those of the enemy, and to be able to manoeuvre in the direction of Paris."

Greatly preoccupied with the interests of Louis XVIII., Wellington judged that each new day of the truce affirmed the power of Napoleon; and, believing in the importance of a Royalist uprising in the Midi, he deemed it necessary to second it by prompt action on the northern frontier.

At Vienna the allied generals were not so eager to begin. They wished to make this war without risks. They desired, in each battle, to be at least three to one, and "to conquer according to the rules of mechanics and the laws of gravitation." In the council of war held on April 19th, and which was presided over by the Czar, it was decided that, in order to give the different armies time to effect their concentration, the campaign should open only on June 1st.

This was one month lost according to Wellington and Blücher; one month gained, according to Knesebeck and Schwarzenberg. The latter intended even to gain another month by the discussion of the strategical plan. It fact, June 10th, at the time when Blücher, who had had, however, the diversion of a revolt of the Saxons, "had become enraged" at remaining inactive, and had said to his soldiers that he was impatient to go to seek his pipe, which he had forgotten in Paris, Schwarzenberg caused to be adopted by the sovereigns a definite plan, the execution of which was to begin only between June 27th and July 1st.

According to these new dispositions, six armies would cross simultaneously the frontiers of France: the Army of the Low Countries (93,000 English, Hanoverians, Brunswickers, and Dutch-Belgians, under Wellington), between Maubeuge and Beaumont; the Prussian Army (117,000 men, under Blücher), between Philippeville and Givet; the Russian Army (150,000 men, under Barclay de Tolly), by Saar-Louis and Saarbrück; the Army of the Upper Rhine (210,000 Austrians, Bavarians, Würtemburgers, and Hessians, under Schwarzenberg; the right wing by Sarreguemines and the main body by Bâle. These four great armies would march concentrically on Paris—the English by

Péronne, the Prussians by Laon, the Russians by Nancy, and the Austrians by Langres.

On the extreme left the Army of Upper Italy (38,000 Austrians and 12,000 Piedmontese, under Frimont) and the Austrian Army of Naples (25,000 men, under Bianchi) would pass the Alps and direct themselves, the first on Lyons, the second on Provence, where the English squadron of the Mediterranean would second its operations.

3

By secret reports from Vienna and Brussels and by the foreign journals—the press was already indiscreet—Napoleon was able to form a general idea of the forces and plans of the enemy. Two plans of campaign presented themselves to his mind.

The first plan consisted in massing under Paris the 1st, 2nd, 3rd, 4th, and 6th Corps, the Guard, the reserve cavalry, and the Army of the Rhine (5th Corps); in concentrating under Lyons the Army of the Alps and the Corps of the Jura; and in permitting the Allies to engage themselves in the net-work of fortresses, well provisioned and defended by nearly 150,000 mobilized National Guards, retired soldiers, cannoneers of the Line, veterans, custom-house officers, *gendarmes*, and urban National Guards. The allied armies, which were not to pass the frontiers until July 1st, would be unable to arrive within the radius of Lyons until the 15th or 18th. and within that of Paris until the 25th. By this time (July 25th) the entrenchments of Paris would be completed; the garrison would number 30,000 regular troops, 18,000 Federate Sharpshooters, and 36,000 National Guards. The army concentrated under Paris would have 200,000 soldiers; and there would remain nearly 80,000 men in the depôts and 158,000 recruits.

As, of the 645,000 Allies who would enter France, 75,000 would manoeuvre in the Lyoness and Provence, and as, on account of the multiplicity of his lines of operations, the enemy would be forced to leave in the rear 150,000 men to protect his communications and besiege or mask the fortresses, the four great armies would have, on arriving between the Oise and the Seine, but 420,000 combatants. To these 420,000 men Napoleon would oppose 200,000 soldiers of the active army and the entrenched camp of Paris. He would recommence the campaign of 1814, but with 200,000 soldiers, instead of 90,000, and with Paris fortified, defended by 80,000 men, and having as Governor the skilful captain of Auerstaedt and Eckmühl, the fierce defender of Hambourg, Davoût.

The second plan—bolder, more conformable to the genius of Napoleon, to the temperament of the French, and even to the principles of great war, but terribly more hazardous—was to attack the enemy before his forces were united. By June 15th the Emperor would be able to concentrate upon the northern frontier an army of 125,000 men. He would enter Belgium, beat there one after the other the English and Prussians; then, after having received reinforcements from the depôts, he would make his junction with the 23,000 men under the command of Rapp, and direct himself against the Austro-Russians.

Doubtless, if the Emperor had had to look only at the military side of the question, he would have adopted the first plan, the success of which appeared certain. But he had no longer his liberty of action of 1805, nor even of 1812. He must, though commander-in-chief, reckon with public opinion. What an impression would have been produced in the country by the abandonment without defence of nearly one-third of the territory, and precisely those departments the most patriotic and the most devoted to the imperial cause! Would it not cause everywhere discouragement and disaffection, excite even to hostility the ill-will of the Chamber, extend in the West and rekindle in 'the Midi the fires of insurrection? The Emperor felt that, in order to raise the courage of the people and impose upon the malcontent and factious, it would be necessary, at the beginning of hostilities, for him to gain a brilliant victory.

Moreover, abandoning himself to his customary illusions, he imagined this victory would be decisive enough to break up the coalition. The Belgians, he thought, would range themselves under the French flag, and the destruction of Wellington's army would lead to the fall of the Tory cabinet, which would be succeeded by one in favour of peace. If it should turn out otherwise, the Army, victorious over the English and Prussians in Belgium, would conquer also in France the Russians and Austrians. At the worst—admitting a check on the Belgian frontier—the Emperor would be able to withdraw under Paris, and operate according to the defensive plan. The Emperor, however, did not conceal from himself the fact that, after a defeat in Belgium, the chances in favour of the success of his first plan, to which it would be necessary to return, would be greatly diminished. He would have lost a great many men, weakened the *morale* of the army and country, provoked the Allies to advance by fifteen days their entrance into France, and, necessarily, on account of not being able to do everything at the same time, neglected somewhat the organization of the defence.

The Emperor meditated for a long time upon these plans. When he had determined in favour of the offensive, he was still undecided for some days upon the point where he would strike his first blows. For the success of his plan, which was to defeat one after the other the two armies occupying Belgium, it was necessary to attack Wellington or Blücher before they had effected their junction. In taking his line of operations on Brussels by Ath, and debouching from Lille or Condé against Wellington's right. Napoleon would drive back the English Army on the Prussians, and would find himself, two days later, before the two united armies.

If, on the contrary, he advanced against Blücher's left by Givet and the valley of the Meuse, he would likewise hasten the junction of the two armies by pushing the Prussians upon the English. By one of his finest strategical conceptions, the Emperor resolved to advance boldly against the very centre of the enemy's cantonments, upon the supposed point of concentration of the Anglo-Prussians. As the route from Charleroi to Brussels formed the line of contact of the two armies, it was upon this route that Napoleon intended to burst, by Beaumont and Philippeville, with the rapidity of a thunderbolt.

4

The orders of concentration were given in the first days of June. The 1st Corps advanced from Valenciennes to Avèsnes; the 2nd, from Avèsnes to Maubeuge; the 3rd, from Rocroi to Chimay; the 4th, from Thionville to Rocroi; the 6th, from Soissons to Avèsnes; and the Imperial Guard, from Paris by Soissons to Avèsnes. The communications with Belgium and the Rhenish provinces were intercepted; in the seaports an embargo was placed on all vessels, even on the fishing barks; and, in order to give no warning to the advance posts of the enemy, some free corps and divisions of National Guards replaced upon the northern and eastern frontiers the troops directed upon the points of concentration.

When Napoleon, who had quitted Paris in the night, arrived at Laon at noon on June 11th, all the troops had effected their concentration. Grouchy alone, whose headquarters were precisely at Laon, had not yet caused his four cavalry corps to budge. Summoned to the quarters of the Emperor, he said that he had received no orders. In fact, it was not until the next day, June 12th, that the Major-General thought of sending him from Avèsnes the instructions of Napoleon! But immediately after having seen the Emperor, Grouchy had sent the order to the four cavalry corps to repair to the frontier by forced marches; himself, without losing an hour, had departed for Avèsnes. The concentration was not delayed, since all the reserve cavalry arrived beyond Avèsnes on the night of the 13th; but many regiments had been forced to make twenty leagues without unbridling—a bad start for horses at the opening of a campaign If only this vexatious incident had called the attention of Napoleon to the negligence of his major-general!

On June 13th the Emperor slept at Avèsnes; and on the evening of the 14th he advanced his headquarters to Beaumont, in the centre of his army. In spite of the unfavourable weather, all the troops bivouacked this night in order to remain well concentrated. At dawn there was read to them in front of their bivouacs the following order of the day of the Emperor:

... Soldiers, today is the anniversary of Marengo and Friedland, which twice settled the destiny of Europe. Then, as after Austerlitz and Wagram, we were too generous. Today, however, leagued against us, the princes whom we have left upon their thrones aim at the independence and the most sacred rights of France. They have begun the most unjust of aggressions. Let us then march to encounter them. Are we not still the same men?

The army occupied the following positions: The 1st Corps (20,731 men, under Drouet d'Erlon), forming the extreme left, between the routes of Avèsnes, at Maubeuge and Solre-sur-Sambre; the 2nd Corps (25,179 men under Reille), between Solre-sur-Sambre and Leers; the 3rd Corps (18,105 men under Vandamme); and the 6th Corps (10,821 men, under Lobau), between Beaumont and the frontier; the 4th corps (15,404 men, under Gérard), between Philippeville and Florenne; the reserve cavalry (13,144 men, under Grouchy), at Valcourt, Bossus, and Gayolle; the Imperial Guard (20,755 men), in front and rear of Beaumont. This army had 370 pieces of artillery. The ground occupied by the bivouacs did not exceed eight leagues in width by ten kilometres in length.

In ten days 124,000 men, separated by distances ranging from twelve to seventy leagues, had united on the frontier, within close cannon range of the enemy's advance posts, without the Allies having taken a single defensive measure. Never had a march of concentration been better conceived, nor, save a few delays, which were quickly repaired, more successfully executed.

While the French Army thus formed a formidable mass, the Anglo-Prussians were still disseminated over a front of more than thirty-five leagues and a medium depth of twelve. On June 14th Blücher's headquarters were at Namur. The 1st Corps (30,800 men, under Ziethen), which formed the right of the Prussian Army, occupied Thuin, Fontaine-Lévêque, Marchienne, Charleroi, Moustiers, Fleurus, Sombreffe, and Gembloux; the 2nd Corps (31,000 men, under Pirch I.), Namur, Héron, and Hannut; the 3rd Corps (23,900 men, under Thielmann), Ciney, Dinant, and Huy; the 4th Corps (30,300 men, under Bülow), Liège and Tongres.

The cantonments of the English Army under Wellington, who had established his headquarters in Brussels, extended from the Lys and the Escault to the little river Haine. The 2nd Corps (27,321 men, under Lord Hill), occupied Leuze, Ath, Audenarde, Ghent, and Alost; the 1st Corps (30,246 men, under the Prince of Orange), Mons, Roeulx, Frasnes, Seneffe, Nivelles, Genappe, Soignies, Enghein, and Braine-le-Comte; the cavalry corps (9,913 men, under Lord Uxbridge), cantoned along the Dender, between Ninove and Grammont; and the reserve (25,597 men, under the immediate command of Wellington), in Brussels and environs.

In the positions which they occupied three days were required for each of the two armies to concentrate on the line of contact and double this time to concentrate on the English right or Prussian left wing. This outrageous extension of the cantonments, so dangerous in front of an adversary like Napoleon, and so favourable to the success of the bold plan that he had conceived, has been criticised by almost all military writers. Wellington has attempted to justify these dispositions by alleging the difficulty experienced in subsisting the troops and the necessity of guarding every point.

As a matter of fact, it was because, while admitting the hypothesis of an attack by Napoleon, and though they had even come to some understanding regarding the method of guarding against such an eventuality, the Allies believed it highly improbable. On June 15th, at the hour when the Emperor had already his foot upon the Belgian soil, Wellington tranquilly stated, in a long letter to the Czar, how he intended to assume the offensive at the end of the month. Some days previous Blücher had written to his wife: "We shall soon enter France. We might remain here a year, for Bonaparte will not attack us."

CHAPTER 3

First Combats

1

On June 15th, at 3:30 p.m., the French advance guards passed the frontier at Leers, Cour-sur-Heure, and Thy. According to the order of march despatched from the Imperial Headquarters on the evening of the day before, the army marched on Charleroi in three principal columns: the left column (corps of Reille and d'Erlon), by Thuin and Marchienne; the central column (corps of Vandamme and Lobau, Imperial Guard, and Grouchy's cavalry reserve), by Ham-sur-Heure, Jamioulx, and Marcinelle; and the right column (Guard's corps), by Florenne and Gerpinnes.

The Emperor had combined everything from a strategical point of view to facilitate the rapid passage of these masses and to spare the men the enervating fatigue of trampling upon the same spot; and he had prepared everything from a tactical point of view to permit of the prompt deployment and mutual aid of the different columns, in case the enemy should offer serious resistance. Thirty minutes were to elapse between the breaking camp of the different army corps. The troops nearest the frontier were to put themselves in motion at three o'clock in the morning, while those the most distant were not to move until eight. Twelve regiments of cavalry reconnoitred the march.

The remainder of the mounted troops were ordered to march on the left of the infantry. The sappers of each army corps were to be united and to march in each corps behind the first regiment of light infantry. Three companies of *pontoniers*, with fifteen pontoons and the same number of boats, were selected to follow immediately the corps of Vandamme; the ambulances were to follow the imperial head-quarters. There was an order to burn every carriage that should slip into the columns, and, until a new order, the baggage and reserve parks were not to approach nearer than three leagues to the army.

The generals in command of the advance, guards were expected to regulate their march so as to remain always abreast of one another; they were to reconnoitre in every direction; interrogate the inhabitants upon the positions of the enemy; seize the letters in the post-offices; communicate to one another any information which they might have; and to address frequent reports to the Emperor, who would be in person with the advance of the central column. All the Army was to have passed the Sambre before noon.

This order of march is justly regarded as a model. Never in the auspicious hours of Austerlitz and Friedland had Napoleon dictated a disposition of march more elaborate or better conceived; never had his genius been more lucid; never had he shown better his application to detail, his broad views upon the *ensemble*, his perspicuity, and his mastery of the art of war.

Unfortunately, the orders were not executed punctually. Drouet d'Erlon took it upon himself to postpone his movement until half-past four o'clock, instead of striking his camp at three, as had been prescribed. Vandamme, who was to have set out at three o'clock, awaited still at five the instructions from the imperial headquarters. During the night the officer who bore the order of march fell from his horse, broke his leg, and remained inert and isolated in the midst of the fields. Vandamme was informed of the march of the Army only by the arrival of Lobau's corps in the rear of his bivouacs. Finally, the troops of Gérard, who were also to set out at three o'clock, were not massed at the point of concentration, abreast of Florenne, until seven o'clock.

The soldiers of the 4th Corps were in great agitation. They had just learned that General Bourmont, commanding the leading division, had passed over to the enemy. This desertion confirmed very inopportunely the fears of treason and the suspicions against the chiefs by which the minds of the soldiers had been troubled for three months. Murmurs and imprecations arose from the ranks. One of Bourmont's brigade commanders. General Hulot, "judging the moment critical," harangued the two regiments under his orders; he swore to them solemnly, sword in hand, "to combat with them the enemies of France until his last breath."

Gérard, in turn, deemed it necessary to pass along the front of the troops and address a few words to them; they replied by acclamations. Gérard himself was greatly troubled by the desertion of his protégé Bourmont, the particulars of which were given to him by Hulot. A little after five o'clock in the morning Bourmont had mounted his horse at Florenne with all his staff—Colonel Clouet, Major Villoutreys, Captains d'Andigné, de Trélan, and Sourda—and an escort of five *chasseurs*. After having passed the French advance posts, he gave to a corporal of chasseurs a letter for Gérard, which he had written at Florenne; and having thus dismissed the escort, he rode rapidly with his officers in the direction of the frontier. He said in his letter to Gérard:

> . . . I do not wish to contribute towards establishing in France a bloody despotism which would ruin my country. ... I would have resigned and returned to my home if I had thought that I would have been permitted to do so. This not appearing probable, I have been forced to assure my liberty by other means. . . . No one shall see me in the ranks of the enemy. He shall obtain from me no information capable of injuring the French Army, composed of men whom I love and for whom I shall never cease to bear a lively attachment.

Two hours after having written this protestation that he was not a deserter and traitor, Bourmont revealed to Colonel von Schutter, commanding the Prussian advance posts along the Sambre, that the French would attack Charleroi in the afternoon. A little later he said to Colonel Reiche, Ziethen's *aide-de-camp*, that the French Army numbered 120,000 men. Finally, when, about three o'clock, he met Blücher near Sombreffe, he would have, no doubt, hastened to answer all the questions asked him. But the old soldier, disgusted at seeing a man wearing the uniform of a general of division deserting on the morning of a battle, hardly deigned to speak to him.

An officer of the Prussian staff having remarked to the field marshal that he should show himself less brusque towards Bourmont, since the latter wore a white cockade, Blücher, without caring whether he was understood by the renegade, who might understand German, said in a loud tone: "What matters the cockade? A traitor will always be a traitor."

2

The enemy had no need of information from the Count de Bourmont. On June 9th Ziethen and General Dörnberg, who commanded the light cavalry brigade detached in front of Mons, were informed of great movements of troops towards the frontier. On the 12th General Dörnberg had forwarded to Wellington, who had transmitted it to Blücher, the information that 100,000 French were concentrating between Avèsnes and Philippeville. On the 13th this same Dörnberg, who had numerous spies along the frontier, wrote direct to Blücher that an attack appeared imminent. On the 14th Pirch II. announced from Marchienne that the French would attack the next day. In the evening the Prussian advance posts were thoroughly informed of the proximity of the Imperial Army. It was in vain that the precaution had been taken to build the camp-fires in the hollows of the ground. The light from these innumerable braziers were reflected upon the heavens, which were illumined by a great white light.

While believing that Napoleon would not take the offensive, Wellington and Blücher, however, in an interview held at Tirlemont on May 3rd, had concerted together in anticipation of this eventuality. Did they decide on this day, as a number of historians state, upon a concentration on the line of Sombreffe-Quatre-Bras? It is doubtful, for they were ignorant whether the French Army would debouch by Philippeville, Maubeuge, Condé, or Lille. It is far more probable that the two commanders-in-chief had agreed only upon a junction in front of Brussels without fixing the precise point—circumstances would dictate this point. Two days after the conference of Tirlemont, Blücher, always zealous for the cause of the Allies, had prescribed to his troops, in order to bring them nearer to the English Army, a general movement on his right.

The 1st Corps concentrated at Fleurus and the 2nd at Namur; the 3rd. Corps marched from Treves on Arlon, then on Dinant and Huy; the 4th came from Coblentz to Malmédy and a little later to Liège. Blücher moved his headquarters from Liège to Namur. Ziethen, commanding the 1st Army Corps, the nearest one to the English cantonments, received the order to remain in close touch with Wellington's army. Blücher wrote to Ziethen on May 5th:

> In case of an attack, you will await at Fleurus the development of the enemy's manoeuvres, and you will inform the Duke of Wellington as well as myself of all that takes place as early as possible.

If not Wellington, who, upon Blücher's promise at Tirlemont to cover the left flank of the English Army, had *echeloned* his forces in such a manner as to protect especially the routes of Ath, Mons, and Nivelles, at least Blücher was prepared to meet an attack from the side of Charleroi. Before noon on June 14th the Field Marshal, informed by the reports of Pirch II. and Dörnberg, began to prepare for the concentration of his entire army at Fleurus.

The advance posts of Pirch II., who covered the front of Ziethen's corps, expected, on the night of the 14th, to be attacked at break of day. They received the French skirmishers with musket-shots; then, in danger of being outflanked, they retired foot by foot, from position to position, as far as the Sambre. In these different engagements, at Thuin, Ham, in the wood of Montigny, and at the farm of La Tombe, the Prussians lost nearly 500 men killed, wounded and prisoners. Continuing to push the enemy in front of them, the French heads of column arrived between nine and ten o'clock on the bank of the Sambre: Bachelu's division of Reille's corps before Marchienne, and Pajol's cavalry in front of Charleroi. The bridges were barricaded and defended by infantry and cannon. The attack of Marchienne—in preparing which a great deal of time was lost—consumed two hours.

It was only a little while before noon that the 2nd Light captured the bridge at the point of the bayonet. Reille at once ordered the 2nd Corps to debouch, but, the bridge being narrow, the four divisions and the cavalry did not finish their movement until the middle of the afternoon. The 1st Corps, which followed that of Reille, did not begin to cross the Sambre until 4 30 p. m. Pajol was also detained quite a while before the bridge of Charleroi. Between nine and ten o'clock the 1st Hussars attempted a hurrah, which failed under the sustained fire of sharpshooters concealed in the houses and behind the barricade.

It required infantry to force the barricade. Pajol resigned himself to await the arrival of Vandamme's corps, which he supposed was following him at a short distance. As we know, this army corps had struck camp four hours late. About eleven o'clock Pajol saw arriving not Vandamme, but the Emperor in person with the sappers of the Guard and the Young Guard of Duhesme. Informed of Vandamme's delay, Napoleon had ordered Duhesme's division to quit its place in the central column and to advance at a rapid pace towards Charleroi by a cross-road. Sappers and marines hurled themselves on the bridge, swept the barricade, and opened the way for Pajol's squadrons. The Prussians having retired, the horsemen, climbing at a rapid trot the steep and winding street which traverses Charleroi from north to south, pursued them along the route of Charleroi.

Not far from Charleroi the road branches off in two directions—the one to the left leads to Brussels, while the other goes to Fleurus. Pajol despatched the 1st Hussars along the Brussels route, and with the main body of his cavalry he advanced along the Fleurus route, by which the Prussians, who had been dislodged from Charleroi, were retreating.

3

It was a little past noon. The Emperor, acclaimed by the inhabitants, traversed Charleroi. He halted at the foot of the crumbling glacis at some hundred yards on this side of the spot where the routes of Fleurus and Brussels branch, near a little tavern called Belle-Vue, from which all the valley of the Sambre may be seen. He dismounted from his horse, ordered a chair to be brought from Belle-Vue, and seated himself on the side of the road. The troops defiled. On perceiving him, cavalry and infantry uttered cheers which drowned the roll of drums and the blare of trumpets. The enthusiasm bordered on frenzy; some of the soldiers issued from the ranks "in order to embrace the horse of their Emperor."

According to an eye-witness. Napoleon soon sank into a deep slumber, from which the noise of the acclamations was insufficient to awaken him. This fact will not appear improbable if we recall to mind that in Paris, in the months of April and May, 1815, the Emperor was often afflicted with these sudden fits of drowsiness, and if we remember that on this day at noon he had already remained seven or eight hours on horseback.

Gourgaud, who had accompanied the 1st Hussars along the route of Brussels, returned about two o'clock to announce that the Prussians showed themselves in force at Gosselies. The Emperor sent him immediately to Marchienne, with the order for Reille to March on Gosselies. Anxious, however, for his left until the execution of this movement, he ordered one of Duhesme's regiments of the Young Guard and a battery of horse artillery to take position on the Brussels route at two kilometres from Charleroi. Soon after he ordered Lefebvre-Desnoëttes to push forward to the support of the 1st Hussars with the light cavalry of the Guard (lancers and *chasseurs*); and he dictated to Soult a letter for d'Erlon, enjoining the latter to march on Gosselies in order to second Reille. This letter had just been despatched—it was a little after three o'clock—when Marshal Ney arrived.

Having arrived by post at Avèsnes on June 14th without his horses and with a single *aide-de-camp*, Ney had found the next day nothing but a peasant's cart to carry him to Beaumont. There, on the morning of the 15th, he had purchased two horses from Marshal Mortier, ill from an attack of sciatica, and had ridden rapidly towards Charleroi, skirting the columns on the march. The soldiers recognized him; they appeared glad to see him again. "Everything is all right now!" they cried; "here is Red-head."

The Emperor, who also wished that "everything should be all right," said to the Marshal: "Good-day, Ney. I am glad to see you. You will take command of the 1st and 2nd Army Corps. I give you also the light cavalry of the Guard, but you must not use it. Tomorrow you will be joined by the *cuirassiers* of Kellermann. Go, push the enemy on the Brussels route, and take position at Quatre-Bras."

On the ground, and in presence of the enemy, the fine strategical plan conceived in Paris by the Emperor takes form and develops itself. He intended only, on this first day, to advance on the presumed point of junction of the two allied armies, so as to forestall them on this point. Now, since his adversaries leave him the time, he will extend his field of action and render it impossible for them to unite. The main body of the English coming from Brussels and that of the Prussians from Namur, the two armies must necessarily effect their junction by the highway leading from Namur to Nivelles, which passes through Sombreffe and crosses at Quatre-Bras the route from Charleroi to Brussels. The Emperor wishes then to push his left wing to Quatre-Bras and his right wing to Sombreffe. He will establish himself at Fleurus, the summit of the triangle formed by these three points, ready to burst the next day with his reserve upon that one of the hostile armies which will approach first. If both of them retreat, he will gain Brussels without firing a cannon.

Grouchy arrived as the Emperor finished giving his instructions to Marshal Ney, who set out immediately to put them in execution. Grouchy had arrived an hour previous, with Exelmans' dragoons, at the bridge of Charleroi, over which the Young Guard was still defiling; impatient to rejoin his 1st Corps of cavalry, which he supposed was engaged with the enemy, he had outstripped the column, and had pushed on to Gilly at a gallop. After having reconnoitred this position, he had returned to obtain the Emperor's orders. The latter, wishing to see for himself, immediately mounted his horse. It was then after three o'clock. The dragoons of Exelmans had finished debouching behind the Guard, and the advance of Vandamme's corps had entered Charleroi.

General Pirch II. had established his division in the rear of Gilly, its front covered by the boggy stream of Grand-Rieux. Four battalions and a battery were stationed upon the acclivities of the wooded heights which command the valley from the Abbey of Soleillemont to Châtelineau; three other battalions were in reserve near Lambusart; and a regiment of dragoons observed the Sambre from Châtelet to Farciennes. Deceived by the extension of this line of battle—extension precisely intended to impose upon the French—Grouchy valued the forces of the enemy at 20,000 men. The Emperor judged, at first glance that there were no more than 10,000. He settled with Grouchy, who had been verbally invested with the command of the right wing, the dispositions for attack. One of Vandamme's divisions, seconded by Pajol's cavalry, would attack the enemy in front, whilst Grouchy, with Excelmans' dragoons, would ford the stream near the mill of Delhatte and take them in flank. Then the Prussians were to be pursued as far as Sombreffe, where the French would take position.

After giving these orders, the Emperor returned to Charleroi in order to hasten the march of Vandamme's corps. It would have been better had he remained at Gilly. In his absence, Vandamme and Grouchy consumed two hours in combining their attack. About 5 30 p. m. the Emperor, surprised at not hearing the cannon, returned upon the ground and ordered Vandamme to plunge headlong against the enemy.

After a short cannonade, which silenced Pirch's guns, three columns, of two battalions each, rushed forward with fixed bayonets. The Prussians posted in the first line did not await the shock. In accordance with Ziethen's order, Pirch put them immediately in retreat. Irritated at seeing these battalions retiring without loss, the Emperor ordered one of his *aides-de-camp*, General Letort, "to charge and crush the Prussian infantry" with the squadrons on duty or serving about his person.

Letort does not take time to unite the four squadrons. He starts with the dragoons alone; the others will follow when they are ready! He crosses the stream to the north of the route, where it is not so deeply embanked; recrosses the route of Sart-Allet in front of Vandamme's columns, and bursts upon the retreating Prussians. Of the four battalions of the enemy two succeed in gaining the wood of Soleillemont; the other two, formed in squares, are overthrown and sabred; the few survivors flee into the woods, the skirts of which are occupied by the first regiment of western Prussia. In pursuing them Letort is struck by a ball in the belly and falls, mortally wounded, from his horse. The soldiers adored this gentle and intrepid chief, and they avenged his death by massacring every Prussian who came within reach of their long swords.

During this combat the dragoons of Exelmans, with the brigades of Burthe and Vincent leading, debouched above Châtelineau, overthrew the dragoon regiment of Colonel Moisky, chased a battalion from the wood of Pironchamp, and threw it back on Lambusart. All the troops of Pirch had rallied there, and the enemy showed a disposition to defend himself. Attacked simultaneously by the dragoons of Exelmans and the light cavalry of Pajol, who had outstripped the columns of Vandamme, he withdrew beyond Fleurus. Grouchy had conducted in person the attack on the right. Although the day was declining, he wished to take possession of Fleurus, occupied only by two battalions, and to push the Prussians as far as Sombreffe, in accordance with the orders of the Emperor.

But Vandamme, who had already commenced to establish his bivouacs between Winage and the wood of Soleillemont, refused positively to go further, saying that his troops were too fatigued, and that, moreover, "he had no orders to receive from the commander of the cavalry." Grouchy, not being able to attack Fleurus without infantry, halted at the distance of two cannon-shots from this village. The corps of Exelmans and Pajol bivouacked in the first line, covering the infantry of Vandamme, between Lambusart and Campinaire.

4

The left wing also did not advance as far as Napoleon would have wished. The 1st Hussars, sent from Charleroi along the route of Brussels, had encountered, about half-past one o'clock, beyond Jumet, the cavalry of Lützow and the skirmishers of the 29th Regiment, which covered the concentration at Gosselies of the division of Steinmetz. Both parties observed each other for some time, then the two cavalries engaged. The *Uhlans* drove back briskly the hussars, when they were charged and repulsed in turn by the lancers of Piré, who formed the advance of Reille's corps. Reille hastened the march of his infantry, arrived about three o'clock within cannon-range of Gosselies, and opened fire against this village.

At the moment when the columns of attack began their movement Marshal Ney arrived with the light cavalry of the Guard, which he had overtaken *en route*, Gosselies, defended by the 29th Prussian Regiment, was occupied after a slight combat. However, the affair was not ended. The larger portion of the division of Steinmetz was still on the march to the west of Gosselies; by the occupation of this village the direct route to Heppignies and Fleurus was intercepted. Without hesitating, Steinmetz pushed several battalions against the French, who had started to debouch from Gosselies, thrust them back, and, under the protection of a strong detachment holding the houses on the northern side of the town, he continued his retreat on Heppignies.

The route of Brussels was open, and there were yet four hours of daylight. But Marshal Ney no doubt thought that, in spite of the formal order of the Emperor to push the enemy, he was already too far advanced with respect to the right wing of the Army. Instead of continuing his march with all his troops, he established the divisions of Girard, Foy, and Jérôme around Gosselies, directed on Mellet the division of Bachelu and the light cavalry of Piré, and only detached towards Quatre-Bras the lancers and *chasseurs* of the Guard.

Arrived, about half-past five o'clock, in sight of Frasnes, the lancers of the Guard were received with cannon-shots. The village was occupied by a battalion of Nassau troops and a horse battery, commanded by Major Normann. This officer, left without instructions, but hearing the cannonade at Gosselies, had at once prepared to defend bravely his post. Lefebvre-Desnoëttes immediately demanded some infantry. A battalion of the 2nd Light, forming the advance of Bachelu's division, and which had arrived abreast of Mellet, continued its route towards Frasnes in accelerating its pace. The skirmishers opened fire on the Nassau troops. Pending the arrival of this reinforcement, Lefebvre-Desnoëttes had directed a part of the lancers to the right of Frasnes, so as to turn the enemy.

The Squadron of the Isle of Elba (Poles), commanded by General Edouard de Colbert in person, pushed as far as Quatre-Bras, which was unoccupied. But Colbert found himself there without support, and very far from the main body of his division; he returned near Frasnes. Meanwhile the battalion of Major Normann had withdrawn along the route, always keeping the French within close cannon-range. It took portion upon the skirts of the wood of Bossu, at two kilometres in front of Quatre-Bras, where at this moment Prince Bernard of Saxe-Weimar arrived with four battalions of Nassau troops. Informed fortuitously at Genappe of the passage of the Sambre by the French, this young Prince had, on his own authority, put his troops on the march to occupy that important strategical point.

On hearing the cannonade. Marshal Ney rejoined his advance guard. He reconnoitred the position. Although the Nassau troops numbered only 4,500 with six guns, they were sufficient to defend Quatre-Bras against the 1,700 lancers and *chasseurs* of Lefebvre-Desnoëttes, supported by a single battalion. Ney contented himself with ordering a few rather feeble charges against the Nassau infantry, in position in front of Quatre-Bras, and directing to the east of this point, on the side of Sart Dame Aveline, a reconnaissance, which did not even approach within musket-range of the enemy's outposts. Then, a little before eight o'clock, he rejoined at Frasnes, where it had established itself, the division of Lefebvre-Desnoëttes, and returned to Gosselies to pass the night.

Colonel Heymès, Ney's *aide-de-camp* during this campaign, has said, in explanation of the Marshal's conduct, "that there was not one chance in ten" of taking possession of Quatre-Bras. As a matter of fact, when Ney arrived within sight of Quatre-Bras, not at ten in the evening, as Heymès pretends, but at seven at the latest, as we have just seen, he could hardly think of carrying this position with two regiments of cavalry and one battalion of infantry; but if at five in the afternoon, being then at Gosselies, he had put on the march along the Brussels route only one-fourth of the troops that had been entrusted to him by the Emperor—that is, two divisions of cavalry, two of infantry, and four batteries—before nine o'clock he would have exterminated in Quatre-Bras with these 14,000 men the 4,500 infantry of Prince Bernard of Saxe-Weimar, the greater part of whom had but ten cartridges.

In halting Reille's corps around Gosselies, Ney, for the first time in his life, had yielded to prudence. He had renounced occupying Quatre-Bras, if not by a cavalry post, in case this point should not be defended. He had judged that it would be compromising his army corps to place it *en flèche*, at four leagues from the right wing, in a position where it might be attacked by all of Wellington's forces. Some strategists have declared that Ney acted according to the true principles of the art of war. This may be possible. But if Prince Bernard of Saxe-Weimar had understood these principles, he would not have obeyed the inspiration to march on Quatre-Bras with four battalions, at the risk of being crushed there by the entire French Army.

Book Two
Ligny and Quatre-Bras
Chapter 1
The Morning of June 16th

1

The occupation of Quatre-Bras and Sombreffe on the evening of June 15th imposed itself only as a complement of the fine strategical operation conceived by Napoleon. The fact that Grouchy and Ney had not seized these two points was only an unfortunate incident. The essential object of the movement of the French Army, which was to advance on the first day upon the line of contact of the English and Prussians, was not the less attained. Almost without striking a blow, and in spite of delays in the march of many columns, the Emperor had passed the Sambre, made seven leagues upon the enemy's territory, and established his army in the very midst of the cantonments of the Allies. He had 124,000 men bivouacked within a triangle of three leagues.

The enemy appeared to be in disorder. During the entire day not an English uniform had been seen. At no point had the Prussians appeared in force; they had feebly disputed the passage of the Sambre, and their half-hearted though skilful and valiant defence of Gilly and Gosselies seemed rather to have been intended to protect a retreat than to cover a concentration.

When the Emperor, who had returned at night to Charleroi, had taken cognizance of the reports of Grouchy and Ney, he imagined that the Allies, disconcerted by his unforeseen aggression, were falling back on their bases of operations—the Prussians towards Liège and Maëstricht, the Anglo-Belgians towards Ostend and Antwerp. The direction pursued by the Prussian advance posts in their retreat from Thuin to Marchienne, from Fontaine-Lévêque and Marchienne to Gosselies, and from Charleroi and Gosselies to Fleurus, was of a nature to confirm this supposition.

If the Prussians had been manoeuvring to unite at once with the English, they would have retired towards the north; as it were, they had retreated towards the northeast, uncovering the route of Brussels. The resolution which Napoleon, judging from appearances, attributed to Blücher and Wellington, assured him the victory. The farther the allied armies departed from each other the more easy it would be to beat them. It was one thing to attack the English when the Prussians were within one march of them, and another thing if Wellington and Blücher were separated by fifteen or twenty leagues.

The Emperor determines upon his plan on the morning of June 16th, probably at six o'clock, perhaps earlier. With Grouchy and the right wing he will advance on Sombreffe and Gembloux. If a Prussian corps is still found in one or the other of these positions, he will attack it. The ground thus reconnoitred or swept on the east, he will recall the reserve, temporarily posted at Fleurus, and will rejoin with it Ney and the right wing at Quatre-Bras. Thence he will move on Brussels by a night march. He reckons that the head of column will arrive in Brussels on June 17th at seven in the morning.

The orders for this double movement were despatched by the Major-General between seven and eight o'clock in the morning; the order for Kellermann to direct himself on Gosselies, in order to be at the disposal of Marshal Ney; the order for Drouot to put the Guard on the march for Fleurus; the order for Lobau to push the 6th Corps half-way from Charleroi to Fleurus; and the order for Vandamme and Gérard to march on Sombreffe with the 3rd and 4th Corps, and to follow henceforth the instructions of Marshal Grouchy, commander of the right wing. Soult wrote to Ney to take position at Quatre-Bras with six divisions of infantry and the *cuirassiers* of Kellermann, and to push his other two divisions of infantry—one to Genappe (five kilometres beyond Quatre-Bras), with the cavalry of Piré, and the other to Marbais, with the cavalry of Lefebvre-Desnoëttes, in order to support eventually the right wing. Ney, finally, was to push some reconnaissances as far as possible along the routes of Nivelles and Brussels. As to Grouchy, he received the order to establish himself at Sombreffe, and to send from there an advance guard to Gembloux and some reconnaissances in every direction.

2

At the imperial headquarters these orders were being expedited when the Emperor received a note from Grouchy, stating that strong columns of the enemy, who appeared to be debouching by the route of Namur, were directing themselves towards Brye and Saint-Amand. While believing that the Prussians were in retreat. Napoleon had admitted the hypothesis of an encounter with them at Sombreffe, but he had been far from thinking that they would come to take position on the outskirts of Fleurus. This movement indicated that, far from withdrawing his troops and separating himself from the English Army, as the direction followed by his advance posts in their retreat the day before had caused him to think, Blücher was manoeuvring with the view of a battle for the same day in conjunction with Wellington. Instead of a rear guard or an isolated corps to be dislodged from Sombreffe or Gembloux, Napoleon would have to fight, north of Fleurus; the entire Prussian Army; and, as Blücher and Wellington would no doubt act in concert, the English would be met with in force on the route of Brussels.

This completely overturned the plan conceived by Napoleon. He could not defeat during the day the army of Blücher on the right, overthrow in the evening the army of Wellington on the left, and march in the night on. Brussels. Napoleon, however, was not disconcerted. With him suppositions changed swiftly into certainties. When he had supposed a thing, this thing must be such as he had supposed it. Fortune had so often declared in favour of his previsions! On the morning of June 16th he believed that Blücher was retreating and the route of Brussels open; then Blücher was retreating and the route of Brussels was open.

The movements reported by Grouchy could be only some demonstrations intended to be misleading. He would give a good account of these few Prussian regiments—merely a screen destined to mask the retreat of their main army. It seemed, moreover, that this was the opinion of Grouchy himself, for in the letter in which he reported the appearance of columns of the enemy in the direction of Saint-Amand he announced that he was uniting his troops in order to march on Sombreffe, in accordance with the orders of the previous day. If since five o'clock in the morning Grouchy had presumed that Blücher's entire army was concentrating to the west of Sombreffe, he would not have prepared for a movement on this village, at the risk of suffering a disastrous flank attack.

The Emperor then made no change in his orders. Far from changing anything in them, he wrote about eight o'clock to Ney and Grouchy in order to reiterate them and to hasten their execution. Knowing that his *aides-de-camp* were better mounted than the officers of the Major-General, he entrusted one of these letters to Flahault, the other to La Bédoyère; in this way he hoped that his two lieutenants would receive his iterative instructions before those even which had just been sent by Soult. In these duplicates the Emperor explained himself more fully upon a few details pertaining to the execution of his orders, and he revealed, what Soult had failed to do, that the object of the double movement on Sombreffe and Quatre-Bras was a night march on Brussels.

Between nine and ten o'clock in the morning, as Napoleon was on the point of setting out for Fleurus, an officer of lancers arrived from the left wing; he said "the enemy presented some masses on the side of Quatre-Bras." Fearing that the presence of these pretended masses might, as the day before, cause Ney to hesitate to march forward, the Emperor deemed it necessary to reassure him and to renew once more his orders. He at once had the major-general to write to him as follows:

> Blücher being yesterday at Namur, it is not probable that he has any troops at Quatre-Bras. Hence you will have an affair only with what comes from Brussels. Unite the corps of Counts Reille and d'Erlon and that of the Count de Valmy; with these forces you should be able to beat and destroy any force that may present itself.

However, in order to be prepared for every emergency, the Emperor ordered Lobau to remain temporarily at Charleroi, so that he could march, if necessary, with the 6th Corps to the assistance of Ney. In accordance with his orders, Adjutant-Commandant Janin, Lobau's assistant chief of staff, was sent to Frasnes in order to judge of the state of affairs.

The Emperor arrived at Fleurus a little before eleven o'clock. He there found Grouchy—not without some astonishment, for he supposed him already on the march for Sombreffe. The Marshal had no difficulty in making him understand that in the presence of the hostile masses, which were taking position to the north of Fleurus, he had been forced to limit himself to the occupation of that village, evacuated at daylight by the Prussians. Napoleon traversed the line of advance posts. In the midst of the plain of Fleurus there rises a mill in the shape of a tower, which dominates all the plain. The Emperor ordered some sappers to prepare, by means of a breach in the roof, a sort of *loggia*, in which he mounted in order to observe the positions of the enemy.

3

Blücher, who had hastened from Namur at the first alarm, had arrived at Sombreffe at four o'clock in the afternoon of June 15th. He flattered himself that he would have, at an early hour on the 16th, his four army corps behind the stream of

Ligny, a position which had been recommended to him two months before by Major von Gröben, and upon which he had then resolved to deliver battle if the French passed the Sambre at Charleroi. He was full of ardour and believed himself invincible.

"With my 120,000 Prussians," he had written to his wife, "I would charge myself with the capture of Tripoli, Tunis, and Algiers, could we but cross the sea."

But on account of the excessive extension of his cantonments the Marshal was to meet with great disappointments. On the 16th, at eleven o'clock in the morning, he had in line only Ziethen's corps, which had been reduced to 28,000 men by the losses of the day before. The corps of Pirch I. (31,000 men) arrived at Sombreffe only at noon, followed at some distance by the corps of Thielmann (24,000 men). As for the 4th. Corps, there had been received at headquarters during the night a letter from Billow, announcing that it would not be assembled at Hannut (forty -two kilometres from Sombreffe) till the middle of the day.

Thus Blücher was about to find himself short of 30,000 bayonets. However, he was determined to accept battle, counting on the more or less prompt, more or less active cooperation of the Anglo-Dutch Army. Had not the two commanders-in-chief agreed on May 3rd, at Tirlemont, to support mutually each other, if Napoleon took the offensive? And had not Wellington just said (evening of June 13th) to Blucher's envoy. Colonel Pfüell, "My army will be concentrated at Nivelles or Quatre-Bras, according to circumstances, twenty-two hours after the first cannon-shot"?

There was a little diplomacy in the promises of Wellington. Blücher's retreat on Liège would have left the English Army alone before Napoleon, and it would have been forced to choose between the alternative of accepting battle with a great inferiority of forces and that of falling back on its base of operations, and thus uncover Brussels. It was then necessary that Blücher should remain in position, and for this Wellington deemed it essential to promise his support. He hoped, moreover, to be able to give him this support—but, like a true Englishman, at his own time and pleasure, and without running the risk of compromising the safety of his army, even though it would be for the good of the common cause. Now, was not the offensive movement of the French towards Charleroi a simple demonstration, intended to attract on this side the Anglo-Prussian masses? Was not the Emperor at this very moment advancing on Brussels with the main body of his army, either by Maubeuge, Mons, and Hal, or by Lille, Tournay, and Ath? Wellington feared that such was the case, and fearing to be drawn into a false manoeuvre, he was unwilling to move a man or cannon before being absolutely certain of the precise point upon which Napoleon would direct his principal attack.

It was in vain that on June 12th, 13th, and 14th numerous reports of the concentration of the French Army upon the frontier had arrived at his headquarters in Brussels; it was in vain that at eight o'clock on the morning of June 15th Wellington had learned by a letter from Ziethen that the Prussian advance posts had been attacked at dawn. On this very day he had yet given no order. Müffling, the Prussian commissioner at the English headquarters, having received a personal letter from Ziethen confirming the first reports, hastened to communicate its contents to the Duke.

"If everything is as Ziethen believes," said Wellington to him, "I shall concentrate on my left wing, so as to act in concert with the Prussian Army; but if a part of the enemy's forces march on Mons, I shall be obliged to concentrate on my centre. I must then await, before coming to a decision, some news from my advance-posts at Mons. However, as the destination of my troops remains uncertain, and as their departure is certain, I shall issue orders in order that they may be ready to march."

According to these orders, despatched only on June 15th, between six and seven o'clock in the evening, the troops were simply to assemble by divisions at Ninove, Ath, Grammont, Brussels, Braine-le-Comte, and Nivelles, and to be ready to march next day at dawn. Thus, at the time when the French left wing had passed Gosselies and the right wing had arrived within sight of Fleurus, Wellington, in place of directing his troops upon the threatened point, contented himself with uniting them in isolated divisions within a parallelogram of ten leagues by nine. In truth, he must have been deluded and paralyzed by the vision of Napoleon attacking in person upon all points at the same time.

At noon Blücher had written to Müffling in order to announce to him the withdrawal of Pirch's division upon the left bank of the Sambre, and that he was about to concentrate his army at Sombreffe, where he intended to accept battle.

"I expect," he added, "prompt news of the concentration of Wellington's forces."

This letter, which arrived about seven o'clock in the evening, and which was immediately shown to Wellington, influenced him no more than had the letters of Ziethen.

"The dispositions of the Field Marshal are very good," said he, "but I cannot decide upon anything before knowing what is passing on the side of Mons." He was, finally, to acquire the certainty that everything was tranquil there. A letter from General Dörnberg, which he received between nine and ten o'clock, informed him in this regard. He then determined, not, as his apologists pretend, on a movement with all his army on Quatre-Bras, but on a partial concentration towards Nivelles.

After having given these orders, which, by reason of the advanced hour and the extent of the cantonments, could not be put in execution before dawn, Wellington said to Müffling: "My troops are about to put themselves on the march. But here the partisans of Napoleon begin to raise their heads. We must reassure our friends. Let us go to the ball of the Duchess of Richmond, and we will mount on horseback at five in the morning."

In Brussels, where, however, there had been festivals every evening, this ball, announced for some time, was discussed almost as much as the early entrance into campaign. It was known that the Duchess of Richmond had made great preparations; that she had turned into a sumptuous hall a vast shed contiguous to her villa; that a military band would furnish the music; and that there had been invited to the *soirée* the *élite* of the English Staff and of the cosmopolite society of Brussels, Russian and German diplomats, English peers, and French *émigrés*. Applications, prayers, and intrigues were multiplied in order to obtain invitations. The Duchess of Richmond received the guests assisted by her eldest daughter, later Lady Ross, at that time seventeen years old.

There were hardly more than two hundred guests—the Prince of Orange, Prince Frederick of the Low Countries, the Duke of Brunswick, the Prince of Nassau, Lord Wellington, the *Burgomaster* of Brussels, Princes Auguste and Pierre d'Arenberg, the Duke and Duchess de Beaufort and their daughter, the Duke and Duchess d'Ursel, the Count and Countess de Mercy-Argentau; Count de La Tour-Dupin, French minister to The Hague, and the Countess de La Tour-Dupin; the Marquis and Marchioness d'Assche, Count de La Rochefoucauld, the dowager Countess d'Oultremont and the Misses d'Oultremont, Lady Fitz-Roy Somerset, Count du Cayla (without his wife), Sir Charles Stewart, Lord and Lady Seymour and their daughter; Count Pozzo di Borgo and Baron de Vincent, ambassadors of Russia and Austria to His Majesty the King of France at Ghent; General Alva, Spanish commissioner, attached to Wellington's staff; General Müffling; Lord Uxbridge, commander-in-chief of the British cavalry; Lord Saltoun, colonel of the Foot Guards; Lord Somerset, commanding the brigade of Horse Guards; Lord Hill, commanding the 2nd English Corps; Generals Clinton, Ponsonby, Picton, Vivian, Byng, Pack, Cooke, Kempt, Maitland, and a great number of colonels, majors, and young captains, lieutenants, and ensigns.

When Wellington, about midnight, entered the home of the Duchess of Richmond, the ball was at its height. Full of life and gaiety, the beautiful young women and handsome officers were intoxicated with the noise and movement. But, as in the funereal dances of the old *frescoes*, Death led the round.

The passage of the Sambre by the French Army was still unknown. Wellington informed the Duke of Brunswick that Bonaparte had entered Belgium, and that in all probability there would be a battle during the day. Brunswick, by a sort of presentiment, felt the chilliness of death. He turned pale and arose with a bound, by this sudden movement letting the little Prince de Ligne, whom he had upon his knees, fall to the floor. Wellington took to one side all the general officers and gave them verbally the orders of march which had just been sent to them in writing. They were not long in quitting the ball. Informed about one o'clock, in the middle of the festivities, by a despatch from Constant Rebecque, that the French had shown themselves at Quatre-Bras, the Prince of Orange set out for Genappe.

By degrees the rumour spread that the army was about to move. But the young officers could not tear themselves from this night of pleasure, "*upon which*," said Lord Byron, "*was soon to rise so bloody a dawn*." It was only when they heard the trumpets and bugles sounding the assembly that they ran, in silk stockings and buckle shoes, to rejoin their companies. The Duchess of Richmond, deeply moved, would have wished to arrest the ball, but the young ladies and the few young men who did not belong to the army continued to dance until daylight.

Wellington did not leave until three o'clock, after having supped. The Duchess awakened her youngest daughter, a true baby Reynolds, who came with her rosy little hands to buckle on the sword of the commander-in-chief.

4

Müffling says that during the ball Wellington was very gay. There certainly was no reason for this gaiety! During the entire day he had persisted in leaving his troops dispersed in their cantonments at four, eight, ten, and fifteen leagues from one another; and the orders of the evening, by which he flattered himself to repair victoriously his great error, were pitiful. His last dispositions tended to nothing less than to uncover the route leading from Charleroi to Brussels in order to protect that of Mons, which was not threatened. If the orders of Wellington had been executed, a gap four leagues wide would have been opened between Nivelles and the Lower Dyle; a gap through which Ney would have been able to advance half-way to Brussels without firing a shot, or, better still, as Gneisenau has said, "to turn back on the rear of the Prussian Army and cause its utter destruction."

Fortunately for the Allies, many of Wellington's subordinates had taken it on themselves to act without awaiting his orders, and others had intelligently disobeyed those which, after so much time lost, he had decided to give. On the day before, Major Normann had defended Frasnes, the Prince of Saxe-Weimar had advanced from Genappe to Quatre-Bras with his brigade, and General Chassé had concentrated his division at Foy. A little later Constant Rebecque, the Prince of Orange's chief of staff, directed, in the absence of the Prince, General Collaert to assemble his cavalry behind the Haine, and General Perponcher to prepare to march on Quatre-Bras.

Finally, at eleven o'clock in the evening, this same Rebecque, not being able to avoid transmitting to the generals of division Wellington's order to concentrate all the Netherland troops at Nivelles—or, in other words, to uncover the route of Brussels—gave them verbal instructions which left them free not to conform to this order. "It is impossible to know at Brussels," he said, "the exact state of affairs."

Perponcher did not hesitate. In place of maintaining at Nivelles the Bylandt brigade and of recalling that of Saxe-Weimar, as directed by Wellington, he marched with Bylandt on Quatre-Bras to support Prince Bernard.

Ah, if Napoleon had had as chief of staff a simple Constant Rebecque and as lieutenants some Perponchers and Bernards of Saxe-Weimar! And what a fine occasion, on the other hand, for professors of strategy like Charras to denounce the fatal indecision, the torpor of mind, and the moral weakness of the Emperor if, on the eve of a battle. Napoleon had remained ten hours without concentrating his troops, had then prescribed a movement in a direction opposite to that of the enemy, and had, finally, passed the night in parading himself at a ball!

But in war, as in play, nothing can prevail against Fortune. When Wellington, who had left Brussels at six in the morning, arrived about ten at Quatre-Bras, he found there the division of Perponcher, when he should have found the advance guard of Marshal Ney. His Grace, appearing to forget the fact that one had acted contrary to his orders, deigned to congratulate General Perponcher and also the Prince of Orange—who had had nothing to do with it—upon the position taken. Then, after having advanced close enough to Frasnes to observe well the French advance posts, he despatched the order to the division of Picton and the corps of Brunswick, which had been halted at Waterloo, to resume their march, and wrote to Blücher that Quatre-Bras was occupied by a division of the Prince of Orange and that the English Army was directing itself on that point. The letter closed as follows:

> I do not see a very large force of the enemy in front of us, and I await some news from your Excellency before deciding upon my course.

Wellington was not long in changing his mind. Believing, rightly or wrongly, that it would be many hours before he was attacked at Quatre-Bras, he decided that in place of awaiting some news, which he would be unable to verify, it would be better to go to see things for himself and to concert verbally with Blücher. About one o'clock he joined the Field Marshal upon the heights of Brye. They ascended upon the roof of the mill of Bussy, situated in front of that village; from there they were able to view all the ground, much better than from the mill of Fleurus, where Napoleon had established his observatory. They saw the French columns debouching; and with their glasses they recognized the Emperor, surrounded by his staff. It seemed evident that they would soon have to combat the entire Imperial Army, the detachment which occupied Frasnes being but a negligible fraction.

"What do you desire me to do?" brusquely said Wellington in French. (He was ignorant of the German language.) Gneisenau proposed that the Duke should direct without delay all his troops in the rear of Brye to act as a reserve for the Prussian Army. This plan, based upon a false appreciation of the distribution of Napoleon's forces, was combated by Müffling. He said in substance that the English should manoeuvre so as to outflank the French left. "You are right," cried Wellington. "I will overthrow what I have in front of me at Frasnes, and I will march on Gosselies."

Gneisenau objected that this movement would be eccentric and of doubtful result, whilst the concentration at Brye would procure a certain and decisive success. The discussion being prolonged, Wellington said, in order to end it: "Well, I will come if I am not attacked myself." With these words, which could not be construed into a formal engagement, the Duke departed from Quatre-Bras, whilst Blucher took his last tactical dispositions.

CHAPTER 2

Battle of Ligny

1

In front of the hill of Fleurus there rises at a gentle incline, beyond an undulating plain, a line of low heights, upon which are situated on the west the village of Brye, on the east that of Tongrinne, and in the centre and somewhat remote the market-town of Sombreffe. These positions in themselves are easily accessible; but at their feet the stream of Ligny, four or five yards wide, deeply embanked and lined with willows, alders, and brambles, pursues its tortuous way through the lowlands. This stream and the rough ground by which one descends to it form a deep trench, which is flanked on the right by the villages of Wagnelée and Saint-Amand and the hamlets of La Haye and Petit Saint-Amand; on the left by the hamlets of Potriaux and Tongrinelle and the villages of Tongrinne, Boignée, and Balâtre.

In the centre there is the village of Ligny, with its two large farms, its old *château*, and its church, situated in the midst of a cemetery, surrounded by breast-high walls. The front of the position was thus constituted by a continuous *fossé* and ten bastions, some in front of this *fossé*, as Petit Saint-Amand, La Haye, Grand Saint-Amand, Tongrinelle, Boignée, and Balâtre, and others in the rear, as Potriaux and Tongrinne. The ninth and most important, Ligny, is traversed in its entire length by the stream of that name.

From the mill of Fleurus, where Napoleon had established his observatory, the Prussian positions appeared less strong than they were in reality. The Emperor was unable to form an exact idea of the lay of the land in the valley. The bottoms, which were cut up with gullies, and through which flows the Ligny, escaped his sight. He seemed to have before him a vast plain covered with grain, shelving slightly downwards in the centre, then rising gently to meet the extreme horizon—a true landscape of Beauce. He ordered brought to him the surveyor of the village, a certain Simon, who informed him as best he could.

At noon the four divisions of Ziethen with the cavalry of Roder were the only forces in line; the corps of Pirch I. and that of Thielmann had just commenced to mass themselves behind Sombreffe and Tongrinne. The Emperor correctly estimated the force in front of him at one army corps. However, he was not deceived as to the intention of Blücher. "The old fox does not take to the open," said he. He conjectured that the Field Marshal had taken up a waiting position, in which he hoped to impose long enough upon the French to give to his other army corps and, according to all probability, the army of Wellington, the time to rejoin. As a matter of fact, if Blücher had had the intention of defending with his sole forces his lines of communication, he would have taken position perpendicular to the route of Fleurus. The extension of his right towards Wagnelée revealed the project of a reunion with the English Army on the march from Brussels.

Resolved to attack immediately, the Emperor was very much disconcerted to learn that the corps of Gérard was not even in sight. He awaited its arrival. Doubtless he then believed that only a single corps of the enemy was opposed to him, and he had at hand the corps of Vandamme, the 1st and the 2nd Corps of cavalry, and, in the second line behind Fleurus, the Imperial Guard. But he apprehended, not without reason, that, in the midst of the action, the mass of the Prussian Army, which in all probability was on the march towards Sombreffe, would put in its appearance.

Soon after noon Gérard, who had outstripped his army corps, arrived upon the line of advance posts with a small escort. In seeking the Emperor, he approached within carbine range of a post of the enemy's cavalry. The Prussians charged. Gérard, thrown from his horse, was in great danger of being captured; he was saved by one of his *aides-de-camp*. Having rejoined the Emperor at the mill, he thought it necessary to say a few words concerning the desertion of Bourmont, who had obtained a command only upon his pressing solicitations. Napoleon interrupted him by saying: "I have often told you, General, that the blue are always blue and the white always white."

It was not until one o'clock that Gérard's column debouched. The order of movement had been sent before eight o'clock; and the distance from Châtelet to Fleurus is but ten kilometres. But in consequence of the non-execution, in the afternoon of the day before, of the Emperor's instructions prescribing the establishment of the 4th Corps upon the left bank of the Sambre, Gérard had been forced in the morning to pass this river over a single bridge with the larger portion of his troops. Hence this long day in the march of the 4th Corps.

It seems that the Emperor had at first thought of attacking by Wagnelée and Saint-Amand in order to throw back the Prussians on Sombreffe. But the exposed position of their right wing suggested the idea of enveloping them in place of driving them back. For this he modified his anterior orders to Ney. According to the instructions sent in the morning, the Marshal was to establish himself at and beyond Quatre-Bras, pending the order to march on Brussels. At two o'clock he ordered Soult to write to Ney:

> The Emperor desires me to inform you that the enemy has united an army corps between Sombreffe and Brye, and that at half -past two Marshal Grouchy with the 3rd and 4th Corps will attack him. His Majesty's intention is that you will attack also what is before you, and after having pressed them vigorously, you will turn back in order to cooperate with us in enveloping the corps of which I have just spoken.

The corps of Vandamme, that of Gérard, and the cavalry of Grouchy were deployed in front of Fleurus, perpendicular to the highway. The Emperor ordered a change of front with the right in advance. By this manoeuvre Vandamme approached Saint-Amand; Gérard advanced within nearly 1,000 yards of Ligny, parallel with the highway; and Grouchy drew up his troops in the form of a square in front of Boignée. The Guard and the *cuirassiers* of Milhaud, left until two o'clock behind Fleurus, ranged themselves in the second line.

From the mill of Bussy, where he was still at two o'clock with Wellington, Blücher had seen this movement taking shape. He hastened to complete his order of battle. The corps of Ziethen, of which only a few battalions had until then occupied the front of defence, took position as follows: four battalions of the division of Steinmetz at La Haye and Le Hameau (or Petit Saint-Amand), the other six in support; three battalions of the division of Jagow in Saint-Amand, the other seven under the mill of Bussy; the division of Henckel in Ligny, with two battalions somewhat in the rear; the division of Pirch II. was drawn up in *echelons* between Brye and the mill of Bussy. Roder's cavalry massed itself in a hollow of the ground on the north of the road leading from Ligny to Sombreffe, with the exception of the 1st Silesian Hussars, which was detached with a light battery on the extreme right upon the old Roman road to reconnoitre the flank of the army. The artillery was established between the villages, upon the lower slopes of the hills. Saint-Amand, La Haye, and Ligny had been hastily fortified; but none of the bridges spanning the Ligny had been cut, as Blücher wished to preserve these debouches in case he should pass to the offensive.

Behind this first line the corps of Pirch I. (divisions of Tippelskirch, Krafft, Brause, and Langen, and the cavalry of Jurgass) was in reserve to the north of Brye, along the route of Nivelles. The corps of Thielmann, which formed the Prussian left, had the divisions of Luck and Kempher at Potriaux, Tongrinne, Tongrinelle, and Balâtre, and the divisions of Borcke and Stulpnagel with the cavalry of Hobe in reserve at Sombreffe and behind

Tongrinne.

This vast deployment had not escaped the vigilant eye of Napoleon. Until past two o'clock—so long as his own manoeuvres had not forced Blücher to unmask all his forces—the Emperor had believed that he would have to deal with but 30,000 men. The extension of the enemy's front, and the masses which he saw in motion, revealed to him the presence of an army! The battle would no doubt be murderous, but he was about to finish with Blücher in a single day. He held him in the hollow of his hand! For in a few hours Ney, taking in reverse the position of Brye, would sound with cannon-shot the death-knell of the Prussian Army. "It may be that in three hours the fate of the war will be decided," said the Emperor to Gérard. "If Ney executes his orders, not one cannon of this army will escape!"

At a quarter-past three a second order—more urgent, more imperative than the preceding—was sent to Ney:

> "I wrote you one hour ago," said Soult, "that the Emperor intended to attack the enemy in the position which he has taken between the villages of Saint-Amand and Brye. His Majesty desires me to say to you that you must manoeuvre immediately so as to envelop the right wing of the enemy and to fall with might and main upon his rear. The Prussian Army is lost, if you act vigorously. The fate of France is in your hands. So do not hesitate a moment in making the movement which the Emperor orders, and direct yourself upon the heights of Saint-Amand and Brye."

At the moment when Soult despatched this order Napoleon received a letter from Lobau, informing him that, according to the report of Colonel Janin, Ney had before him at Quatre-Bras nearly 20,000 enemies. The Emperor reflected that these 20,000 men might make a defence sufficiently tenacious to prevent the Prince of the Moskowa from effecting in time the movement against the Prussian Army. His fine tactical combination was in danger of miscarrying. He did not flatter himself, as he has been wrongfully accused, with gaining two battles in one day. The important thing for him was not to gain a half-victory over Blücher and a half-victory over Wellington; it was to contain the English and to exterminate the Prussians.

The Emperor thought that Ney with the single corps of Reille would suffice to contain the English, and that the single corps of d'Erlon would be sufficient to turn the right of Blücher. He decided to entrust to this general the execution of the movement previously assigned to Ney and from which he expected such decisive results. There was not an instant to be lost. He sent directly to Count d'Erlon the order to advance with his army corps in the rear of the Prussian right wing. Colonel Forbin-Janson, charged with transmitting to him this order, was also to communicate it to Ney.

At the same time the Emperor, desiring to have all his forces well in hand, wrote Lobau, who had been detained temporarily at Charleroi, to march on Fleurus.

2

Battle was joined. About three o'clock three cannon-shots, fired at equal intervals by a battery of the Guard, had given the signal for the assault.

Without deigning to prepare the way with his artillery, Vandamme launched against Saint-Amand the division of Lefol. With the band of the 23rd Regiment playing the air "La *Victoire en chantant*," the division advanced, formed in three columns, each column preceded by a swarm of skirmishers. Before the enemy's front the ground, entirely bare of trees or hedges, formed a sea of ripening grain, already four or five feet high. The march through it was slow and laborious, and if the corn almost concealed the skirmishers, the columns were perfectly visible. The batteries opened a heavy fire on them, and as many as eight men were cut down by one ball.

The Prussians were sheltered in the houses and behind the embankments and quickset hedges which surrounded the orchards. At fifty yards from the village the soldiers of Lefol leaped over the enclosures. The point-blank discharges did not arrest their *élan*; and in less than fifteen minutes of furious combat the enemy was driven from the orchards, the houses, the cemetery, and the church. But the Prussians of Jagow rallied upon the left bank of the stream, and soon, supported by four battalions of Steinmetz, they prepared for a counter- attack. The division battery of Steinmetz turned its fire against Saint-Amand, starting many fires, and the 24th Prussian regiment passed the stream at La Haye in order to take the French in flank.; Vandamme deployed the division of Berthezène on the left of Lefol; and, in accordance with the anterior instructions of the Emperor, he ordered the division of Girard, in position to the north of Wangenies, to attack Le Hameau and La Haye.

Whilst Lefol was engaged in the attack of Saint-Amand, Pécheux's division of Gérard's corp. attacked Ligny in three columns under the fire of the Prussian batteries. The left and centre columns carried the hedges and enclosures on the outskirts of the village, but, decimated by the heavy and rapid fire of musketry which came from the old chateau and the first houses, they fell back. The 30th of the Line, composing the column on the right, pushed farther. It entered the hollow road, crowned by the farm of La Tour, a building with walls like a fortress, and from which the bullets rained in a perfect hail; it penetrated even as far as the church square.

There the regiment, completely surrounded by the enemy concealed in the houses, in the cemetery, and behind the willows along the stream, found itself in the centre of a quadrilateral of fire. In an instant the entire head of the column was swept away; twenty officers and nearly five hundred men fell dead or wounded. The survivors retired in disorder and went to rally in their first positions.

Two new attacks succeeded no better. Some batteries of twelve-pounders reinforced the artillery of Gérard, which until then had only replied to that of the enemy. They opened fire on Ligny. The balls demolished the houses and ricocheted in the streets; the roofs of the cottages caught fire and fell in, starting a conflagration upon ten different points. For the fourth time the division of Pécheux, seconded by a brigade of Vichery's division, marched against the Prussians. In an ardent combat, a succession of assaults against each house, the French obtained possession of most of the upper village.

Ligny is composed of two streets running parallel with the Ligny and separated by this stream—the Rue d'En-Bas on the north and the Rue d'En-Haut on the south. Between the two streets are a few scattered cottages, the church square, and a vast communal meadow, which shelves downwards like a glacis to the Ligny. Dislodged from the farm of La Tour and the Rue d'En-Haut, the Prussians resumed their positions in the cemetery, in the church, and in the houses surrounding the square. The soldiers of Pécheux advanced valiantly under a murderous cross-fire; some broke into the houses, while others escaladed' the wall of the cemetery.

At this moment a large force of the enemy, which had rallied behind the church, charged the French, who had become disorganized by these numerous assaults. Upon this little square, too narrow for the number of combatants, French and Prussians engaged in a terrible and murderous hand-to-hand struggle, in which, after having discharged their muskets, they used their bayonets, the butt-ends of their muskets, and even their fists. The carnage was abominable.

"The men massacred one another," says a Prussian officer, "as if they had been animated with a personal hatred. It seemed as if each man saw in his opponent a mortal enemy, and that he rejoiced at finding the opportunity to wreak his vengeance. No one thought of fleeing or of asking quarter."

The Prussians finally fell back. They abandoned the houses, the church, the cemetery, and retired in disorder over the two bridges of the Ligny. The French pursued them with the bayonet. More than one Prussian was hurled into the boggy bed of the stream. Upon the left bank, however, the enemy, reinforced by the two remaining battalions of Henckel's division, re-formed and renewed the fight. Some of the Prussians opened fire from the hedges and clumps of willows which lined the bank of the stream, whilst others fired, over the heads of their comrades, from the houses of the Rue d'En-Bas and from loopholes made in the walls of the large farm on the left bank. In spite of this terrible fire in tiers, some soldiers of the 30th and 96th Regiments crossed the bridges and drove back the Prussian sharpshooters against the houses.

But Jagow brought four battalions to the support of Henckel. The Prussians threw back the assailants upon the right bank; they even attempted to recross the two bridges. It was the turn of the French to defend the stream. French and Prussians fired at each other from one bank to the other—a distance of four yards—through the smoke. The weather was tempestuous, and the suffocating heat was still further increased by the musketry and fires started by the shells. Amidst the noises of the combat were heard the horrible cries of the wounded who were being roasted alive under the burning ruins.

Grouchy, on his side, had commenced his attack against the Prussian left. His cavalry had driven from Boignée the enemy's posts, and Hulot's division of Gérard's corps, which had passed under his immediate command, threatened Tongrinelle and skirmished before Potriaux with the Prussians of Luck.

Upon all points new batteries entered into action, and the fusillade increased in violence. From La Haye to Tongrinelle, the battle raged upon both banks of the Ligny, from which arose, as from an infernal river, a curtain of fire and smoke.

3

About four o'clock the action had extended still further west. Girard had launched his division against Le Hameau and La Haye. The assault was so prompt, so resolute, so ardent, that the Prussians were terrified and gave ground almost without firing a shot. Blücher, solid in his centre, intact on his left, saw his right outflanked. He wished to disengage it by a vigorous counter-attack. It was necessary for him at any price to give himself air on this side, for it was from here that he intended to debouch later with the English, whose cooperation he still expected. The

Field Marshal unhesitatingly drew upon his reserve. The division of Pirch II., the only one of Ziethen's corps which had not been under fire, would march from Brye against La Haye and Saint-Amand, whilst the cavalry of Jurgass, of the corps of Pirch I., and the division of Tippelskirch, of the same corps—in all, forty-seven squadrons and nine battalions—would advance on Wagnelée, from whence they would burst on the flank of the French.

Formed in columns of battalions, the infantry of Pirch II. attacked with the bayonet the soldiers of Girard, who had already debouched from La Haye in order to turn Saint-Amand, where the Prussians of Steinmetz had returned in force and occupied many points. The division of Girard fell back under the attack of the fresh troops, retired into La Haye, and, after a stubborn fight, abandoned half of this hamlet. But with a chief like Girard it was only for a short time. He re-formed in the streets, swept by balls and bullets, his decimated battalions, and hurled them again against the enemy. He led them in person, sword in hand. He fell mortally wounded, but he saw his soldiers throw back for the second time the Prussians out of La Haye upon the left bank of the stream.

The flank movement attempted by Jagow and Tippelskirch was less successful than the counter-attack of Pirch II. Habert's division and Domon's cavalry, which Vandamme had until then held in reserve, were deployed in front of Wagnelée with two battalions as skirmishers in the com. The head of Tippelskirch's column, which advanced in order of march and without reconnoitring, was surprised by the heavy and well-directed fire which issued from the corn. It fell back in disorder, spreading confusion among the battalions which it preceded, and in which there were a great many recruits. Without hesitating, Habert ordered a bayonet charge against these disunited troops and drove them back into Wagnelée. Stupidly dispersed and intimidated by the evolutions of General Demon's horse *chasseurs*, Jurgass' cavalry took scarcely any part in the action.

During these combats Blücher had descended from the mill

of Bussy in order to direct in person the execution of the manoeuvre from which he promised himself such immense results. He arrived within close cannon-range of La Haye, just at the moment when the division of Pirch II. was driven from this village by the mortal effort of the intrepid Girard.

Without giving the men time to recover their breath, Blucher ordered Pirch II. to lead them back into the fire and to reoccupy La Haye, regardless of the cost. Reanimated by the presence of old *Vorwärtz*, the soldiers cheered, crossed the stream, and penetrated into La Haye with fixed bayonets. Girard's division, reduced from 5,000 to 2,500 men, its chief mortally wounded and its two brigadiers *hors de combat*—it was Colonel Matis, of the 82nd of the Line, who had taken the command—resisted desperately. Forced to yield to numbers, it retired from house to house, from orchard to orchard, and from hedge to hedge, as far as Le Hameau, where it massed itself and awaited the assault.

The enemy was about to leave it some respite, for the French had thrust back Tippelskirch into Wagnelée, they held firm in Saint-Amand and they occupied half of Ligny. Blücher was compelled to relieve before Saint-Amand the division of Steinmetz, which had lost half of its effective, to send a reinforcement to Henckel in Ligny, to give Tippelskirch time to rally in Wagnelée, and, in view of the new manoeuvre which he meditated, to send to the south of Brye the corps of Pirch I.

The Emperor also makes his preparations for the great movement which he has had in view since the beginning of the battle. It is half-past five; he had written to Ney at two o'clock; at six he will hear the cannon of the Marshal thundering in the rear of the Prussian Army; then he will launch his reserves, still intact, against the centre of the enemy, will overthrow it, cut off its retreat towards Sombreffe, and push it under the steel and fire of Vandamme and Ney. Of the 60,000 Prussians of Ziethen and Pirch, not one will escape.

The Imperial Guard, horse and foot, and the *cuirassiers* of Milhaud had already commenced to form for the attack, when there arrived an *aide-de-camp* from Vandamme with the intelligence that a hostile column of 30,000 men was reported at the distance of a league upon the left, and appeared to be directing itself on Fleurus with the purpose of turning the army. Vandamme added that the troops of Girard, having discovered this supposed hostile column, had abandoned La Haye, and that he himself would be forced to evacuate Saint-Amand and to retreat unless the reserve arrived in time to arrest this column.

Napoleon was amazed at this intelligence. He at first had an idea, as Vandamme also had had for a moment, that the column was the French division which, in accordance with his orders of eight o'clock in the morning, should have been sent by Ney to Marbais. But a division has not 20,000 or 30,000 men, and troops who show themselves to the south of Villers-Perwin cannot debouch from Marbais. Was it then Ney who arrived with all his forces, according to the new instructions sent at two o'clock and renewed at three? Or was it d'Erlon who arrived with the 1st Corps, in conformity with the despatch of half-past three? But d'Erlon, like Ney, had orders to turn back by the heights of Saint-Amand on the rear of the enemy and not to come to Fleurus. To march on Fleurus was to cause the plan of the Emperor to miscarry.

Neither Marshal Ney nor Count d'Erlon could be guilty of such an error! Then it must be either an English corps, which had turned Ney's right, or a Prussian corps, which had operated by the old Roman road a vast turning movement. The Emperor hastened to send one of his *aides-de-camp* to ascertain the strength and intentions of the hostile column. Meanwhile he suspended the movement of the Guard against Ligny and caused it to resume its first position in front of the mill of Fleurus with its regiments deployed. Duhesme's division of the Young Guard and the 2nd, 3rd, and 4th Foot Chasseurs of the Old Guard, detached from the reserve, advanced at an increased pace to the support of Vandamme.

These reinforcements did not arrive any too soon. Hardly recovered from a panic caused by the approach of the hostile column—panic which General Lefol had been able to arrest only by turning his guns against the fugitives—the corps of Vandamme was about to suffer the combined attack of the greater part of the Prussian right wing. A little before six o'clock the reserve batteries of the enemy entered into action and prepared the way for the assault. Tippelskirch debouched from Wagnelée upon Le Hameau, his right supported by the numerous squadrons of Jurgass. The skirmishers of the 1st St Pomeranian Regiment opened so brisk and sustained a fire that in a few minutes they had emptied their cartridge-boxes; the hussars who flanked them brought them their own cartridges.

The division of Pirch II., seconded by the fresh troops of the division of Brause and a part of the division of Krafft, assailed Saint-Amand on three sides. The French withdrew. The debris of Girard's division abandoned Le Hameau; Lefol and Berthezène yielded all the northern part of Saint-Amand; and Habert recoiled as far as his first position on the left of this village. From the mill of Bussy, where he had returned, Blücher witnessed the success of his troops. He already believed himself master of the road of Fleurus and soon free to go to attack in flank the French reserve, a manoeuvre which he had had in view for a long time.

But the Young Guard of Duhesme advances at the charging step. It passes the division of Habert and attacks with superb ardour the Prussians of Tippelskirch. The latter, roughly handled, retire, partly into Wagnelée and partly into Le Hameau. Held in check by the *chasseurs* of Domon and the lancers of Alphonse de Colbert, whom the Emperor had just sent from the right to the left of the battle-field, the cavalry of Jurgass can only protect the retreat of Tippelskirch without attempting anything against the Young Guard.

The indefatigable division of Girard, whose four intrepid regiments, the 11th and 12th Light and the 4th and 82nd of the Line, well deserve to be named, bursts again upon Le Hameau, from whence it drives the Prussians for the third time. Lefol and Berthezène force Pirch II. out of Saint-Amand. The French are once more masters of all the ground as far as the first houses of

La Haye.

"What soldiers!" writes a Royalist *émigré* present in the battle. "They were no longer the feeble *débris* of Arcis-sur-Aube. They were, according to the point of view, a legion of heroes or demons."

On the right wing the cavalry of Grouchy occupied Tongrinelle, and the infantry of Hulot vigorously attacked Potriaux. In the furnace of Ligny the battalions of heroes melted like gold in the crucible. Gérard had thrown himself into this village with his last reserve, the second brigade of Vichery. Blücher had relieved there the division of Henckel by the larger part of the division of Krafft. Both sides fought with the same rage— Prussians and French passing and repassing in turn the stream— for the possession of the church, the cemetery, the farm d'En-Bas, and the castle of the Counts de Looz, in which, in spite of the flames which surrounded them, two companies of Silesian sharpshooters intrepidly held out.

Many soldiers fell from exhaustion. Krafft no longer hoped to maintain his position much longer. He informed Gneisenau that he and Jagow were on the point of being surrounded in Ligny. "Hold out for a half -hour longer," replied Gneisenau. "The English Army is approaching." Illusion or lie! for Blücher was soon to or had already received a despatch from Müffling, informing him that Wellington, fighting with an entire army corps, would not even be able to send him a single squadron.

Nothing discouraged the intrepid soul of Blücher. If Müffling's letter contained "disagreeable news," according to the moderate expression of Grolemann, it at least informed him that Napoleon had not all his army with him, as he had thought, and gave him the assurance that he would not be attacked in reverse, since Wellington would contain the French corps detached upon the route of Brussels. He received simultaneously a report from Pirch II. and one from Thielmann announcing that the attack of the French seemed to slacken towards La Haye and Potriaux. After having begun its advance, the Old Guard had returned to its first position. This counter-march, which had been seen from the mill of Bussy, seemed to indicate some hesitancy on the part of Napoleon. It was the moment to act, if one did not wish to permit the victory to escape. Blücher still possessed confidence. He clung to the idea of gaining the battle all alone by throwing back the French left upon its centre. For this it would suffice that his lieutenants hold Ligny. He would charge himself with the rest. He ordered his last reserves to advance, save two battalions, which he posted in Brye and near the mill. He sent to Ligny to reinforce Jagow and Krafft a part of the division of Langen, and also summoned Thielmann to send there the division of Stulpnagel. Then, taking with him the last battalions of Langen and the debris of the division of Steinmetz, which had retired into the second line about five o'clock in the evening, the ardent old man—he was seventy-three years old—led them towards Saint-Amand.

On his way he rallies all the men whom he meets returning from the fight—there a company, here a section, farther on a group of fugitives. With these seven or eight battalions he rejoins the exhausted divisions of Brause, Pirch II., and Tippelskirch, and orders a new attack.

"My men have burned all their cartridges and emptied the cartridge-boxes of the dead," said Pirch to him; "they have no longer a single shot to fire."

"Have at them with the bayonet!" cries Blücher. And brandishing his sabre, spurring forward his magnificent white horse, a gift of the Prince Regent of England, he leads on his electrified soldiers. Supreme effort of brave men at the end of their strength! They retake Le Hameau, but then wave breaks against the steel dike of the 2nd, 3rd, and 4th Chasseurs of the Guard, deployed by regiments on the left of Saint-Amand.

The Prussians had returned in confusion into La Haye. Blücher at least hoped to sleep on his positions. He thought the battle ended, for night had come. It was not night. At half-past seven, during the June solstice, the sun still shines on the horizon. It was a tempest. Great black clouds swept up from the edge of the horizon and accumulated overhead, covering with a dark pall the entire field of battle. The rain began to fall in large drops. It thundered violently, peal on peal; but the rumbling of the thunder was soon drowned by the noise of the frightful cannonade which burst forth suddenly towards Ligny.

4

About half -past six o'clock the *aide-de-camp* sent to ascertain the strength of the hostile column which had debouched from the wood of Villers-Perwin on the flank of Vandamme had reported to the Emperor that this pretended English column was the corps of d'Erlon. Napoleon should have surmised as much. A false manoeuvre, a confusion of orders, an eccentric march, are things not so rare in war that he could not admit of their possibility. Greatly disconcerted by the threatening march of this column, he had not thought of the corps of d'Erlon, which, however, he himself had just called upon the battle-field. If his habitual presence of mind had not failed him, the abortive movement would have yet been feasible.

It would have sufficed to send by the *aide-de-camp* charged with reconnoitring the column the pressing order to d'Erlon to manoeuvre so as to turn the Prussian right. Napoleon had not thought of this. And when the *aide-de-camp* returned, he rightly judged that the movement could no longer be made in opportune time. In order to operate this enveloping march, two hours would have been required. Besides, the Emperor had probably been informed by the *aide-de-camp* that the 1st Corps was disappearing. Had Ney, in peril, recalled it, or had d'Erlon, having discovered that he had taken a wrong direction, moved to the west of Wagnelée to manoeuvre in the rear of the Prussian lines, in accordance with the order borne by Forbin-Janson?

The Emperor quickly made up his mind. If, in consequence of orders badly understood or poorly executed, it appeared that he could no longer count on the cooperation of a part of his left wing, at least he was freed from the uneasiness occasioned by the presence of the supposed hostile column on his flank. He was free once more to act. He could no longer gain the decisive victory of which he had dreamed since the afternoon, but he could yet win the battle and throw back Blucher far from Wellington. He issued his orders for the final assault.

The reserve batteries open fire against the hills which dominate Ligny; the Old Guard deploys in columns of divisions; the squadrons of the Emperor's escort, the 2nd cavalry division of the Guard and the *cuirassiers* of Milhaud, form for the attack; whilst the corps of Lobau debouches from Fleurus. The cannonade ceases, the charge beats, and all this mass moves under the warm rain with cries of "Long live the Emperor!" The first column of the Guard (2nd, 3rd, and 4th Grenadiers) penetrates to the west of Ligny; the second (1st Chasseurs and 1st Grenadiers) attacks the village on the east. Led by Gérard, the soldiers of Pécheux and Vichery cross the stream of Ligny, and finally wrest from the Prussians the farm d'En-Bas and all the houses on the left bank.

The debris of the divisions of Jagow and Krafft and the battalions of Langen endeavour to re-form upon the first acclivities, above the ravine. But Pécheux rushes from the midst of Ligny, followed by Vichery and the first column of the Guard; from the right of the village debouch the 1st Grenadiers and the 1st Chasseurs, followed by the *cuirassiers* of Milhaud; from the left, with the Emperor, advance the squadrons of his escort and the heavy cavalry of the Guard. The Prussians yield on all points. In order to describe the rapidity and the impression of this irresistible attack, Soult wrote to Davoût: "It was like the transformation scene at the theatre."

Blucher arrived from La Haye at full speed. The rain had ceased and the wind had dispersed the clouds. By the last rays of the sun, which reappeared for an instant above the hills of Brye, he saw his troops in full retreat, and, in the wide breach made in his front of battle, the bear-skin caps of the Old Guard, the horse grenadiers, tall as towers, the dragoons manoeuvring to charge, and, in a scintillation, the 3,000 *cuirassiers* of Milhaud.

Old Blücher, according to the words of Major von Grolemann, "never regarded himself as defeated so long as he could continue the combat." To check the French, he counted on the cavalry of Roder, in reserve between Brye and Sombreffe; on the *débris* of the division of Henckel, which, at six o'clock, had been relieved in Ligny; and on the divisions of Stulpnagel and Borcke, which Thielmann had detached from his corps. But, on account of orders badly interpreted, Henckel was already near Sombreffe, and Stulpnagel still far from Ligny. As for the troops of Borcke, Thielmann could not deprive himself of this last reserve; he was pressed too vigorously on his front by Grouchy—the division of Hulot had carried Potriaux and threatened Sombreffe, and the dragoons of Excelmans (brigade of Burthe) had overthrown the cavalry of Lottum, captured its guns, and were advancing towards the route of Namur.

The thirty-two squadrons of Roder alone remained available. Blücher hastened to them and ordered the charge. Lützow, the celebrated partisan chief of the War of 1813, fell with the 6th Uhlans upon a square which he believed was composed of mobilized National Guards, on account of the dissimilarity of their uniforms. It proved to be the 4th Grenadiers of the Guard. The *Uhlans* were received by a file-fire at close range, which stretched upon the ground eighty-three men. Lützow, overturned with his horse, was made prisoner.

A charge of the 1st Dragoons and of the 2nd Landwehr of Courmache, another of the *Uhlans* of Brandenburg and the Dragoons of the Queen, and a fourth of all the squadrons together, succeeded no better. Some were repulsed by the Old Guard, which had relieved in the first line the divisions of Gérard, and the others were roughly handled by the dragoons of the Guard and the *cuirassiers* of Milhaud. Until nightfall Prussian and French squadrons gyrated and clashed together upon the acclivities of the hills, in front of the squares of the Guard, which advanced slowly but surely towards the mill of Bussy.

Struck by a ball, the horse of Blücher sank under his rider. The *aide-de-camp* Nostiz, who charged by the side of the Field Marshal, saw him fall and dismounted to assist him. They found themselves in the midst of the *Cuirassiers* of the 9th Regiment, who had just overthrown the Prussians, and who, in the darkness, passed without perceiving these two officers. A few minutes later the *cuirassiers*, being driven back, in turn repassed near them—almost over them—still without seeing them. Nostiz hailed the Prussian dragoons. Blücher was disengaged, all bruised, and in a half-swoon, from beneath his horse, placed upon the horse of a subaltern, and led far from the field of battle in the midst of the torrent of fugitives. They were innumerable. On the next day 8,000 of them were stopped at Liège and Aix-la-Chapelle.

The Prussian centre was overthrown and broken. Save a few battalions, which withdrew in good order and resisted intrepidly the *cuirassiers* of Delort, who unfortunately were not supported by the second division of Milhaud's corps, all the infantry fled in confusion. Thanks to the desperate charges of Roder's cavalry, which delayed the march of the French, Krafft, Langen, and Jagow saved a part of their artillery, and were able to rally the debris of their divisions between Sombreffe and the Roman road.

But if Blücher's centre had been pierced, he still held his positions on the wings. Ziethen and Thielmann had begun to retreat only when they had learned of the abandonment of Ligny. The Prussians massed around La Haye gained slowly the last summits of the hills, arresting by offensive returns the infantry of Vandamme when it pressed them too closely; their rear guard maintained itself in Brye until dawn. Thielmann withdrew his corps in the rear of Sombreffe, which he continued to occupy during the night by a strong detachment. At half-past nine there was still skirmishing along the line of Brye-Sombreffe.

The Emperor returned about eleven o'clock to Fleurus, whither the 2nd, 3rd, and 4th Chasseurs of the Guard were recalled from Saint-Amand. Save these regiments and the reserve batteries, all the Army bivouacked upon the left bank of the stream—the corps of Lobau, which had taken no part in the action, in the first line, near the mill of Bussy; the corps of Vandamme in front of La Haye; the corps of Gérard, the Old Guard and the cavalry of the Guard, before Ligny; the *cuirassiers* of Milhaud to the right of this village; the division of Hulot and the cavalry of Grouchy between Tongrinne, Potriaux, and Sombreffe. In front of Brye and Sombreffe the French outposts were within close musket-range of those of the Prussians. The French felt themselves so near the enemy that, although they were in the second line, the grenadiers of the Guard bivouacked without fire, in battalion squares.

During the night the wounded were cared for, but the ambulances, too few in number and badly organized, were not sufficient for the task; 12,000 Prussians and 8,500 French lay dead or wounded on the plain and in the villages, which had been transformed into charnel-houses.

CHAPTER 3

The Battle of Quatre-Bras

1

In the course of this day the Emperor had sent nine despatches to Marshal Ney. But, as he said at St. Helena, "Ney was no longer the same man." The most ardent of the Emperor's lieutenants, he who in so many battles—notably at Jena and Craonne—had attacked the enemy before the appointed hour, had become circumspect and temporizing, even to inertia.

On the day before, assailed by strategical scruples, the Marshal had directed towards Quatre-Bras only a detachment, which was too weak to carry that position. On the morning of June 16th he did nothing to make up for the time lost. Admitting that he was right in awaiting new instructions from the Emperor before attacking, he should at least have prepared everything to act on the receipt of the first order. His troops were *echeloned* from Frasnes to Thuin, over a line of seven leagues.

At daybreak he ought to have massed at Frasnes the divisions of Bachelu, Jérôme Bonaparte, and Foy, and all the cavalry, and summoned to Gosselies the corps of d'Erlon. This movement could have been completed before nine o'clock in the morning, save the division of Allix, which would have re-joined only two hours later. Thus by nine o'clock Ney would have found himself in position to attack Quatre-Bras, at the' first order, with 19,000 bayonets, 3,500 sabres, 64 guns, and a reserve of 20,500 men. But the Marshal took no preparatory measures. He left his divisions dispersed, his soldiers in bivouac, and awaited, inert, the orders of the Emperor.

About half-past six o'clock the Marshal received a first letter from Soult. It was not, indeed, an order of march, but it was a warning that his troops would soon have to put themselves in motion. Soult announced to him the early arrival at Gosselies of Kellermann's *cuirassiers*, and asked him if the 1st Corps had operated its movement in that direction. It was then still a question of Ney pushing straight ahead along the route of Brussels. If the Emperor had wished to recall the Marshal on his left, apparently he would not have sent him a reinforcement of eight regiments of heavy cavalry.

Ney, however, did not issue from his apathy. He contented himself with addressing to Soult the information demanded. Then, about seven o'clock, he set out for Frasnes without even directing Reille to cause his troops to take up arms. He confined himself to saying to him: "If there arrives an order from the Emperor during my absence, you will execute it at once and communicate it to Count d'Erlon."

At Frasnes Ney remained inactive and careless, as at Gosselies. He did not think to examine closely the positions of the enemy, and to push towards Quatre-Bras an offensive reconnaissance, which would have caused his adversary to unmask his forces. We might even say that he neglected to interrogate his generals and the commanders of his advance posts, or that he did not listen to what they reported to him. Lefebvre-Desnoëttes, or Colbert, certainly informed him that the Netherlanders appeared to have received reinforcements; that since morning they had extended and advanced their front; and that at six o'clock their skirmishers had driven back the French advance posts upon the edge of the wood of La Hutte.

After this skirmish, it is true, the combat had degenerated into a desultory firing, but the *ensemble* of the enemy's dispositions led to the presumption that his intention was to make a stand at Quatre-Bras. Ney believed nothing of the kind. They were only vain demonstrations, intended to impose upon the French and prepare for a retreat. At most, "we will have an affair with that handful of Germans who were sabred yesterday."

The Marshal was so convinced of this that about eleven o'clock, when Flahault delivered to him the letter of the Emperor which directed him to take position at and in front of Quatre-Bras, he dictated without hesitating the following order:

> The 2nd Corps will put itself on the march at once to take the following positions: The 5th Division in the rear of Genappe upon the heights; the 9th Division in the second line, to the right and left of Bauterlez; and the 6th and 7th Divisions at Quatre-Bras itself. The three first divisions of Count d'Erlon will take position at Frasnes. The right division will establish itself at Marbais with the 2nd Division of cavalry. The 1st Division of cavalry will cover our march arid reconnoitre in the direction of Brussels and on our flanks. The two divisions of the Count de Valmy will establish themselves at Frasnes and Liberchies. The cavalry division of the Guard will remain in its present position at Frasnes.

This was not a disposition for battle; it was a simple order of march. The mind of Ney is clearly revealed therein. He counted on occupying Quatre-Bras without striking a blow; at the worst, after a very short resistance. His instructions were merely a transcription of the Emperor's orders. Like Napoleon, he imagined that the route of Brussels was free. But he was on the spot!

To make matters worse, Ney, who had served the Emperor badly, was served in like manner by Reille. He enjoined this general to execute immediately any orders which he might receive from the Emperor. Now, when Flahault passed through Gosselies at ten o'clock and communicated to Reille the instructions of which he was the bearer, the latter, troubled by a report from General Girard, deemed it advisable to await a positive order from Ney before putting his troops on the march.

"General Flahault," he wrote to the Marshal, "has communicated to me the orders which he has for you. I would have commenced my movement on Frasnes as soon as my divisions would have been under arms, but, according to a despatch from General Girard, which reports two bodies of the enemy, of six battalions each, coming by the route of Namur, and whose advance guard is at Saint-Amand, I shall hold my troops in readiness to march pending your orders. As, no doubt, they will reach me in a short time, there will be only a short delay."

This "short delay" was one of two hours. Reille did not move his troops until the receipt of Ney's order—that is to say, about noon. His head of column hardly reached Frasnes before half-past one o'clock. In vain, during this interval of time, Ney had received another letter from the Major-General reiterating the first instructions. With a single battalion and the chasseurs and lancers of the Guard, he was constrained to await the infantry of Reille before beginning the attack. Besides, he thought that he had plenty of time to establish himself at Quatre-Bras, for he still laboured under the impression that the enemy, being few in number, would offer no great resistance.

The Prince of Orange, it is true, had at hand only the division of Perponcher—7,800 men and 14 guns. But, impressed with the strategical importance of Quatre-Bras, he was determined to hold this position at any cost until the arrival of the English.

The position was favourable to the defence. The hamlet of Quatre-Bras,. consisting of a group of three large farms and of two houses, situated at the crossing of the roads leading from Charleroi to Brussels and from Namur to Nivelles, commands on all sides the multiple undulations of the ground. On the east, the route of Namur, raised above the level of the ground, forms a natural entrenchment, in front of which arises, like a redoubt, the farm of Piraumont.

On the southwest access to Quatre-Bras is protected by the farm of Pierrepont and the coppice of Bossu, which extends for the space of 2,000 yards, on the left of the route of Charleroi. Finally, in a sort of valley, at the distance of half a league to the south of the hamlet, the large farm of Gemioncourt, constructed near the route, constitutes another advance work.

Although a division numbering less than 8,000 men was insufficient to line this front of more than three kilometres and occupy solidly all its positions, Perponcher, in order to impose on the French and delay as long as possible the attack of Quatre-Bras, feared not to scatter his force. Two battalions with three guns remained in reserve at Quatre-Bras and along the route of Namur; the others were distributed as follows: on the left, one battalion with five guns in front of Gemioncourt and another occupying this farm; on the right, four battalions and the horse battery upon the eastern skirt of the wood of Bossu and in front of Pierrepont.

2

About half-past one o'clock Reille, who marched with the advance guard of Bachelu's division, rejoined Ney. "There is only a very small force in the wood of Bossu," said the Marshal. "It is necessary to carry this position at once."

Reille, on this day, was not in a very enterprising humour; he replied: "This may be a Spanish battle, in which the English will show themselves only when it is time. It would be prudent, before attacking, to wait until all our troops are massed here."

Ney, impatient, replied: "Nonsense! Two companies of *voltigeurs* will suffice for this work!" Nevertheless, Reille's remarks had caused him to reflect; he delayed the attack until the arrival of Bachelu's second brigade and of Foy's division.

At two o'clock these troops, debouching from Frasnes, formed in columns of battalions—Bachelu on the right of the route and Foy upon and to the left of it; the *chasseurs* of Piré flanked the right of Bachelu's division, and the lancers remained in the rear of the interval between the two divisions. In the second line were the cavalry of the Guard, in column upon the highway, and the first brigade of Kellermann's *cuirassiers* deployed on the left. The division of Jérôme Bonaparte was still on the march between Gosselies and Frasnes, and the three other brigades of Kellermann had taken position at Liberchies, in accordance with

Ney's orders.

The Marshal did not wish to delay longer his attack; but, troubled by the words of Reille, he judged that the troops whom he had in hand would not be sufficient to attack the position in front. He resolved to direct his efforts against the left of the enemy. (He hoped that the defenders of Pierrepont would fall back as soon as they saw themselves outflanked, but Prince Bernard, having a line of retreat on Hautain-le-Val, had no fears of being cut off from Quatre-Bras.) After a short cannonade, the Marshal launched in the direction of Piraumont the division of Bachelu, the cavalry of Piré, and the brigade of Jamin of Foy's division. The second brigade of Foy (General Gauthier) remained temporarily in reserve. The division of Bachelu and the cavalry of Piré advanced between the wood of La Hutte and the highway towards Piraumont.

The Netherlanders posted in the second line were not in sufficient force to meet this attack. Bachelu drove back without difficulty the 27th Chasseurs as far as Piraumont. Arrived abreast of the farm of Lairalle, Jamin's brigade, led by Foy, took the lead on the left, drove back the 2nd Battalion of Nassau, and dislodged from Gemioncourt the 5th Battalion of militia, whose *débris* re-formed on the west of the route, and fell back towards the wood of Bossu. Ney then ordered them to be charged by the lancers of Piré, who overthrew them. The Prince of Orange, closely pressed, owed his safety only to the swiftness of his horse; one of his *aides-de-camp* was wounded and captured. Save on the right, where the four battalions of Prince Bernard of Saxe-Weimar had not yet been molested, the French were masters of the advanced positions of the enemy.

It was nearly three o'clock. Wellington, who had returned from the mill of Bussy, judged the situation critical, almost desperate. In a very short time he would be forced in Quatre-Bras by Foy, already on the march to attack this hamlet on the south, and by Bachelu, who would soon be in position to attack it on the east. But just at this moment reinforcements arrived—the brigade of Van Merlen (Dutch hussars and Belgian dragoons), by the route of Nivelles; and the division of Picton (eight English and four Hanoverian battalions), by the route of Brussels. Wellington was especially uneasy for the right of his line—almost disgarnished and threatened by Bachelu, in possession of the farm of Piraumont and its dependencies. The division of Picton, by a prompt movement "'towards the left, in line of battle," advanced upon the route of Namur; the brigades of Kempt and Pack in the first line, kneeling in the wheat; the Hanoverian brigade, in the second line, sheltered behind the talus of the highway.

During the deployment of the English the Prince of Orange launched in succession his hussars and dragoons against the column of Foy, whose sharpshooters had approached Quatre-Bras. Before reaching this infantry the enemy's squadrons were broken by the lancers of Piré and driven back at a quick pace beyond the cross-roads. Wellington was jostled and drawn in the rout as far as the Brussels highway. In turning back by a wheel to the right towards Gemioncourt, the lancers of Piré overthrew a battalion of militia and captured eight cannon.

The action had opened also to the south of the wood of Bossu. At three o'clock the division of Prince Jérôme had debouched from Frasnes, and Ney had at once directed it against the farm of Pierrepont, whilst the brigade of Gauthier rejoined General Foy. Dislodged from Pierrepont, the enemy withdrew into the wood, whither the skirmishers penetrated behind them. They advanced there very slowly; besides this wood being well defended, the undergrowth was so thick that in certain spots it became necessary to cut a passage with the sabre.

At this stage of the combat, a little before four o'clock, the Marshal received Soult's letter, written at two, ordering him to push the enemy vigorously and to turn back upon the Prussian corps in position at Brye, so as to envelop it. Enlightened henceforth as to the projects of the Emperor and the importance of the occupation of Quatre-Bras, Ney ordered a general advance. Bachelu moved from Piraumont towards the enemy's left; Foy marched from the lowlands of Gemioncourt towards Quatre-

Bras, with one column on the highway and the other to the right of it; Jérôme threw the brigade of Soye into the wood of Bossu and advanced with the brigade of Bauduin between the highway and the wood, to meet the corps of Brunswick—a new reinforcement which had reached Wellington.

Under this combined and vigorous attack the Allies gave ground on their right and centre. The brigade of Soye rendered itself master of most of the wood of Bossu and threw back its defenders on Hautain-le-Val, with the exception of one battalion, which maintained itself in the northern corner, near Quatre-Bras. Foy's division and Bauduin's brigade, which marched on its left, drove back the black battalions of Brunswick. A charge of Brunswick cavalry, led by the Duke of Brunswick in person, broke itself on the bayonets of the 1st Light. Frederick William was struck by a ball in the belly; transported into a house of Quatre-Bras, he died there during the evening. His father, the author of the manifesto of 1792, had been mortally wounded at Auerstaedt. They were both ardent enemies of France.

On the right the column of Bachelu had traversed the little valley which separates the heights of Gemioncourt from those which crown the route of Namur; it had just scaled this slope when it received, almost at point-blank range, the fire of Picton's first line, concealed in the wheat. The column halted, wavered. Picton, seeing the hesitation of the French, caused them to be charged with the bayonet by the brigade of Kempt, which drove them back rapidly, near Piraumont.

There, however, riddled with grape from the batteries of Bachelu and scourged by the musketry of the 108th of the Line, which had been left in reserve, the English were arrested in turn and forced to regain their first positions. In their retreat they were subjected to the charges of the 1st and the 6th Chasseurs (Piré's division.) The skirmishers were sabred, but the battalions, rapidly formed in squares, remained unbroken. The square of the 28th, attacked on two rides, seemed on the point of breaking, when Picton, in order to reanimate his soldiers, cried: "Twenty-eighth, remember Egypt!"

The 42nd (Highlanders) and 44th Regiments, which formed the right of Pack, were less fortunate. The lancers of Piré, galloping in pursuit of the Brunswickers, discovered the Red-coats in line of battle at the angle of the two routes; they rushed straight on them and broke without, however, over- throwing them. A furious *mêlée* of bayonets against lances took place; the flag of the 44th was taken and retaken. Colonel de Galbois with the 6th Lancers pierced as far as the route of Namur, where he cut to pieces a Hanoverian battalion.

3

To second his attack, Ney counted on the 20,000 men of Count d'Erlon, who were soon expected to debouch from Frasnes. But—by a concatenation of fatalities, or, rather, by the logical consequences of delays in the preparatory dispositions, of orders badly understood and executed, and of inopportune counter-orders—this corps was about to fail him, as it had failed Napoleon.

In the morning d'Erlon had concentrated his five divisions at Jumet (a half-league in the rear of Gosselies), where he was in person since the evening of the day before with the divisions of Durutte and Donzelot. Reille's corps, upon which he was to close up, not having budged from Gosselies, he awaited instructions. A little before eleven o'clock he received notice from Reille to prepare to follow the movement of the 2nd Corps. Reille also informed him that he himself would remain in his position until a new order. D'Erlon could only do as much. About a quarter-past twelve the order from Ney to advance to Frasnes was transmitted to him, either directly or through the intermediary of Reille; but, before putting himself on the march, he was compelled to await the movement of the entire 2nd Corps, which preceded his. Jérôme's division having scarcely quitted its bivouacs, to the south of the wood of Lambuc, before one o'clock, the advance guard of the 1st Corps did not reach Gosselies till between half-past one and two o'clock.

There d'Erlon halted his troops until the return of a strong reconnaissance which he had sent from Jumet towards Chapelle-Herlaymont, where the presence of an Anglo-Belgian corps, threatening his left, had been falsely reported to him by some peasants. In spite of Ney's order of eleven o'clock, written according to the instructions of the Emperor of eight o'clock; he neglected sending to Marbais one of his divisions. He intended, probably, to detach this division towards this village as soon as he attained Frasnes. He did not resume his march until three o'clock.

Between four and a quarter-past four o'clock half of the column had passed the Roman road, when d'Erlon was overtaken by Colonel de Forbin-Janson, of the Imperial Staff. Forbin-Janson had left Fleurus a quarter of an hour after the officer charged with Soult's message; but, by cutting across the country by way of Mellet, he had gained nearly .an hour upon the latter. He bore an order from the Emperor ordering Count d'Erlon to direct the 1st Corps upon the heights of Saint-Amand, in order to burst on Ligny.

Anxious to second the views of the Emperor, General d'Erlon at once ordered his column to turn to the right. Unfortunately, he had read wrong this order, scrawled in pencil, which Forbin-Janson, an officer who owed his position solely to favour, and without any knowledge of the combinations of war, was unable to explain to him. The order stated, "*sur la hauteur de Saint-Amand*" ("upon the height of Saint-Amand"); d'Erlon had read or understood, "*à la hauteur de Saint-Amand*" ("abreast of Saint-Amand").

Consequently, instead of taking the direction of Brye and Ligny, in order to attack the Prussians in reverse, he directed himself on Saint- Amand and Fleurus, so as to prolong the Emperor's left. This movement was precisely contrary to the instructions of Napoleon; so we can, in a measure, explain why the Emperor, on being informed of the advance of a column and its threatening position on his left flank, had not thought of d'Erlon, whom he was far from expecting on this point, and why he, as well as Vandamme, had taken this column for a Prussian or English corps.

In confiding an order of such importance to a staff officer as inexperienced as was Count Forbin-Janson, Napoleon acted contrary to his usual method in such instances. Until 1814, when he had raised in the *Nièvre* a partisan corps, which took part in only a few slight skirmishes, Forbin-Janson had seen no service. In 1815 the Emperor introduced him into the Army with the rank of colonel and attached him to his staff. He had no knowledge whatever of the duties of an *aide-de-camp*. Not only was he unable to explain to d'Erlon the prescribed movement, but when he had transmitted to him the order, either that he had badly understood or had forgotten the subsidiary recommendation of the Emperor, or for some other cause, instead of going to communicate this order to Marshal Ney, he rejoined at a rapid pace the Imperial Staff. Count Forbin-Janson, at least, deserves credit for having lost no time in going and returning.

The Prince of the Moskowa learned of d'Erlon's movement only from General Delcambre, chief of staff of the 1st Corps Whilst on the march along the Roman road with his troops, d'Erlon, filled with misgivings, had sent this officer to inform the Marshal of his march towards the other battlefield. Ney flew into a great passion. His rage was still further increased a few minutes later when the officer arrived bearing Soult's order, dated a quarter-past three o'clock:

> You must manoeuvre immediately so as to envelop the right of the enemy and to fall with might and main upon his rear. This army (the Prussian) is lost if you act vigorously. The fate of France is in your hands. So do not lose an instant in making the movement ordered by the Emperor, and direct yourself upon the heights of Saint-Amand and Brye.

Seeing the masses of the enemy increasing—the advance of Alten's division had just debouched from Quatre-Bras—Ney understood more fully that it would be necessary to oppose to them all his forces. Besides, at the very moment when the

Emperor's letter suggested to him the fine manoeuvre by which the Prussian Army could be exterminated, he recognized the impossibility of executing it. Ney was exposed to the fire of a battery; the balls struck the ground and ricochetted around him. He was heard to exclaim: "Would that these English cannon-balls would strike me dead!"

Exasperated and blinded by rage, Ney did not stop to reflect that the 1st Corps would no longer be able to arrive in useful time at Frasnes, and that in recalling it there he crossed the plans of Napoleon and acted in direct contravention with his will. He sent back General Delcambre with the imperative order for d'Erlon to bring back his troops to the right wing.

4

And yet these words of Napoleon's letter, "The fate of France is in your hands," troubled and fascinated the Marshal. This movement, which he had directed d'Erlon to interrupt, he had not entirely abandoned the idea of executing himself. Perhaps by a desperate effort he might yet, in spite of the disproportion of forces, throw back the English beyond Quatre-Bras, and once master of this point, operate against the Prussian Army, with the aid of d'Erlon, the manoeuvre awaited by Napoleon. All the troops had been engaged, with the exception of the *cuirassiers* of Kellermann and the cavalry of the Guard. He summoned Kellermann. "My dear general," said he to him in an excited tone, "it is a question of the safety of France. An extraordinary effort is necessary. Take your cavalry and throw yourself in the midst of the English. Crush them, ride them down!"

The intrepid Kellermann had never discussed an order to charge. However, he thought it his duty to say to Ney that the Anglo-Dutch were thought to number more than 20,000 men, and that he had with him but one brigade of *cuirassiers*, his three other brigades having remained in the rear, in accordance with the order of the Marshal.

"What does that matter!" cried Ney. "Charge with what you have! Ride them down! I will cause you to be supported by all the cavalry here present.... Go!..."

Kellermann could do nothing else but obey. He rejoined Guiton's brigade (8th and 11th *Cuirassiers*), formed it in columns of squadrons, each squadron separated by a distance double that of its front, and led it at a rapid trot as far as the summit of the hill which rises between Gemioncourt and Quatre-Bras. There he gave the command, repeated at once from front to rear of the column: "Prepare to charge!... Gallop!... Forward!... Charge!"

"I hastened," says he in his report to Ney, "in order not to give to my men the time to recognize the full extent of the danger."

The trumpets sound the charge. In an irradiation of steel and a rain of pebbles thrown up by the feet of the horses the *cuirassiers* descend the slope like an avalanche. At each stride the pace increases. The ground trembles and a cloud of dust arises. The men in the first rank, bending forward over the necks of their horses, hold their blades straight before them; the others brandish their glittering swords. Kellermann, sword in hand, charges twenty steps in front of the leading squadron.

In the valley the four battalions of Colin Halkett's fresh brigade are drawn up in line or formed in squares. Motionless, resolute, and calm, the English, reserving their fire, await the *cuirassiers*. The 69th Regiment, posted in the first line, between the wood of Bossu and the highway, delivers its fire at thirty yards. The *cuirassiers* pass through the balls and smoke like a flash of lightning through the clouds. They attack the 69th, overthrow and crush it and, take its flag. They then charge the square of the 30th and overthrow the 33rd. Then, without giving their horses time to blow, they scale the opposite slope, sabre in passing the cannoneers of a battery, break a square of Brunswick, and penetrate as far as Quatre-Bras.

The first and second lines of the enemy were pierced, and a bloody breach was opened. Unfortunately, the *cuirassiers* were not supported. Offended by Ney, who seemed to doubt his resolution, Kellermann had delivered his charge too soon. His mind still unbalanced by his rage against d'Erlon, the Marshal had badly coordinated this supreme effort, had delayed to issue orders, and had forgotten the cavalry of the Guard in reserve near Frasnes. The columns of infantry and the lancers and *chasseurs* of Piré had just begun to move, whilst the two regiments of *cuirassiers*, reduced to 500 men, disunited by the very impetuosity of the charge, and their horses blown, found themselves alone in the midst of Wellington's army.

They were at the apex of a triangle of fire, fusilladed from the wood of Bossu by the Dutch, from the embankment of the route of Namur by the English, from the houses of Quatre-Bras by the sharpshooters of Brunswick, and cannonaded from the route of Brussels by the batteries of Major Kulmann. Count de Valmy fell under his dead horse. This was the signal for flight. It was in vain that he arose and attempted to re-form his squadrons; the *cuirassiers* no longer listened to his commands. They wheeled about, buried their spurs in the flanks of their horses, and, in small groups, in disorder, but still with threatening point, re-traversed under a hail of balls the two lines of the enemy, bearing off as a trophy the flag of the 69th English.

These horsemen, panic-stricken and retreating at headlong speed, jostled and drew with them in their flight many battalions of Foy's division and the brigade of Bauduin. Bachelu, who had just begun his advance from Piraumont, saw at a distance the rout and also arrested his movement. Alone, the cavalry of Piré continued its charge against the enemy. At a rapid gallop it hurled itself upon the battalions of Kempt. The English squares, opposing their bayonets and flanking fire to this cavalry, rendered unavailing its multiplied charges.

At this moment Commandant Baudus, who had been sent by the Emperor, joined Marshal Ney, who, having had two horses killed under him, was standing on foot "at the most exposed point." Baudus transmitted to him the words of Napoleon: "It is absolutely necessary that the order given to Count d'Erlon should be executed, regardless of the situation in which Marshal Ney may find himself. I attach no great importance to what is passing today where he is. The important affair is here, where I am, because I wish to finish with the Prussian Army. As for the Prince of the Moskowa, he must, if he can do no better, confine himself to holding in check the English Army."

Ney, wild with rage, his face purple with passion, brandished his sword like a madman. He hardly listened to the words of Baudus, and cried that he had just sent to d'Erlon the order to return to Frasnes. Baudus vainly attempted to get him to rescind this order. The Marshal quitted him abruptly to throw himself in the midst of his routed infantry. He quickly rallied it and led it against the brigade of Pack, which was advancing offensively.

From six until seven o'clock Wellington had received new reinforcements—namely, the artillery of Brunswick, the brigades of English Guards of Maitland and Byng, and the Nassauers of Kruse. It was his turn to attack—to attack safely, as he loved to do. Maitland and Byng entered the wood of Bossu; Halkett and Pack, supported by the corps of Brunswick and Nassau, marched on the right and left of the highway in the direction of Gemioncourt; and the English and Hanoverians of Kielmansegge converged on Piraumont. The French yielded the conquered ground only foot by foot and under reiterated attacks.

More than an hour was necessary to drive Jérôme from the wood of Bossu. Foy, driven from position to position as far as Gemioncourt, held out for a long time around this farm. Bachelu abandoned Piraumont only after a fierce fight. Past eight o'clock a battalion of Maitland having debouched from the southwest corner of the wood in order to retake Pierrepont, the division battery of Foy stopped it short by its fire; then the indefatigable lancers of Piré charged it, threw it in disorder, and pursued it as far as Gemioncourt; it escaped by re-entering the wood. At the same time the *cuirassiers* overthrew the 7th Belgian Battalion to the northwest of Pierrepont. Everywhere the piles of dead and wounded—4,300 French and 4,700 Anglo-Netherlanders—testified to the fury of the fight.

At nine o'clock, when the battle was lost, or rather had terminated without result, for both armies had resumed the positions which they had occupied in the morning, the 1st Corps debouched from Frasnes.

Having been rejoined about six o'clock, at the distance of a long cannon-shot from Saint-Amand, by General Delcambre, d'Erlon had hesitated between the first instructions of the Emperor and the imperative order of Ney. In spite of the advice of Generals de Salle and Garbé, and to the intense indignation of the soldiers, who saw the Prussians and burned to attack them, he had finally determined upon a counter-march. "I judged," said he, "that to recall me in spite of the will of Napoleon the Marshal was in extreme peril."

But d'Erlon did not stop to think that, being within three kilometres of Fleurus and at three leagues from Quatre-Bras, he would be able to aid the Emperor very efficaciously, whilst he would be unable to arrive in time to support Ney. As a matter of fact, when he reached Frasnes, when it was quite dark, with his troops, "indignant and humiliated at having done nothing on this day," the Marshal no longer had need of them.

Count d'Erlon brought back but three divisions. The idea having occurred to him at the beginning of the counter-march that it was necessary to fill the gap existing between the right and left wings, he had left Durutte in sight of Wagnelée with the 4th Division of infantry and the cavalry of Jacquinot. Durutte not having been able to obtain any definite instructions from d'Erlon, save the recommendation to "act with extreme prudence," advanced slowly between Villers-Perwin and Wagnelée. To the northwest of this last point Jacquinot had a slight engagement about eight o'clock with the cavalry of General Marwitz, which covered the right of Blücher.

A little later Durutte turned back on Wagnelée, which he occupied after having dislodged a feeble rear guard. These feints against the flank of the Prussians were not made in time nor were they pushed far enough to annoy in any way whatsoever the retreat of the vanquished army. At Wagnelée, however, Durutte had plainly seen the Prussians retiring from Le Hameau and La Haye on the heights of Brye. Impassive, he had permitted them to defile within range of his guns. He was paralyzed by the instructions of d'Erlon, who had recommended him to act with extreme prudence. One of Durutte's brigadiers, General Brue, exasperated by this forced inaction, exclaimed: "It is something unheard of for one to witness with grounded arms the retreat of a beaten army, when everything indicates that it would only be necessary to attack in order to destroy it."

"It is very fortunate," replied Durutte, "that you are not responsible."

"Would to God that I were!" answered Brue. "We would already be fighting."

CHAPTER 4

The Retreat of the Prussian Army

1

On the evening of the battle of Ligny the Emperor had not deemed it prudent to pursue the enemy farther than the line of Brye-Sombreffe. The Prussian Army, whose right and left wings had retired in rather good order, and which continued to occupy these two villages with detachments, still seemed capable of offering a serious resistance. It was also to be feared that a reserve corps debouching by the route of Namur would arrive upon the scene. Finally Napoleon was without news of his left wing. During the entire day the Prince of the Moskowa had not written him a single despatch. The Emperor had learned in an indirect way that there had been a battle at Quatre-Bras. But had Marshal Ney been victorious? The presumptions were rather that he had been held in check, if not repulsed, since the orders prescribing a movement in the rear of the Prussian Army had not been executed. There were many reasons for not risking the chances of a night pursuit.

The Emperor then contented himself with directing Grouchy, who, in accordance with his instructions, had come about eleven o'clock to Fleurus for orders, to cause the enemy to be followed at early dawn by the cavalry corps of Pajol and Exelmans.

About seven o'clock on. the morning of June 17th Flahault returned from Frasnes and informed the Emperor, who was lunching, of the battle of Quatre-Bras. Almost at the same time there was received at headquarters a despatch from Pajol, dated

Balâtre, at four o'clock in the morning, stating that he was pursuing the enemy, who was in full retreat towards Liège and Namur. Pajol added that he had already made many prisoners.

Thus, between seven and eight o'clock at the latest, the Emperor was informed regarding the movements of the Prussians as well as the English. The first were retreating towards Liège and Namur; the second still held their positions at Quatre-Bras. But was this information sufficiently complete and exact? Was it the main body of the Prussian Army, or an isolated corps, that was retreating towards Namur? Was it a rear guard that occupied Quatre-Bras, or was it the entire army of Wellington? Napoleon did not judge that he was well enough informed to come to a decision. Grouchy had come for orders; he told him to remain in order to accompany him upon the battle-field of Ligny, whither he was preparing to go to visit his troops. At the same time he caused Soult to write to Ney as follows:

> ...The Emperor is going to the mill of Brye, by which passes the main highway leading from Namur to Quatre-Bras. It is then hardly possible that the English Army will do anything in front of you, for if it attempted to do anything, the Emperor would march against it by the route of Quatre-Bras, whilst you would attack it in front, and this army (English) would be instantly destroyed. So inform His Majesty of what is passing in front of you...
>
> His Majesty's intention is that you will take position at Quatre-Bras; but if this is impossible, you will inform him at once of everything in detail, and the Emperor will go there, as I have told you. If, on the contrary, there is only a rear guard there, you will attack it and take up position there. Today is needed to terminate this operation and to supply ammunition, rally the stragglers, and call in the detachments.

From this we see that the plans of the Emperor for the day of the 17th were confined to the occupation of Quatre-Bras by

Ney and the revictualling of the Army. Doubtless, if Wellington should remain in his exposed position at Quatre-Bras, he would profit by this fortunate chance to march against the English and exterminate them; but he doubted very much if his cautious adversary would commit such a fault. Ney would dislodge without difficulty from Quatre-Bras the rear guard, which still remained in that position, and the French Army would remain inactive in its bivouacs during the entire day.

There were better ways in which to employ the day after a victory. So Napoleon did not long persist in the idea of giving so much rest to his troops and such a respite to the enemy. This was his intention at 8 o'clock, as is shown by the letter of Soult to Marshal Ney; but at half-past eight, before entering his carriage, he meditated other projects. He sent to Lobau the order to send to the assistance of Pajol on the route of Namur the infantry division of Teste with its battery, and he caused to be directed on Quatre-Bras a cavalry reconnaissance, to ascertain if the English still occupied in force that position.

He then quitted the Château of Fleurus, thoroughly determined to return there no more. Already, in the Imperial entourage, it was said that the Prussians were to be followed towards Namur and the English towards Brussels. The Emperor, in fact, had conceived this double manoeuvre, but he had not as yet determined upon its mode of execution. He wished to obtain further information; he went to await it upon the battle-field of the day before, in the midst of his soldiers, to whom he knew that he could never show himself too often.

A little before nine o'clock the Emperor entered his carriage; but, unable to bear the severe jolting of his heavy berlin over the furrows, he left it, "fatigued as he was," says Grouchy, and mounted his horse. He traversed Ligny, Saint-Amand, and the outskirts of La Haye. A great number of wounded Prussians were still lying upon the ground pell-mell with the dead. The Emperor spoke to them, ordered brandy and money to be distributed to them, and gave the most positive orders for them to be picked up at once and shown the same attention as the

French. A Prussian officer of rank lay, horribly mutilated, on the very spot where he had fallen the day before. The Emperor called a peasant who was standing at some steps from him and said to him in a serious tone: "Do you believe in hell?" The Belgian, terribly frightened, answered in the affirmative.

"Well, if you do not wish to go to hell, take care of this wounded man whom I entrust to you; otherwise, God will cause you to burn; He desires us to be charitable."

"This recommendation," concludes an eye-witness of this scene, "was not useless, for the Belgians showed as much eagerness in caring for our wounded as they manifested aversion in succouring the Prussians, who had rendered themselves obnoxious."

Arrived on a line with the mill of Bussy, the Emperor passed along the front of the troops drawn up before their bivouacs. He halted to congratulate the chiefs of the corps, the officers, and soldiers. At sight of him these last broke forth in resounding cheers that were heard at a distance of more than three kilometres by General von Gröben, in observation before Tilly. This tour finished, the Emperor dismounted from his horse and conversed for quite a while with Grouchy and many generals on the state of opinion in Paris, the Legislative Corps, Fouché, and the Jacobins.

Some of his auditors admired the freedom of mind which he preserved in such critical circumstances; others were a little uneasy at seeing him lose time in talking politics and bewildering his mind with subjects foreign to those which it seemed should occupy him exclusively. Grouchy, however, dared not sound the Emperor upon the operations planned for the day. Already, on his departure from Fleurus, he had demanded some orders of him, and Napoleon had sharply replied: "I will give them to you when the time comes."

2

The Emperor was not so absorbed with the plots of the Liberals of the Chamber that he forgot the enemy. He had received new information. It was at first a letter from Ney, stating that the English, in position in front of Quatre-Bras, held the wood of Bossu, Gemioncourt, Piraumont, and showed eight regiments of infantry and two thousand horse. The Emperor could not doubt that these masses were the first line of Wellington, present with his army, and not a rear guard. Soon after, between ten and eleven o'clock, the officer commanding the reconnaissance sent towards Quatre-Bras reported that the English still occupied that point, their left covered by the cavalry with which he had had an engagement. There also arrived some information regarding the retreat of the Prussians. A despatch from Pajol stated that he had captured, in front of Mazy, upon the route of Namur, eight guns and numerous wagons; and a message from Exelmans made known that he was marching with his two divisions of dragoons and his horse batteries on Gembloux, "where the enemy had massed his forces."

It was nearly eleven o'clock. The Emperor finally took his last dispositions. He ordered Lobau to send the 6th Corps to Marbais, in order to second the attack of Marshal Ney upon Quatre-Bras by outflanking the English left. Drouot received an order to follow this movement with all the Guard.

The Emperor then said to Marshal Grouchy: "While I am marching against the English you will put yourself in pursuit of the Prussians. You will have under your orders the corps of Vandamme and Gérard, the division of Teste, and the cavalry corps of Pajol, Exelmans, and Milhaud."

From the very first Grouchy felt the responsibility rather than the honour of this mission. In the course of his long career he had never exercised a great command. It was as a general of cavalry that he had accomplished his fine feats of arms and won his renown. He had the *coup d'œil* of the battlefield, the lucid and prompt vision of weak points, the conception of sudden and decisive movements; but he was the man of a single hour, a single manoeuvre, a single effort; he was a tactician, but a tactician momentary, local and special, and not made for the conduct and the responsibilities of strategical operations. To make matters worse, he was conscious of his inferiority as commander of an army acting independently. This sentiment was soon to paralyze him. Besides, he knew or suspected that Gérard and Vandamme especially, with whose intractable character he was acquainted, were displeased at being put under his orders. What authority could he have over some lieutenants who lacked confidence in him? But, as a marshal of France, Grouchy could not, nor even did he wish, through respect for himself, to decline the mission from which he augured already nothing but difficulty and danger. A refusal was at the bottom of his mind; he dared not formulate it.

If, as he pretends, he observed to the Emperor that it would be very difficult to discover in what direction the Prussians had gone and to baffle their designs, since they had begun their retreat in the night or at break of day, Napoleon could not have failed to reply to him something like the following: "Pajol has been in pursuit of the enemy since three o'clock; he has taken from him, on the Namur route, since five o'clock, men, baggage, and guns. Exelmans, who has followed a Prussian corps now massed at Gembloux, has certainly, by this time, regained contact with the enemy. Then, if Blücher's heads of columns have eight or ten hours the start of you, your cavalry is in close pursuit of his rear guard."

It is even possible that the Emperor may have added, as Grouchy affirms: "All the probabilities lead me to believe that it is upon the Meuse that Blücher is effecting his retreat. So you will direct yourself on that side."

The reports from Pajol and Exelmans seemed, in fact, to confirm the assumption that, in accordance with the principles of strategy, the Prussians were withdrawing upon their base of operations.

Grouchy having departed in order to issue his orders, the Emperor decided that it would be better to have more cavalry with the principal fraction of the army. He determined to retake from his lieutenant Domon's division of Vandamme's corps and Milhaud's corps of *cuirassiers*. In the absence of the major-general, still at Fleurus, he dictated to Bertrand an order for Grouchy, enjoining the latter to direct without delay on Marbais these three divisions of cavalry.

A few minutes after (probably between 11:30 and 11:45 a.m.) the Emperor thought it best to develop and explain more fully in writing the verbal instructions which he had just given to Marshal Grouchy. Soult had not yet arrived. Bertrand again took the pen and wrote under the Emperor's dictation:

> Go to Gembloux with the cavalry corps of Pajol and Exelmans, the light cavalry of the 4th Corps, the division of Teste, and the 3rd and 4th Corps of infantry. You will reconnoitre in the direction of Namur and Maëstricht, and you will pursue the enemy. Explore his march and inform me of his movements, in order that I may be able to penetrate what he intends doing.
>
> I am carrying my headquarters to Quatre-Bras, where the English still were this morning. Our communications then will be direct by the paved route of Namur. If the enemy has evacuated Namur, you will write to the general commanding the 2nd Military Division at Charlemont to cause that town to be occupied by some battalions of the National Guard."
>
> It is important to discover what Blücher and Wellington are intending to do; whether they propose to unite their armies in order to coyer Brussels and Liège, in trying the fate of another battle. In all cases keep constantly your two corps of infantry united in a league of ground, having many avenues of retreat. Post intermediate detachments of cavalry, so as to be able to communicate with headquarters.

According to this letter, Marshal Grouchy was, first, to concentrate all his forces at Gembloux, an intermediate between Namur, Liège, and Wavre; second, to explore all the country in the direction of Namur and Maëstricht, directions which it was probable, but not certain, that the enemy was following in his retreat; third, to put himself on the traces of the Prussians and penetrate their designs in pursuing them; and fourth, to know whether Blücher's object was to unite with the English. Doubtless the Emperor did not trace for his lieutenant, as he might have done, the conduct to be followed under all circumstances; but he could not doubt that Grouchy, who by his very position upon the flank of the army, was manifestly destined to cover it against an offensive return of the enemy, would manoeuvre so as to interpose himself between the army and the Prussians.

Napoleon had provided for Blücher. There remained Wellington. He ordered Soult, who had just rejoined the Imperial Staff, to write to Ney that he must attack the English at once and that he (Napoleon) would second him. It was noon. By this time the heads of columns had no doubt reached Marbais. The Emperor mounted his horse and took the road to Quatre-Bras, whither the soldiers of Lobau, all the Guard, the divisions of Domon and Subervic, and the *cuirassiers* of Milhaud were on the march, eager for the fray.

3

Napoleon, Soult, Grouchy, and all the staff thought the Prussians were retreating towards the Meuse; it was in the direction of the Dyle that they were falling back. On the day before, at night, whilst their troops were rallying between the route of Namur and the Roman road, Ziethen, Pirch I., and other generals, no longer receiving any orders, hastened to Brye, where they expected to find Blucher. At this moment the dragoons, who had picked up Blucher from the battlefield, bore him all bruised from his fall and in a half-swoon into a cottage of Mellery. His staff was without news of him; it was ignorant if he were a prisoner or free, dead or living.

Consternation reigned supreme; every eye was fixed with expectancy on Gneisenau, to whom, in Blücher's absence, belonged the command by reason of his seniority of rank. What course would he take? Would he abandon his lines of communication with Namur to try once more to unite with the English by a parallel march, or, in order to fall back on his base of operations, would he leave Wellington alone against the French Army and overturn the plan of campaign decided upon for two months? Gneisenau sat his horse in the middle of the road which joins to the north of Brye the route of Namur; by the light of the moon he consulted with difficulty his map. After a short examination, he cried: "Retreat on Tilly and Wavre."

Some days later Wellington wrote emphatically to the King of the Low Countries:

It was the decisive moment of the century.

likewise the German military historians have exalted the retreat on Wavre as the equal of the finest strategical conceptions. We think this is putting it a little extravagantly, to say the least. This determination marks in Gneisenau firmness in reverses and an understanding of the necessities of war; but when he ordered this movement, he certainly did not foresee the immense consequences that were to result from it. At that time he had no intention of rejoining the English Army in order to cover Brussels. If he thought that at Wavre the Prussians would again find themselves in the same sphere of operations with the English, he had no assurance that such would be the case, as it was dependent upon the line of retreat that would be chosen by Wellington and upon other eventualities.

At all events, he did not count on resuming the offensive thirty-six hours after his defeat. It was especially as a temporary position, as a point of concentration, that he indicated Wavre, whose defence was rendered easy on account of the River Dyle. The movement was not as audacious as the Germans have pretended. If Gneisenau abandoned his lines of communication with Namur and Liège, it was to open new ones, by way of Tirlemont and Louvain, with Maëstricht, Cologne, Wesel, Munster, and Aix-la-Chapelle.

On the morning of June 17th couriers had been sent to these places to collect munitions, and the order had been sent to Liège to direct the siege park on Maëstricht. Gneisenau had then not "broken the bridges behind him," as General von Ollech says, or rather, he had broken them, but with the certainty of establishing others the next day.

The corps of Ziethen and Pirch I. bivouacked between Tilly, Mellery, and Gentinnes; three battalions of Jagow remained at Brye as an outpost under the command of Quartermaster-General Grolemann. Notice of the retreat on Wavre was sent to Thielmann, who had withdrawn his troops to the north of Sombreffe, though continuing to occupy this position by a strong detachment, and to Bülow, who, knowing already that the battle was lost, had halted his army corps upon the Roman road with his advance guard at Baudeset. On arriving at Mellery, Gneisenau had there found Blücher. He was stretched upon some straw in a remote cottage, taking from time to time a few swallows of milk.

At dawn on the 17th all the army decamped. The corps of Ziethen and Pirch, which had just rallied the three battalions of the outpost at Brye, marched on Wavre by way of Gentinnes,. Villeroux, and Mont Saint-Guibert; Colonel Sohr was left temporarily behind Tilly with two regiments of cavalry. Having arrived before Wavre between eleven o'clock and noon, Ziethen passed with his troops upon the left bank of the Dyle and established them in Bierges and environs. Pirch halted his corps upon the right bank; it bivouacked between Aisernont and Saint-Anne.

From Sombreffe, Thielmann had at first advanced to Gembloux; judging his troops to be very much fatigued, he took position a little beyond this village and, very imprudently, remained motionless from seven in the morning until two in the afternoon. He finally resumed his march, passed through Corbaix, crossed only at eight o'clock the bridge of Wavre, and camped at La Bavette (a half-league to the north of Wavre). The cavalry of Lottum and the division of Borcke, which formed the rear guard of this corps, did not even arrive in sight of Wavre until long past midnight; they were forced to bivouac upon the right bank of the Dyle.

Bülow, whose troops were in column upon the Roman road, had orders to establish himself at Dion-le-Mont (a league to the southwest of Wavre). He marched so slowly that at ten in the evening his movement was unfinished.

4

The retreat of the Prussian outpost established at Brye, and consequently those of the corps of Pirch and Ziethen, escaped absolutely the notice of the French *videttes* in position in front of the mill of Bussy. During the entire morning the cavalry posts made no movement, not a reconnaissance, not a patrol. On the French right, towards Tongrinne, the hussars of Pajol showed more vigilance. At half-past two in the morning they warned their general that the enemy was abandoning his positions. Pajol at once ordered to mount the two regiments which he had under his immediate command, and launched himself in pursuit of the Prussians along the route of Namur.

Unfortunately, this was a false direction. He believed himself to be on the traces of Thielmann's corps, when it was only a few stragglers, a convoy, and a stray battery that he was following. Beyond Mazy, about five or six o'clock in the morning, he overtook this column, sabred a squadron of the 7th Uhlans which had joined it, and captured the guns and wagons. He pushed no farther than Les Isnes on the route of Namur, no longer seeing anything in front of him. Very uncertain as to what he ought to do, he sent reconnaissances in different directions, and halted in person at the point where the road of Saint-Denis crosses the main highway.

At twelve o'clock, informed by false reports that the enemy was not retreating on Namur, but on Saint-Denis and Liège— or, in other words, on Louvain—he directed himself on that side. Thanks to the arrival of the 1st Hussars, which had rejoined about nine o'clock, and the division of Teste, which had just been sent him by the Emperor, his forces then amounted to three regiments of cavalry, four of infantry, and two batteries.

Berton's brigade of dragoons of Exelmans' corps had put itself in motion soon after the rear guard of Thielmann had evacuated Sombreffe. But instead of entering this village and taking the route of Gembloux, Berton followed Pajol along the route of Namur. However, he did not cross the stream of Orneau, as some peasants had informed him that the Prussian Army was retreating by way of Gembloux and that there were still a great many troops in that village. Berton hastened to transmit this information to General Exelmans, and awaited further instructions. He ought to have also communicated it to Pajol, who was fifteen hundred yards in front of him. The order to advance on Gembloux soon reached Berton. He resumed his march, and arrived in front of the village at nine o'clock. Some Prussian videttes were posted on the left bank of the Orneau; and beyond Gembloux masses of the enemy were discovered taking their rest.

Exelmans soon rejoined Berton, bringing with him his three other brigades of cavalry. He rather judiciously estimated at 20,000 men the Prussians bivouacked behind Gembloux. Exelmans had 3,000 dragoons and two horse batteries; and Pajol was six kilometres to the right with 1,400 hussars, 3,000 infantry, and two batteries. Exelmans did not think to inform him that the Prussians occupied Gembloux—information which would have saved his comrade an eccentric march of twenty kilometres (going and returning) in the direction of Leuze. He made no demonstration to compel the Prussians to unmask their designs. He did not fire a cannon-shot at (these masses, not even a musket-shot at the *videttes*. He limited himself to observing the enemy—very heedlessly, as we shall see farther on. Finally, with a negligence truly unpardonable, he neglected to inform at once Grouchy or the Emperor that he was in touch with one of Blücher's corps.

In spite of these faults, affairs were not seriously compromised. At noon, at the moment when the Emperor reiterated in writing to Grouchy the order to pursue the Prussians, their army was divided. The corps of Ziethen and Pirch were concentrated at Wavre, the corps of Bülow on the march from Baudeset had not yet passed Walhain, and the corps of Thielmann had halted near Gembloux, within cannon-range of Exelmans. The negligence of the French *videttes*, the carelessness of the officers commanding the outposts, the time lost in the morning, and the false indications of the Prussian line of retreat, all could have yet been repaired if Exelmans had been vigilant and active and if Grouchy had thoroughly understood his mission.

5

On quitting the Emperor, about half-past eleven o'clock, near the mill of Bussy, Grouchy sent by Colonel de Blocqueville the order to General Vandamme, at Saint-Amand, to advance quickly with the 3rd Corps to Point du Jour, at the intersection of the roads of Namur and Gembloux. At the same time he despatched to Exelmans, towards Gembloux, another *aide-de-camp*. Captain Bella, to obtain information. He then went to Ligny, wishing to give in person his instructions to Gérard.

On his way there he met Marshal Soult, who was on his way to rejoin the Imperial Staff. He had with Soult a short interview, which bore only upon the divisions of cavalry which, according to the first order of Bertrand, which he had just received, he was to detach from his army and direct on Marbais. When he had departed, Soult said to one of his *aides-de-camp*: "It is a fault to divert so large a force from the array which is marching against the English. In the state in which their defeat has put the Prussians, a feeble corps of infantry, with the cavalry of Pajol and Exelmans, would suffice to follow and observe them." Soult, who, moreover, was deceived as to the disorder of the Prussian Army, blamed the too great strength of the detachment placed under the orders of Grouchy, but he did not criticise the direction given to the pursuit of the enemy.

At Ligny, Grouchy found Gérard in a bad humour, he was, it appears, greatly vexed at not receiving the Marshal's baton after the battle, and doubtless, somewhat dissatisfied at seeing himself detached under the orders of Grouchy. In conformity with the second despatch of Bertrand, which had reached him, the Marshal ordered Gérard to follow the 3rd Corps to Gembloux. It does not appear, whatever Grouchy may say, that the irritation of Gérard had led the latter to defer with a bad intention the movement prescribed. Before he could put his troops on the march, he was forced to wait until the entire corps of Vandamme had finished defiling. Now, the defile of an army corps of three divisions of infantry, with artillery, engineers, and train, lasted at least an hour at this time, when the distance between the divers elements of the column was less, however, than it is today. If there was any delay in the departure of the 4th Corps, the fault must be attributed to Grouchy himself.

As the 3rd and 4th Corps were to follow the same route, and as the corps of Vandamme was at Saint-Amand, 2,000 yards, as the crow flies, to the left of Ligny, where the corps of Gérard was stationed, it was Gérard, and not Vandamme, that Grouchy should have first put on the march. In this way more than an hour would have been gained. It has been said that Grouchy wished to spare the self-love of Vandamme, whose ill-nature he feared. A fine reason! Grouchy must have, indeed, felt himself invested with but little authority! On the day before and the one previous to that, on the left wing, the 2nd Corps had formed the head of column instead of the 1st Corps; and in the Guard it was customary to march with the left in advance, without the grenadiers feeling humiliated.

The corps of Vandamme marched with incredible slowness. From Saint-Amand to Point du Jour, by way of Ligny and Sombreffe, it is nearly four miles. Now the advance of the 3rd Corps, which had decamped from Saint-Amand before noon, did not reach Point de Jour until three o'clock. It had then marched at the rate of two kilometres per hour.

Grouchy arrived at Point du Jour almost at the same time as the advance of Vandamme. What he had done since quitting Gérard at Ligny, scarcely a league distant from Point du Jour, cannot be explained. At all events, he had not thought to send a few squadrons on a reconnaissance in the direction of Gentinnes. Yet the Emperor had said to him: "It is for you to discover the direction taken by the enemy."

The *aide-de-camp* Bella, on returning from his mission to Exelmans, rejoined Grouchy either at Point du Jour or Sombreffe. Exelmans had given him at Gembloux, between one and two o'clock, a letter for the Marshal, stating that he was in touch with the enemy's army, massed upon the left bank of the Orneau, and that he would follow the Prussians as soon as they would put themselves on the march. It was necessary to hasten to profit by this important information.

Grouchy, who was an excellent handler of cavalry, ought to have hastened at full speed to Gembloux, to see with his own eyes what was going on and to direct in person the movements of the four brigades of dragoons. He contented himself with proceeding there at a snail's pace with the entire corps of Vandamme, which was followed by that of Gérard. The troops continued to march very slowly. It is seven kilometres from Point du Jour to Gembloux. Vandamme did not arrive there till seven o'clock, and Gérard at nine. Notwithstanding the dilatory march of these corps, they would have been able to reach Gembloux two hours earlier and simultaneously if Grouchy had ordered them to move on this village in two columns. Gérard would have taken the road to Point du Jour and Vandamme would have gained the Roman road above Sombreffe.

The corps of Thielmann had been gone for some time, and Exelmans, whose *videttes* were separated from those of the enemy only by the stream of the Orneau, had permitted the Prussians to march away on his left without discovering their retreat in time. Thielmann had struck camp to the north of Gembloux at eight o'clock; Exelmans did not enter the village with the dragoons until three. The Prussians were still close by, and he might have yet discovered their traces lost by his fault. But he knew not how to repair his very culpable lack of vigilance. Instead of pushing some parties in every direction and of following with the main body of his cavalry the one which would have again found the traces of the enemy, he went simply to take position at Sauvenierre, a short league to the north of Gembloux, satisfied with having captured near there a park of four hundred beeves. During this afternoon Grouchy had shown little activity. He put off until the next day the pursuit of the Prussians. The corps of Vandamme had made only thirteen kilometres and that of Gérard hardly ten. Now, although there were still nearly two hours of daylight, Grouchy halted his troops. He ordered the infantry of Vandamme to bivouac around Gembloux and that of Gérard in the rear of that village. The Marshal has alleged as an excuse the bad condition of the roads and the rain, which fell in torrents. But on the side of Wavre and Dion-le-Mont the roads were no better, and the Prussians marched under the beating rain.

Exelmans, however, had determined about six o'clock to send the brigade of Bonnemains on a reconnaissance to Sart-à-Walhain and the 15th Dragoons to Perwez. Bonnemains went beyond Sart-à-Walhain, and threw out some detachments towards Nil Saint-Vincent and Tourinnes. This last village was still occupied by a Prussian rear guard. After having observed for nearly an hour this infantry, which made no movement, the dragoons fell back and established themselves in bivouac at Ernage. There, about ten o'clock, a peasant informed Bonnemains that the enemy had evacuated Tourinnes, and was marching in the direction of Wavre. Bonnemains reported this information. On returning from Perwez, the colonel of the 15th Dragoons also reported that the Prussian troops were retreating on Wavre.

These reports did not reach Grouchy until late at night. But since six o'clock he knew by a letter from Pajol that the hostile column, which at first seemed to be directing itself on Namur, had marched towards Louvain; and between seven and eight o'clock he had himself gathered at Gembloux important information. If these reports did not all agree—if, according to some, the Prussians were marching by Perwez on Liège and Maëstricht—according to the greater part, they were directing themselves on Wavre, in order to unite with Wellington towards Brussels.

From the despatch of Pajol, together with the information

given by the inhabitants of Gembloux, it was evident that, in the first place, the enemy was not retreating on Namur, as had been believed in the morning; in the second place, that he was marching either on Louvain, Maëstricht, or Liège, or on Wavre, but far more probably on this last point, with the design of uniting with the English Array.

Under these circumstances, it was necessary, by all means, to proceed towards Wavre, for if the Prussians were falling back towards Liège, Maëstricht, or Louvain, they would put themselves outside of the sphere of operations for at least two days; whilst, if they rallied at Wavre with the view of a junction with Wellington's army, there was imminent danger for the Emperor. Then Grouchy ought to and could have, since eight o'clock in the evening, sent the cavalry of Exelmans to Walhain and Sart-à-Walhain, the corps of Vandamme to Ernage, and that of Gérard to Saint-Géry.

Not only by this movement would he have established his army on the same evening at a league nearer Wavre, but by immediately causing the 4th Corps to double upon the 3rd in order to send it to Saint-Géry, he would have given himself the faculty of marching the next day, without loss of time, in two parallel columns. Besides, at Saint-Géry the 4th Corps would have found itself well placed to gain rapidly Mont Saint-Guibert and the bridges of Mousty and Ottignies, if Grouchy at sunrise had believed it necessary to move on Wavre by the left bank of the Dyle.

Grouchy did not understand that Wavre was his immediate objective, and that he ought to sacrifice the doubtful hope of overtaking the Prussians, if they were retreating towards Liège, to the necessity of covering the flank of the Imperial Army, if they manoeuvred to unite with the English. At ten in the evening he wrote to the Emperor:

> . . . It appears, according to all the reports, that, having arrived at Sauvenierre, the Prussians have divided themselves into two columns; one has taken the route to Wavre, and the other appears to be directing itself on Perwez.

One may perhaps infer from this that a portion are going to join Wellington, and that the centre, which is Blücher's army, is retiring on Liège, while another column with artillery is making its retreat on Namur. General Exelmans has orders to push this evening six squadrons on Sart-à-Walhain and three squadrons on Perwez. According to their reports, if the main body of the Prussians is retiring on Wavre, I shall pursue them in that direction, in order that they may not be able to reach Brussels, and to separate them from Wellington. If, on the contrary, my information proves that the principal Prussian force has marched on Perwez, I shall direct myself by way of that town in pursuit of the enemy.

Although Grouchy says in this letter that he was preparing, according to the news of the night, to march either on Wavre or towards Liège, he took no measure in view of the first of these movements. His orders for the next day—orders to Exelmans and Vandamme to march on Sart-à-Walhain; order to Pajol to direct himself from Mazy on Grand Leez; order to Gérard to follow the 3rd Corps to Sart-à-Walhain and to send his cavalry to Grand Leez, "the enemy retiring on Perwez"—testify that, forgetting Wellington and neglecting Wavre, it was in the direction of Liège that he persisted in seeking the enemy.

Chapter 5

The Retreat of the English Army

1

On the side of Quatre-Bras, French and English remained motionless in their positions during the morning of June 17th. Ney did not learn the result of the battle of Ligny till after nine o'clock. As for Wellington, he had remained all night without hearing from his allies. The last message which he had received from Blücher, on the day before, stated that the Field Marshal had resumed the offensive and "that all was well."

A little later Gneisenau had, indeed, despatched an officer to inform him of the retreat; but this officer, severely wounded *en route* by French sharpshooters, had not been able to carry out his mission. Wellington thought that the battle, which had been indecisive, would be renewed the next day all along the line. Therefore he ordered his troops to bivouac at Quatre-Bras and summoned there reinforcements. The cavalry of Lord Uxbridge arrived in the evening and during the night; and on the morning of the 17th the brigade of Ompteda, the divisions of Clinton and Colville, and the reserve artillery put themselves on the march to rejoin.

Wellington, who had gone to Genappe to sleep, returned early in the morning to Quatre-Bras. Anxious to hear from Blücher, for it had been reported at Genappe that the Prussians had met with defeat, he sent towards his left his *aide-de-camp*, Colonel Gordon, with a detachment of the 10th Hussars. Gordon, avoiding the French *videttes* at Marbais, pushed as far as Tilly, where he had the good fortune to find still General Ziethen with the rear guard of the 1st Corps. He learned from the General that the Prussian Army was retreating on Wavre. On returning to Quatre-Bras at half-past seven o'clock, he transmitted this information to Wellington, who, in order to deceive his impatience, was walking with long strides along the road of Charleroi in front of Quatre-Bras.

Affairs assumed a different aspect. Wellington could no longer remain at Quatre-Bras, exposed to a combined attack from Ney in front and from Napoleon on his left. At first, somewhat troubled, he thought of retreating at once. "Old Blücher," said he, "has received a d——d good mauling, and has fallen back eighteen miles in the rear. As he has fallen back, we must fall back also. I suppose they will say in England that we have been thrashed."

Müffling observed to him that the situation did not appear so serious. "The Prussian Army," said he, "having marched on Wavre, you can easily put yourself again in the same sphere of operations with it. You can fall back on some point on a line with Wavre; there you will obtain news of the Field Marshal, information regarding the state of his troops, and you will be able to come to a decision as to what is best to be done under the circumstances."

Wellington determined to go to occupy the plateau of Mont Saint-Jean, a strong defensive position, which he had reconnoitred the preceding year at the time of his passage through Brussels. But should he decamp at once, or should he wait until his troops had breakfasted, at the risk of having a warm rear-guard affair? There was from time to time some firing at the advance posts, but the troops of Ney made no movement.

"I know the French," said Müffling. "They will not attack before having made their soup." Wellington decided that the retreat should commence only at ten o'clock. He sent to Lord Hill the order to fall back to Waterloo with the divisions on the march for Quatre-Bras. Then, after having read his paper, which had just been brought him from Brussels, he enveloped himself in his cloak and stretched himself upon the ground to sleep. On awakening, about nine o'clock, he threw a glance at the French positions. Seeing that Ney made no preparations for an attack, he said: "Are the French retiring? It is not at all improbable."

At this moment a Prussian officer, Lieutenant Massow, arrived from Mellery. He had been sent by Gneisenau to inform Wellington of the proposed concentration of all the Prussian Army at Wavre, and to ask him what he intended to do. The Duke replied in presence of Müffling: "I am going to establish myself at Mont Saint-Jean. I shall await Napoleon there in order to deliver battle to him, if I have the assurance of being supported, even by a single Prussian corps. But if this support cannot be rendered me, I shall be forced to sacrifice Brussels and take up a position behind the Escault." Massow left immediately to return to the Prussian head-quarters.

The English began their movement. The divisions of Cook and Picton, the Dutch-Belgians of Perponcher, the division of Alten, and finally the corps of Brunswick, marched successively by the route of Brussels. The numerous squadrons of Lord Uxbridge were deployed in the second line, so as to mask and then to cover this retreat. At one o'clock this corps of cavalry alone remained in position. Ney giving Lord Uxbridge plenty of leisure, the latter seated himself with his *aide-de-camp* upon the edge of the road. Uxbridge having remarked that the French would soon attack, the *aide-de-camp* replied, laughing: "They are eating." A short time after this Uxbridge was informed that large masses of troops were to be seen on the march towards the left. The imperial advance guard was approaching by the route of Namur.

2

From the mill of Bussy, near Ligny, the Emperor, with the light cavalry of Domon and the *cuirassiers* of Milhaud, had repaired to Marbais, whither he had previously directed the corps of Lobau, the cavalry division of Subervic, and the Guard. Having arrived there a little before one, he halted a short time, awaiting news from Ney, or the noise of cannon. Impatient, he determined to march in person on Quatre-Bras. At nearly a league from this point the scouts of the 7th Hussars, who reconnoitred the Army, fell back before the English *videttes*.

The Emperor arrayed his troops in line of battle, with the artillery in the centre, the infantry in the second line, the *cuirassiers* on the right, and the light cavalry of Domon, Subervic, and Jacquinot on the left. At the same time he detached towards Frasnes, in order to communicate with Ney, the 7th Hussars, who, mistaking for the English the red lancers of the Guard, posted on the extreme right of the Marshal's position, opened fire upon them.

The scouts had made prisoner an English *vivandière*. On being brought before the Emperor, she told him that the only troops at Quatre-Bras were the cavalry of Lord Uxbridge, charged with the duty of covering the retreat of the English Army. As for the French who had fought the day before, she knew nothing of them; she believed that they had passed the Sambre. Greatly vexed that Wellington should escape from his clutches, the Emperor wished at least to give a good account of the fine English cavalry. The *cuirassiers*, the *chasseurs*, the lancers, and the horse-batteries moved forward at a rapid trot. The Emperor, in his impatient haste, outstripped them with the squadrons of his escort.

Lord Uxbridge, at first notice of the approach of the French, had hastened to the route of Namur. He there found Wellington. The French were still a great way off, and only the reflection of the sun upon burnished steel could be seen. "They are bayonets," said Wellington. But, having taken General Vivian's field-glass, he recognized the *cuirassiers*. After having exchanged a few words with Lord Uxbridge, he decided to retreat. He charged Uxbridge with the command of the rear guard and departed. Whilst the brigades of English dragoons followed by the route of Brussels, the hussars of Vivian and Grant deployed perpendicular to the route of Namur, with the horse batteries in position along their front.

It was a little more than two o'clock. Great black clouds, driven by a furious wind, accumulated overhead. The tempest coming from the northwest, Quatre-Bras was already shrouded in darkness, whilst on the side of Marbais the weather remained clear. Lord Uxbridge was on horseback near the light battery of Captain Mercer, whose guns enfiladed the route of Namur. Suddenly there was seen, issuing from a fold of the ground, a horseman, followed by a small escort. His face, body, and horse, lighted up in reverse, appeared black as night—a statue of bronze, standing out from a luminous background, through which pierced the rays of the sun.

From the silhouette Lord Uxbridge recognized Napoleon "Fire!" cried he, "and aim well." The cannon roared. The Emperor ordered a horse battery of the Guard to advance. The English, judging the danger too great in continuing this duel of artillery, limbered up their pieces. The horsemen of Jacquinot and Subervic rushed forward. English hussars and cannoneers fled in confusion in the midst of blinding flashes and under the torrential rain which had commenced to fall.

"It seemed," said Mercer, "that the first cannon-shots had rent asunder the clouds."

Marshal Ney had given no sign of life. The Emperor sent some orders direct to the commanders of the army corps in position in front of Frasnes. D'Erlon appeared finally with the advance guard of his infantry. To the reproaches that were addressed to him by the Emperor for having arrested the day before his movement against the Prussian right, he replied that, being under the direct command of Marshal Ney, he had been forced to obey the orders of his immediate chief. The Emperor judged that time was too valuable to be lost in discussion; he ordered Count d'Erlon, with the 1st Corps, to follow the cavalry immediately along the route of Brussels.

Soon after this Ney arrived. In his letter of eight o'clock Napoleon had already expressed his dissatisfaction that he had, on the day before, manoeuvred so unskilfully. He did not return again to this subject; but he manifested very plainly his surprise at the non-execution of the orders that he had sent him the same morning, touching the occupation of Quatre-Bras. Ney excused himself by saying that he still believed that he had in front of him the entire army of Wellington. At least the Marshal ought to have assured himself if such were the case by a vigorous offensive reconnaissance. Now, he had not even pushed a single squadron beyond his lines. He had shown himself as negligent, as careless, and as apathetic as on the morning of the 16th and evening of the 17th.

Marshal Ney, in truth, had remained all night, through the carelessness of the Major-General, in ignorance of the victory of Ligny. He would have been able to take the offensive only after having received the order of eight o'clock. Furthermore, this order was conditional. Had Ney even attacked then, it is probable that the English would have none the less effected their retreat without disorder, thanks to their numerous cavalry. They would have only put themselves in motion an hour earlier, and Ney would have occupied Quatre-Bras at noon—a sterile result. However, there would have been a chance that Wellington, vigorously assailed, would have determined to fight upon his positions.

But Marshal Ney had done nothing to provoke this combat. The Emperor blamed him for this. Furthermore, he no doubt reproached himself for not having sent, at seven in the morning, from Ligny to Quatre-Bras, the Guard and Lobau's corps. He had thus permitted to escape the opportunity of exterminating the English Army. Wellington, most of whose troops were in position, his line of retreat on Genappe compromised, and attacked in front by Ney, would have been forced to accept a battle, virtually lost in advance.

While speaking to Ney at Quatre-Bras, the Emperor had a vision of this lost victory. He wished to re-seize it. He imagined that, by hastening his march, he might yet overtake Wellington and compel him to fight. He ordered Reille, then Lobau, and finally the Guard, to follow rapidly the 1st Corps and the light cavalry along the route of Brussels; they would be flanked on the right by the chasseurs of Domon and the *cuirassiers*. Himself, with the squadrons of his escort, and a horse battery of the Guard, gained at a gallop the head of the column, in order to render the pursuit more impetuous.

3

"This pursuit," says Captain Mercer, "was conducted with the speed of a fox-chase." The English rear guard fled in the greatest disorder—hussars and cannoneers galloped pell-mell, going like mad, blinded by the lightning-flashes and lashed by the rain, which fell in such torrents that it was impossible to distinguish the colour of the uniforms. Lord Uxbridge performed the duties of a comet of horse. He hastened along the column, crying to his men: "Faster! Faster, for God's sake! Gallop, or you will all be captured." The lancers of Alphonse de Colbert clung sometimes so closely to the English hussars that, amidst the noise of the horses and the thunder, their peals of laughter and insults reached the fugitives.

Some of the English passed the Dyle over the bridge of Genappe, others over a bridge above this village, and a few at a ford. To the north of Genappe there rises at a gentle incline a range of hills. In order to delay a little the impetuosity of the pursuit, Lord Uxbridge established half-way up the ascent, in two lines, the greater part of his cavalry and two batteries. When the 1st Lancers debouched from the village, in pursuit of Vivian's brigade, it was saluted by a volley of grape, then charged by turns by the 7th English Hussars and the 1st Regiment of Life Guards. The lancers broke without difficulty the hussars; but they were driven back into Genappe by the Guards, who penetrated into the village with them.

Uxbridge led this charge in person. In the narrow and winding street which formed at that time almost all of the village there took place a body-to-body combat, in which the lancers lost all the advantage of their long weapons. In the midst of Genappe, the 2nd Lancers, debouching in companies of fours from a transversal street, fell upon the Guards and threw them back far beyond the first houses. On the route of Brussels, the English were again charged by the hussars of Marbot, who had turned the village by the right. Thrown into disorder, they regained the heights under the protection of their artillery.

At this moment the Emperor issued from Genappe with the squadrons of his escort and a horse battery. Mounted upon "Désirée," a very swift white mare, he had galloped from Quatre-Bras to rejoin the advance guard. His gray *surtout*, made of very thin material—a sort of duster—was penetrated by the rain. The water streamed over his boots. The clasps of his hat were broken by the violence of the rain and the corners had fallen down in front and behind—he found himself coifed like Basil in the *Barber of Seville*. He superintended in person the placing of the guns in battery, crying to the gunners in accents of rage and hatred: "Fire! They are English!"

In the street of Genappe, Colonel Sourd, of the 2nd Lancers, was surrounded by many Life Guards, and had his right arm hacked so as to render its amputation necessary. Larrey amputated it at once. During the operation Sourd dictated the following letter to the Emperor, who had just promoted him to be a general:

> .. The greatest favour that you can render me is to leave me colonel of my regiment of lancers, which I hope to conduct again to victory. I refuse the rank of general. Let the great Napoleon pardon me! The rank of colonel is everything to me.

Then, before the bandage had hardly been placed upon his bloody stump, he remounted his horse and galloped along the column to rejoin his dear regiment. The armies of the Republic and Empire had many men of this stamp.

Past Genappe, the march became extremely slow. The English did not show less haste, nor the French less ardour; but under the continuous action of this great rain the ground became more and more difficult. Along the road, reserved for the artillery and infantry, the water ran like a mill-race; in the ploughed lands, the horses sank up to their knees.

Towards half-past six Napoleon attained with the head of column the heights of La Belle Alliance. The infantry of Brunswick, in the greatest disorder, and the rear guard of the English cavalry traversed the valley which separates these heights from the plateau of Mont Saint-Jean. The hussars of Marbot followed them. They began to skirmish, when from the edge of the plateau an enemy's battery opened fire upon the main body of the cavalry, which had halted near La Belle Alliance. The rain had ceased, but the atmosphere was still saturated with water. Through this curtain of fog the Emperor indistinctly perceived masses of cavalry and infantry. Was it all of Wellington's army ready to deliver battle, or only a strong rear guard, which had taken position to protect the retreat? The Emperor wished to ascertain the truth. By his orders, four light batteries opened fire, whilst the *cuirassiers* of Milhaud deployed as if to charge. The enemy's cannon thundered loudly; the English unmasked themselves. All their army was there.

4

Night approached, and most of the infantry were still far in the rear. The Emperor ordered the fire to cease. During the cannonade he had remained near La Belle Alliance, exposed to the cannon-balls which Captain Mercer, who had recognized him, directed upon the staff. Napoleon pointed out to the troops the positions for their bivouacs. The corps of d'Erlon (save the division of Durutte, which did not rejoin until next morning), established itself between Plancenoit and the farm of Montplaisir, its front and right flank covered by the cavalry of Jacquinot. The *cuirassiers* of Milhaud, the light cavalry of Domon and Subervic, and the cavalry of the Guard bivouacked in the second line, abreast of Rossomme. The corps of Reille and Lobau and the *cuirassiers* of Kellermann halted in Genappe and environs. After having traversed this village at dark, the Foot Guard left the main highway, which was encumbered with the artillery and baggage train, and attempted to gain the imperial quarters.

Only two or three regiments arrived near there, at the village of Glabais, between eleven and twelve o'clock at night. The others having lost their way, the men disbanded and wandered in search of the farms and isolated country houses. They did not rejoin their colours until the next morning.

It was indeed a villainous night of bivouac! The troops arrived in the darkness, broken with fatigue, streaming with water, and "each man dragging two or three pounds of mud with his shoes." A great many of the soldiers marched barefooted, having lost their shoes in the heavy ploughed lands. They were compelled to stretch themselves out in the midst of the rye, which was more than three feet high and drenched with water. "It was like entering a bath." The men could not think of erecting shelters; the wood cut in the copses of Vardre, Chantelet, and Caillou served to make fires, which were lighted with great difficulty, were continually going out, and produced more smoke than heat.

The rain ceased only at rare intervals. In order to receive less water and regain a little warmth, ten or twelve of the soldiers would group themselves together and sleep standing, closely pressed one against the other. The most stoical, or the most fatigued, extended themselves in the mud. There are times in war when one would sleep upon bayonets. After having picketed their horses, a number of horsemen mounted again in the saddle and, enveloped in their long mantles, slept bent over their horses' necks. Of the four days' bread carried in the haversacks, all was consumed. The men suffered greatly from hunger. In most of the regiments the distributions were made only at midnight and even in the morning. We can imagine the dissatisfaction of the troops, as well as the frenzied marauding of which the Belgian peasants were the victims.

The Guard, which during a part of the night had wandered through the fields and along the country roads, was especially furious. Never had the grumblers grumbled so much. With the murmurs and oaths were mingled imprecations against the generals; the men accused them of having purposely led them astray in these unknown roads. And, remembering 1814, these old soldiers said: "This smells of treason." But in the Guard, as well as in the Line, there was neither demoralization, nor even discouragement; the men preserved in their hearts the hope of vengeance and faith in victory. In spite of and before everything, it was the English, the Red-coats, the "Goddams," whom they blamed for this night under the rain, without bread and without fire. And they promised themselves to make them pay dear for it the next day.

The English were not much better off upon the plateau of Mont Saint-Jean. Nevertheless, the infantry, having commenced its retreat at ten o'clock, had reached its positions before night. The leading divisions had even arrived before the storm. The soldiers established themselves upon ground still dry, made for themselves comfortable beds of straw by bending down the rye, and kindled fires; finally, the service of food being well assured, they tranquilly prepared their supper. Alone, the cavalry of Lord Uxbridge, which had bivouacked after night, suffered severely from the inclemency of the weather.

5

The Emperor returned to spend the night at the pretty little farm of Caillou, situated on the edge of the road, at 2,700 yards from La Belle Alliance. The farmer Boucqueau and his family had fled in order to escape the pranks of the Brunswickers, who, in their retreat, had fired some shots through the windows, burst in the door, and finally pillaged the house. The Emperor ordered a great fire to be kindled; and, pending the arrival of his baggage, he dried himself as best he could in front of the chimney.

About nine o'clock General Milhaud informed him verbally that, in his march from Marbais to Quatre-Bras, his right flankers had discovered a column of Prussian cavalry which, from Tilly, had withdrawn in the direction of Wavre. It is possible that the Emperor immediately wrote to Grouchy, from whom he had as yet received no message, to inform him of the direction of this column and to enjoin him to advance on Wavre so as to draw near the Imperial Army. But if the order was sent, it never reached its destination. The officer who bore it did not overtake the Marshal, either because he had been captured or killed *en route* by the Prussian scouts, or for some other cause.

Besides, it does not appear that the Emperor was alarmed by Milhaud's report. Since noon he had manoeuvred with the idea that Blücher's army was retreating on Namur or Maëstricht, or was falling back to the north, in order to unite with the English Army in front of Brussels. The march of a Prussian column on Wavre only confirmed one of his previsions. Furthermore, this column might be only a stray corps, cut off from its line of retreat. But at the worst, if all the Prussian corps should seek to concentrate at Wavre, Grouchy would overtake them in time to combat them. If they marched immediately towards Brussels by the route from Wavre to that city, they would not be immediately dangerous. As to supposing that Blücher, thirty-six hours after a defeat and having 33,000 French on his traces, would risk a flank march, from Wavre to Plancenoit or Ohain, in order to resume the offensive, such a hypothesis never entered the mind of the Emperor.

On the evening of June 17th Napoleon was less preoccupied with the movements of the Prussians than with the plans of the English. He feared that Wellington had only made a simple halt at Mont Saint-Jean, and that he would slip away during the night to go to take up a position in front of Brussels, where he would be joined by the Prussians. If such was the object of the enemy, the Emperor regarded the game as greatly compromised, for though he was certain of exterminating the English at Mont Saint-Jean, he regarded it as very hazardous to debouch from the Forest of Soignes before the two united armies.

However, all this was only a matter of conjecture with the Emperor, for he still doubted if the main body of the Prussians was falling back towards Brussels or Liège. And among the crowd of contradictory thoughts that struggled with one another in his brain, there survived the hope that even should Blücher manoeuvre to approach Wellington, the Prussian Army, defeated, cut in twain, and demoralized by the battle of Ligny, would be in no condition to enter again into line before many days.

The uncertainties of the Emperor touching the plans of Wellington were, indeed, justifiable, for, even far into the night, the Duke himself did not know what course he would take. This depended on Blücher. As he had said in the morning to the orderly officer of Gneisenau, Lieutenant Massow, he would accept battle at Mont Saint-Jean, if he had the assurance of being supported by at least one of the four Prussian corps; otherwise, he would continue his retreat.

Now, since eleven o'clock Wellington had remained without news from the Prussian headquarters. Blücher had, indeed, been informed by Massow, on the latter's return, of the eventual plan of the English general, and he burned to co-operate therein. But before formally pledging himself to second Wellington the next day, Blücher was forced to wait until his army was concentrated and revictualled. Things did not proceed with the rapidity that he would have wished. In the afternoon of June 17th the 1st and 2nd Corps alone were massed at Wavre; and, besides, they were lacking in munitions and food. The great park had been directed by way of Gembloux on Wavre; but would it avoid the French cavalry? For the 3rd and 4th Corps, they might be followed so closely by the French, that it would be necessary to halt and deliver battle.

About five o'clock, as the noise of the cannonade of Genappe diminished in violence, the great park arrived. Three hours later the 3rd Corps passed through Wavre on the way to La Bavette. Finally, at eleven o'clock, a report from Bülow announced that he was at Dion-le-Mont with the head of the 4th Corps. Blücher received at the same moment a despatch from Müffling confirming the information that Wellington had taken eventually at Mont Saint-Jean some positions for battle. Gneisenau still hesitated. "If the English are defeated," he objected, not without reason, "we run the risk of being completely destroyed."

Blücher finally succeeded in convincing his all-powerful chief of staff. "Gneisenau has yielded!" said he, with a triumphant air, to Colonel Hardinge, the English military attaché. "We are going to rejoin the Duke."

He wrote to Wellington:

> The corps of Bülow will put itself on the march tomorrow at dawn in your direction. It will be followed immediately by the corps of Pirch. The 1st. and 3rd. Corps also will hold themselves in readiness to advance towards you. The exhaustion of the troops, a part of whom have not yet arrived, will not permit me to begin my movement earlier.

This letter reached Wellington about two in the morning at his headquarters at Waterloo, a village situated a league in the rear of the first English lines. Assured, henceforth, of the cooperation of the Prussians, Wellington determined to accept battle. Fortune declared once more in his favour; but he had none the less remained too long in expectation. The want of news from Blücher should have caused him to think that the Prussians would be unable to second his army, and, though he wished to fight only with their support, he had yet made, at one in the morning, no preparations for retreat.

At the very moment when Wellington reached his conclusions Napoleon penetrated them. The Emperor had retired rather late at Caillou. Before retiring he had dictated an order of battle, based upon the hypothesis of a great battle, for the next day. He had also caused to be read to him the journals which had arrived from Paris, and had dictated many letters, "necessitated," says Davoût, "by the *ennui* and embarrassment occasioned by the intrigues of the Chamber of Representatives." Awakened after a short nap, the Emperor arose about one in the morning in order to make the entire round of his advance posts. He was accompanied only by General Bertrand.

The rain had set in again; it fell in torrents. When Napoleon had attained the crests of La Belle Alliance, the English bivouacs appeared before him at the distance of a short cannon-shot. Silence reigned in the camps of the enemy, and the Allied Army seemed buried in sleep. On the horizon, the Forest of Soignes, upon which were reflected, through a veil of rain and smoke, the innumerable fires lighted by the soldiers, looked like an immense conflagration. The Emperor judged that the English would stand on their positions. If they had been intending to retreat during the night or even at sunrise, as he had feared, there would have been already some preparatory movements in their camp. The Emperor returned to Caillou as the day dawned.

He there found the letter that Grouchy had written from Gembloux, on the day before, at ten in the evening. The courier had arrived at Caillou about two o'clock. This despatch stated that the Prussians seemed to be falling back in two columns—one in the direction of Liège and the other towards Wavre—and that, if the march of the Prussian columns on Wavre was confirmed by the reports of the night, Grouchy "would follow them in order to separate them from Wellington." Confiding in the promise of his lieutenant, the Emperor did not deem it necessary. to send him, just then, new instructions. It is not for us to say if he acted wisely.

Soon after some spies, then some officers sent on reconnaissances, and Belgian deserters, came by their reports to confirm the previsions of the Emperor. The English did not budge. The battle would take place at Mont Saint-Jean.

The Emperor felt sure of victory. The wan sun that appeared through the clouds "would witness the destruction of the English Army." Napoleon, however, was troubled by his inability to attack as early as he would have liked, and as was necessary. On the evening of the day before, in the doubtful hope that Wellington would await him at Mont Saint-Jean, he had indicated the positions to be occupied by the different army corps, so as to be able to begin the action at an early hour.

Unfortunately, the rain had soaked the ground to such an extent that, in the opinion of the artillery generals, it would be impossible to manoeuvre the guns. It is true the rain had ceased; but many hours would be required to dry and harden the ground. About five o'clock the Emperor, judging, no doubt, that it would no longer be necessary to occupy so early the position of battle, and that it would be better to give the troops time to rally, clean their arms, and prepare their soup, determined to wait until nine o'clock to begin the attack. He dictated to Soult this order, which modified that of the day before:

> The Emperor orders that the Army be ready to attack at nine in the morning. The corps commanders will rally their troops, cause them to clean their arms, and permit the soldiers to prepare their soup. They will also cause the soldiers to eat in order that at nine o'clock sharp each corps may be ready and in line of battle, with its artillery and ambulances, in the position of battle which the Emperor has indicated in his order of yesterday evening.

Book Three
Waterloo
Chapter 1

Blucher and Grouchy

1

In accordance with his promise, Blucher had made ready to second vigorously his allies. Some orders despatched during the night enjoined Bülow to march at dawn on Chapelle Saint-Lambert, distant from Mont Saint-Jean some seven kilometres, as the crow flies, and Pirch to follow the movement of Bülow's corps. At Chapelle Saint-Lambert these generals were to act according to circumstances. If the action did not appear to be seriously engaged, they were to remain in that position and to conceal their presence; in the contrary case, they were to attack the right flank of the French Army.

As for the corps of Ziethen and Thielmann, they were to remain until a new order in their cantonments on the left bank of the Dyle. Blucher intended to lead them also to the support of the English; but before doing this it was necessary that he await the morning reports. He could not completely disgarnish the line of the Dyle without having positive information regarding the march and strength of the French corps which had been reported at Gembloux.

Well conceived as was this disposition, it had one initial fault. As Bülow's corps had not been engaged at Ligny, Blücher wished to engage it first. He sacrificed to this pre-occupation, which, moreover, was legitimate, rapidity of movement. The corps of Ziethen and Thielmann were bivouacked at Bierges and La Bavette (eight and nine kilometres, respectively, from Chapelle Saint-Lambert); the corps of Pirch and Bülow were at Aisemont and Dion-le-Mont (ten and fourteen kilometres from Chapelle Saint-Lambert.)

Manifestly, the troops nearest the field of battle should have been sent there first, whilst those farthest away should have come to occupy temporarily the line of the Dyle. At all events, the Prussian staff ought to have foreseen that Pirch's corps must remain motionless under arms during the defile of Bülow's corps. It was then Pirch who ought to have made the head of column. If one had acted in this manner, half of the Prussian Army would have found itself concentrated at Chapelle Saint-Lambert long before noon.

As it was, things were very different. The division of Losthin, Bülow's advance guard, did not arrive in front of Wavre till seven in the morning. It lost a great deal of time in crossing the bridge and climbing the main street of the village, which was narrow and very steep. When it had debouched, a violent conflagration, entirely fortuitous, broke out in this street and barred its access. The bulk of Bülow's corps was forced to await until the fire was extinguished. The march of the 4th Corps thus suffered a delay of more than two hours; the rear guard division did not reach until near three o'clock the environs of Chapelle Saint-Lambert. The 2nd Corps (Pirch) had taken up arms at five o'clock. But, as it was necessary to permit the 4th Corps to defile, the troops remained motionless in front of their bivouacs at Aisemont till past noon. At two o'clock half of Pirch's corps was still upon this side (right bank) of the Dyle.

Between seven and eight o'clock in the morning Count Gröben, on returning from the advance posts, had reported that the French, in position at Gembloux, had yet made no movement, and that he estimated their strength at 15,000 men. "I cannot affirm," he had added, "whether the French are not more numerous, but even should they number 30,000 men, a single one of our army corps will suffice to guard the line of the Dyle. It is at Mont Saint-Jean, that the fate of the campaign is to be decided. It is necessary to send there every man possible."

This was, indeed, the opinion of Blücher; but Gneisenau and Grolemann still hesitated to disgarnish the line of the Dyle.

"This question," said Grolemann, with the formal assent of Gneisenau, "will be resolved at noon; if, from now until then, the enemy does not appear before Wavre in too great strength, the 1st Corps will follow the 2nd and 4th, and perhaps the 3rd will march also."

Meanwhile Blucher wrote to Müffling:

> I pray you to say in my name. to the Duke of Wellington that, sick as I am, I shall put myself at the head of my troops to fall upon the right wing of the enemy as soon as Napoleon will have engaged battle. If the day passes without an attack from the French, I am of the opinion that we should both attack them tomorrow.

Before forwarding this letter which Blucher had dictated to him, the *aide-de-camp* Nostitz communicated its contents to Gneisenau. On the day before and the morning of the battle of Ligny the latter had somewhat mistrusted the promises of Wellington, whom he regarded as "a great knave." The day of June 1 6th, during which the Duke had sent to Brye neither a man nor a cannon, had confirmed and increased the prejudices of Gneisenau. He feared that the English would fall back without combat on Brussels. In this event the Prussian Army would be exposed to a disaster, taken *en flagrant délit* of march, and attacked in front by Napoleon and in flank or reverse by the corps of Grouchy. Gneisenau caused this postscript to be added to Blücher's letter:

> General Gneisenau is in perfect accord with the Field Marshal; but he prays your Excellency to penetrate the secret thoughts of the Duke of Wellington and to learn if he is fully determined to fight in his present position, or if it is only a mere demonstration, which might greatly

endanger our army.

Time passed; the ardent Blucher wished to be present at the opening of the battle. Leaving Gneisenau free to control the movements of the other army corps, he quitted Wavre at eleven o'clock to rejoin Bülow towards Chapelle Saint-Lambert. "In spite of all that which I suffered from my fall," said he later, "I would have had myself tied on my horse rather than to have missed the battle."

2

If Grouchy, on the evening of June 17th, was. still doubtful as to the concentration of the Prussian Army at Wavre, the information that reached him during the night ought to have dissipated this doubt. Between eleven and twelve o'clock at night he received a report from General Bonnemains and another from the colonel of the 15th Dragoons, both announcing the march of the Prussians on Wavre. Towards three in the morning there was transmitted to him from Walhain, or Sart-à-Walhain, notice that there had been seen passing on the day before three army corps which were directing themselves on Wavre, and that, according to the words of the officers and soldiers, these troops were going to concentrate near Brussels in order to deliver battle.

All this information, which confirmed that of the preceding evening, only half convinced Grouchy. He no longer doubted that the enemy was directing himself on Wavre; but, taking to the letter, without reflecting, the words of the Prussians, he imagined that their army had made there not a strategical concentration, but a simple halt, and that it would march from there towards Brussels by the main highway. He knew that the Emperor had foreseen a battle with the English in front of the Forest of Soignes, and he never stopped to think that instead of gaining Brussels, the Prussians might, from Wavre, join directly their allies by a short lateral march.

He did not see that, in order to prevent this junction, it was not necessary to follow the Prussians by way of Walhain and Corbaix, but to make a flank pursuit by way of Saint Géry and

Mousty. There was every advantage and no danger in passing the Dyle at the nearest point and in manoeuvring by the left bank of this little river. If the Prussians remained at Wavre, which is situated on the left bank of the Dyle, that position could be attacked more easily from the left bank than by the right. If they directed themselves towards Brussels, the French could follow them after having reached Wavre. If they marched directly to join the English, the appearance of 33,000 French on their flank would arrest, or at least retard, their movement.

Finally, if they had already effected their junction with the English and threatened to crush the Imperial Army under their united masses, the French would be, at least, upon the left bank of the Dyle, and near enough to the Emperor to be able to assist him in the midst of the battle. Grouchy had no idea of all this. He made no change in his orders of the day before. He even permitted, although he had at that time decided to march on Wavre, the corps of Pajol and the cavalry of Vallin to operate the eccentric movement on Grand Leez which he had ordered. He wrote to the Emperor that, as all the information confirmed the march of the Prussians by way of Wavre on Brussels, "in order to concentrate there or to deliver battle after having united with Wellington," he was starting for Wavre.

Grouchy had under his hand 33,000 soldiers and 116 guns. In attaching himself servilely to the traces of the Prussian rear guard, instead of manoeuvring, on the morning of June 18th, by the left bank of the Dyle, he committed a gross strategical error. In leaving, under circumstances so pressing and so grave, his troops in bivouac a part of the morning, he was guilty of an irremediable fault. On June 18th day dawns at half-past two; at three it is light enough to march. Now, Grouchy had directed Vandamme and Gérard to put themselves on the march at six and eight o'clock, respectively. Unfortunate man!

In consequence of the delay in the distribution of food, the troops did not even set out at the hour prescribed. The dragoons of Exelmans, who had passed the night at Sauvenierre and were to form the advance, did not mount until six o'clock. The corps of Vandamme did not put itself *en route* from Gembloux until between seven and eight, and the corps of Gérard did not quit its bivouacs on the right bank of the Orneau until the same hour. Another cause of the delay was that all these troops followed the same route. By marching in two columns—one by Sauvenierre and Walhain, and the other by Ernage and Nil Pierreux—the two army corps would have been massed at the same time at Corbaix.

Grouchy, it appears, did not leave Gembloux before eight or nine o'clock. He proceeded slowly and rejoined the advance of the 3rd Corps a little on this side of Walhain. Having reached about ten o'clock the outskirts of this village, he allowed the columns of infantry to file by, and entered the house of the notary Hollërt, in order to write to the Emperor.

It appears that his *aide-de-camp*, Pontbellanger, who had been sent upon a reconnaissance upon the banks of the Dyle, towards Mousty, had reported to him that no hostile troops had been discovered in that region; and an inhabitant of Walhain, who claimed to have formerly served in the French Army in the capacity of an officer, had given him new and important information. He assured the Marshal that the main body of the Prussians, who had passed through Wavre, was camped in the—plain of La Chyse, near the road leading from Namur to Louvain (three leagues, as the crow flies, to the northeast of Wavre).

This false information, which the old officer "declared was positive," was most satisfactory to Grouchy. Not only was the army of Blücher not seeking to effect its junction with Wellington by a flank march, but, instead of advancing directly on Brussels, it had commenced by making a long detour in order to concentrate first in the direction of Louvain. Thus the enemy had put himself for the time being outside of the sphere of operations. Grouchy could congratulate himself upon having manoeuvred so skilfully. If he had not overtaken the Prussians, he was on their traces and had driven them away from the English, which was the principal object of his movement. By evening all his troops would be massed at Wavre, in position between the two hostile armies; and on the next day he would be free either to go to combat the Prussians in the plain of La Chyse, or to attack them in their flank march if they directed themselves towards Brussels, or to advance towards this city in order to unite with Napoleon's forces. The Marshal hastened to write to Napoleon, in order to transmit to him this new information. He closed this letter by saying:

> ...This evening I expect to be concentrated at Wavre, and thus find myself between Wellington, whom I presume to be in retreat before Your Majesty, and the Prussian Army. I have need of ulterior instructions in order that I may know what Your Majesty wishes me to do. The country between Wavre and the plain of La Chyse is very difficult, intersected with ravines, and partly marshy. I can easily reach Brussels before the Prussian force, which has halted at La Chyse....Vouchsafe, Sire, to send me your orders; I can receive them before beginning my movement tomorrow.

"Tomorrow!" It was indeed a question of tomorrow!

Grouchy gave this letter to Major La Fresnaye, a former page of Napoleon, who set out at once. As to the Marshal, free henceforth from anxiety, and thinking that he had an entire day before him in which to reach a determination, he seated himself tranquilly at dinner.

3

Grouchy was eating some strawberries (to eat strawberries is not, moreover, a hanging matter, even on a morning of battle), when Gérard, who had outstripped by two or three kilometres the vanguard of the 4th Corps, entered the room where he was dining. Soon after Colonel Simon Lorière, Gérard's chief of staff, was introduced. While walking in the garden of the notary Hollërt, he had heard the cannon growling in the distance; he hastened to inform his chiefs of this fact. It was a little more than half-past eleven. Grouchy and Gérard descended into the garden. General Baltus, commanding the artillery of the 4th

Corps, General Valazé, commanding the engineers, and Inspector of Reviews Denniée were there with numerous officers of the staff—all very attentive to the noise of the cannonade. Many of them were kneeling, with ear to the ground, in order to ascertain the direction of the sound.

Gérard listened for some minutes, and said: "I think that we should march to the sound of the cannon."

Grouchy objected that it was probably only a rear-guard affair. But the fire increased in violence. "The earth trembled," relates Simon Lorière. It could no longer be doubted that two armies were fighting. Towards the west clouds of smoke arose above the horizon.

"The battle is at Mont Saint-Jean," said a peasant whom Valazé had taken as a guide. "We could reach there in four or five hours' march."

The notary Hollërt, summoned by Gérard, confirmed the words of the guide "It is in front of the Forest of Soignes," said he. "The distance from here there is nearly three and a half leagues."

"We should march to the sound of the cannon," repeated Gérard.

"We should march to the sound of the cannon," said in turn General Valazé.

Grouchy has admitted that he was "vexed" at hearing his subordinates publicly giving him advice. This is one reason why he did not heed it. There was another—the fear of responsibility. Rather than to follow the dangerous advice of his generals, would it not be better to follow blindly the instructions of the Emperor, which would cover him, whatever might happen?

He said: "The Emperor told me yesterday that his intention was to attack the English Army, if Wellington accepted battle. So I am not at all surprised at the engagement which is taking place at this moment. If the Emperor wanted me to take part in it, he would not have sent me away from him at the very time when he was advancing against the English. Besides, on account of the condition of the roads, drenched by the rain of yesterday and of this morning, I would not be able to arrive in useful time upon the battlefield."

General Baltus coincided with the views of Grouchy. He said: "The roads are in very bad condition and the artillery would be unable to pass over them."

"With my three companies of sappers," replied General Valazé, "I pledge myself to remove every difficulty."

"I would arrive with the ammunition-chests!" cried Gérard Valazé, having again consulted his guide, who affirmed that the march would be an easy thing, resumed: "The sappers can open many passages."

Gérard became more and more animated. "*Monsieur le Maréchal,*" said he, "it is your duty to march to the sound of the cannon."

Offended at Gérard for permitting himself to read him a lesson, and that in a loud voice in the presence of a score of officers, Grouchy replied in a severe tone, so as to close the discussion: "My duty is to execute the orders of the Emperor, which direct me to follow the Prussians; to follow your advice would be an infringement of his instructions."

At this moment there arrived an *aide-de-camp* of Exelmans, *Commandant d'Estourmel*; he announced that a strong Prussian rear guard was in position in front of Wavre. This officer was also directed to say that, according to every indication, the enemy's army had passed the bridge of Wavre during the night and morning in order to draw near the English Army, and consequently General Exelmans thought of advancing by way of Ottignies upon the left bank of the Dyle. This new information and the advice expressed by Exelmans were so many reasons in support of Gérard's counsel.

But for Grouchy, still persuaded that the Prussians had gained Wavre in view of a retreat towards La Chyse, the presence of their rear guard in that town confirmed this supposition. He congratulated himself on having resisted Gérard, since the orders of the Emperor were to follow the Prussian Army, and since he was finally on the point of overtaking this unseizable army.

Having said to d'Estourmel that he would give his orders to Exelmans in person, the Marshal called for his horse.

As Grouchy was preparing to mount, Gérard risked a last attempt: If you do not wish to advance towards the Forest of Soignes with all the troops, at least permit me to make this movement with my army corps and the cavalry of General Vallin. I am confident that I can reach the battlefield in time to be of assistance to the Emperor."

"No replied Grouchy; "it would be committing an unpardonable military fault to divide my troops and cause them to operate upon both banks of the Dyle. I would expose both of these bodies, which would be unable to support each other, to the danger of being crushed by forces two or three times more numerous."

He set his horse at a gallop. Those officers of his staff who had witnessed the discussion from a distance and who heard the cannon believed that he was about to manoeuvre in order to draw near the Imperial Army.

CHAPTER 2

The Battle of Waterloo - Morning

1

The plateau of La Belle Alliance and Mont Saint-Jean, each of an average altitude of 396 feet, extend almost parallel with each other in an easterly and westerly direction. They are separated by two twin valleys, which are crossed perpendicularly, from south to north, by the great highway from Charleroi to Brussels, These two valleys are narrow and of slight depth; from the inn of La Belle Alliance to the crests of Mont Saint-Jean the distance is 1,300 yards, as the crow flies, and the depth of the lowest valley is about 330 feet.

East of the great highway there is the valley of Smohain, which, very rough, gradually contracts itself, becomes a ravine, and finishes by confounding itself with the bed of the stream of Ohain; on the west there is the valley of Braine l'Alleud, which also presents multiple undulations, and through which passes diagonally the route of Nivelles. This route runs in an S.S.W. and N.N.E. direction. After having reached the plateau of Mont Saint-Jean, it joins, at the hamlet of the same name, thus forming an acute angle, the main highway, which traverses, at nearly a league beyond this point, the village of Waterloo, built in a hollow in the Forest of Soignes, and continues towards Brussels through the forest.

As seen from La Belle Alliance, the great highway of Brussels, which ascends and descends in a straight line, appears very steep. This, however, is an illusion of the perspective. In reality the slope has not so great an inclination. A horseman can climb the hill at a sustained gallop without urging or blowing his horse. But on the right and left of the highway the very uneven ground falls abruptly in many spots. It is an infinite succession of hills and valleys, swales and hummocks, furrows and ridges. Nevertheless, in looking from the heights, the double valley presents the appearance of a plain extending without marked depressions between two hills of slight elevation. It is necessary to pass through the fields in order to see these incessant and undulating movements of the ground, similar to the waves of the sea.

The road from Ohain to Braine l'Alleud, which skirts the crest of the plateau of Mont Saint-Jean, and there intersects at right angles the route of Brussels, covers with a line of natural obstacles almost all of the English position. East of the great highway, this road is even with the ground; but a double row of quickset hedges, tall and stiff, renders it impassable to cavalry.

On the west side, on account of a sudden rise of the ground, the road of Ohain extends between two banks from five to seven feet high; it thus forms, for the space of 400 yards, a redoubtable shelter-trench; then it rises again to the surface and continues its course without presenting other obstacles than a few scattered hedges. In the rear of the crest which forms the screen the ground slopes downward towards the north, rendering the position very favourable to the defence. The troops of the second line and the reserves are concealed from the enemy and partly protected from his fire.

Spread over a radius of 3,500 yards, half-way up the hill and in the valleys, the Château of Hougoumont, with its chapel, its vast commons, its park enclosed with walls, its orchard surrounded by hedges, and the coppices which, defends its southern approach; the farm of La Haye Sainte, a massive stone building, flanked by an orchard bordered by hedges and a terraced garden; a mound surmounting the excavation of a sand-pit and protected by a hedge; finally, the hamlet of Smohain—form so many bastions, galleries, and redoubts in front of the position.

The horizon is limited on the north by the green masses

of the Forest of Soignes, against which the steeples of Mont Saint-Jean and Braine l'Alleud stand out in bold relief. On the northeast extend the woods of Ohain and Paris, and farther on the wood of Chapelle Saint-Lambert. On the east the woods of Vardre and Hubermont line the tops of the hills which crown the ravine of Lasne, which has its source near the village of Plancenoit. All the rest of the ground is open. The summits of the plateaux, the hillsides, and the valleys, were everywhere covered with tall rye, which had begun to ripen.

In short, a vast rampart (the plateau of Mont Saint-Jean), rising above the valleys of Smohain and Braine l'Alleud; two rows of hedges, then a double wall like a parapet (the road of Ohain), from whence all points of approach are commanded by a plunging fire; six advanced works (Hougoumont, La Haye Sainte, the sandpit, Papelotte, La Haye, and Smohain); some *débouchés* suitable for counter-attacks; and in the rear of the parapet a sloping ground, hidden from view of the enemy, crossed by two great highways, favouring the rapid movements of supports and of artillery reserves—such was the position chosen by Wellington.

2

The English had bivouacked in some disorder over all the extent of the plateau. Awakened at dawn, they began to kindle the fires, to prepare their breakfast, and to clean their arms and uniforms. Instead of drawing the charges from the guns, the greater number of the soldiers discharged them in the air. There was a continual fusillade, giving the illusion of a combat. The outposts of Napoleon were either lacking in vigilance or well inured to war, for no French relation mentions the false alarm caused by this fusillade. About six o'clock, to the discordant summons of trumpets, *pibrochs*, and drums, sounding and beating on all sides at the same time, the troops assembled. The inspection over, battalions, squadrons, and batteries, guided by staff officers, marched to occupy their positions of combat.

The English brigades of Maitland and Byng (Guards) and Colin Halkett, the Hanoverian brigade of Kielmansegge, and the Anglo-German brigade of Ompteda, established themselves in the first line along the road of Ohain—the right (Byng), near the route of Nivelles; and the left (Ompteda), resting on the route of Brussels. East of this route, and also along the road of Ohain, were stationed the English brigades of Kempt and Pack (Picton's division), the Dutch-Belgian brigade of Bylandt, and the Hanoverian brigade of Best.

These nine brigades formed the centre or, more correctly speaking, almost the entire front of the Allied Army; for, in Wellington's order of battle, there was, properly speaking, no centre. There were a right and left centre, separated by the route of Brussels, and the two wings. The right wing, composed of the English brigades of Adam and Mitchell, of the Hanoverian brigade of William Halkett, and the Anglo-German brigade of Duplat, was *en potence* between the route of Nivelles and Merbe Braine; on the extreme right the Dutch- Belgian division of Chassé occupied the ground in front of Braine l'Alleud. The left consisted only of the Nassauer brigade of the Prince of Saxe-Weimar and the Hanoverian brigade of Wincke; these troops were stationed above Papelotte, La Haye, and Smohain, with detachments in these positions. On the extreme left the English cavalry brigades of Vandeleur and Vivian flanked the army in the direction of Ohain.

The reserve formed upon the plateau in two lines, the second line near the farm of Mont Saint-Jean. It comprised, behind the right centre, the Nassauer brigade of Kruse, the entire corps of Brunswick (infantry and cavalry), the Anglo-German cavalry brigades of Grant, Dörnberg, and Arenschild, the Horse Guard brigade of Somerset, the brigades of Trip and Van Merlen (Dutch-Belgian *carabineers* and hussars); and behind the left centre, the English brigade of Lambert, the English brigade of dragoons of Ponsonby, and the Dutch-Belgian brigade of dragoons of Ghigny.

The artillery was disposed as follows: four batteries along the front of the right centre; the same number at the centre of the line of battle, at the intersection of the route of Brussels and the road of Ohain; four along the front of the left centre; two on the right wing; two on the extreme left with Chassé; two foot and seven horse batteries in the second line, behind the right centre; and three batteries in reserve, near the farm of Mont Saint-Jean.

Against the impetuous onslaught of the French columns Wellington had employed in Spain and Portugal a very peculiar kind of tactics. He placed his first line of infantry in the rear of the crests, so as to conceal it from the view and from the blows of the enemy during the preparatory period of the assault and even during the assault itself. It was only when the assailants, disunited by the ascension under the fire of the chains of sharpshooters and of the batteries established upon the crests, that the English battalions, which until then had not suffered, unmasked themselves, delivered a point-blank discharge, and charged with the bayonet. The ground of Mont Saint-Jean favoured this kind of tactics.

"Form in the usual manner," said Wellington to the general officers. Thus, with the exception of the Belgian brigade of Bylandt and a chain of sharpshooters which were posted on the slopes—so to speak, in the advance line—all the infantry took position at 20, 100, and 200 yards behind the road of Ohain. These troops were completely masked, some by the banks and quickset hedges of the road, and others by reason of the interior declivity of the plateau. This declivity also favoured the reserves by preventing them from being seen from the opposite height. The batteries were established along the front, in front of and behind the road of Ohain, according to the nature of the ground and the extent of the field of fire. Embrasures had been opened for the guns in the banks and hedges.

The farms and the unevenness of the ground, forming advanced works, had been put in a state of defence. A barricade had been erected across the route of Brussels on a line with La Haye Sainte; and an abattis closed the route of Nivelles. Hougoumont was occupied by seven companies of the 1st and 2nd (Coldstreams) and 3rd Regiments of English Guards, a company of Hanoverians, and a battalion of Nassauers; La Haye Sainte, by five companies of the German Legion; the sand-pit and its approaches, by a battalion of the 95th; and Papelotte, La Haye, and the first houses of Smohain, by detachments of the Prince of Saxe-Weimar.

Wellington had confidence only in his English troops. This is why the troops of his nationality alternated along the line of battle with the different allied contingents. He desired the latter to be everywhere solidly encircled.

After deducting the losses suffered on June 16th and 17th, the Duke had in line 67,700 men and 184 pieces of artillery. He would have been able to concentrate at Mont Saint-Jean a greater number of combatants; but, still uneasy for his lines of communication with the sea, and fearing that a French corps would turn his right, he had left inactive between Hal and Enghien—four leagues, as the crow flies, from Mont Saint-Jean—nearly 17,000 men and 30 guns, under Prince Frederick of the Low Countries.

What a capital fault was this detachment on the eve of a battle, to guard against a chimerical danger! As General Brialmont has very aptly said, "One has never been able to explain how Wellington could have attributed to his adversary a plan of operations which must hasten the junction of the allied armies, when, from the beginning of the campaign, Napoleon had evidently manoeuvred to prevent this junction."

Whilst the troops were taking up their positions, Wellington, accompanied by Müffling and a few officers, traversed the line of battle. He examined carefully all the positions and descended as far as Hougoumont. Often he levelled his glass upon the heights occupied by the French. He was mounted upon his favourite horse, "Copenhagen," a superb pure-blooded bay, that had been trained at Vittoria and Toulouse. Wellington wore his ordinary field uniform—pantaloons of white buckskin, boots with tassels, dark blue coat, and short cloak of the same colour, white cravat, small hat without plumes, ornamented with the black cockade of England and three others, of smaller size, of the colours of Portugal, Spain, and the Low Countries. He was very calm. His face reflected the confidence inspired by the assured cooperation of the Prussian Army.

3

The orders of the Emperor prescribed that all the army corps should be by nine o'clock sharp upon their positions of battle, ready to attack. But the troops who had passed the night at Genappe, Glabais, and in the scattered farms of the neighbourhood were a long time in rallying, cleaning their arms and making soup. Besides, they had only the great highway of Brussels by which to debouch. The corps of Reille did not arrive on a line with Caillou until nine o'clock. The Foot Guard, the *cuirassiers* of Kellermann, the corps of Lobau, and the division of Durutte were far in the rear. To begin the action, the Emperor wished rightly or wrongly to have all his force under his hand, and besides, it does not appear that the condition of the ground yet permitted of the manoeuvring of the artillery. At least, this was the opinion of Napoleon and Drouot.

About eight o'clock the Emperor had breakfasted at the farm of Caillou with Soult, the Duke of Bassano, Drouot, and many general officers. After the repast, which had been served in vessels of silver bearing the imperial arms, the maps of Ferrari and Capitaine had been unfolded upon the table. The Emperor said: "The enemy's army is superior to ours by more than a quarter. We have, none the less, ninety chances out of a hundred in our favour."

Ney, who entered at this moment, heard these words. He had just come from the advance posts, and had taken some movement of the English for the beginning of a retreat; he exclaimed: "No doubt, sire, if Wellington were simple enough to wait for you. But I come to announce to you that his retreat is pronounced, and that, if you do not hasten to attack, the enemy will escape you."

"You have seen wrong," replied the Emperor; "the time is gone for that. Wellington would expose himself to certain destruction. He has thrown the dice, and they are for us."

Soult was anxious. He apprehended the arrival of the Prussians upon the battlefield no more than did the Emperor—he judged that the French were rid of them for many days. But he regretted that Marshal Grouchy with 33,000 men had been detached to pursue Blücher, when a single corps of infantry and a few thousand cavalry would have sufficed. Half of the troops of the right wing, he thought, would be far more useful in the great battle which was to be fought with the English Army, so firm, so stubborn, and so formidable.

As Lefebvre's chief of staff, Soult had carried by assault, July 9, 1794, this same plateau of Mont Saint-Jean, and had thrown back from the Forest of Soignes the Imperialists into Brussels. But he knew that the English infantry was far more tenacious than the Austrian; so, on the previous evening, he had advised the Emperor to recall a part of the troops put under the orders of Grouchy. During the morning he had reiterated his advice.

Napoleon, impatient, brutally replied: "Because you have been beaten by Wellington you regard him as a great general. I tell you that Wellington is a bad general, that the English are bad troops, and that this will be a very small affair."

"I hope it may," said Soult.

Soon after, Reille and Jérôme entered. The Emperor asked Reille his opinion of the English Army, which this general must well know, from having so often fought it in Spain. Reille replied: "Well posted, as Wellington knows how to do, and attacked in front, I regard the English infantry as invincible on account of its calm tenacity and the superiority of its fire. Before attacking it with the bayonet, it may be expected that half of the assailants will be struck down. But the English Army is less agile, less supple, and less skilful than our army. If it cannot be defeated by a frontal attack, it may be done by manoeuvring."

For Napoleon, who had never fought a pitched battle with the English, the advice of a veteran of the Spanish wars was worthy of consideration. But, irritated, perhaps, because Reille had spoken so frankly, at the risk of discouraging the generals who listened, he appeared to attach no importance to it. He broke off the interview by an exclamation of incredulity.

The weather had cleared up and the sun shone; a rather stiff wind—a drying wind, as one says in venery—began to blow. Some of the artillery officers reported that they had gone over the ground, and that the guns would be able to manoeuvre. Napoleon called for his horses. Before starting he received with kindness the farmer Boucqueau, who with his family had returned from Plancenoit on learning that the Emperor was at Caillou. The old man complained of having been pillaged the day before by the enemy's stragglers.

Napoleon, who appeared to be deeply absorbed, seemed to be thinking of something more important than these grievances. He finished by saying: "Be tranquil; you shall have a safe-guard." This did not appear superfluous, for the imperial quarters were to quit Caillou during the day. It was said that the Army would sleep in Brussels.

The Emperor, skirting at a rapid trot the flank of the columns which were still debouching from Genappe, advanced in front of La Belle Alliance, upon the very line of sharpshooters, to observe the enemy's positions. A Fleming named Decoster was his guide. This man kept a small inn on the side of the road between Rossomme and La Belle Alliance; he had been taken from his house at five in the morning and brought to the Emperor, who had called for someone who knew the country. As the maps which Napoleon used in his campaigns only indicated in a general and summary manner the undulations of the ground, he nearly always took a guide.

Decoster had been watched closely, for he seemed anxious to escape; and on leaving Caillou he had been lifted and bound upon a troop-horse whose saddle was attached by a halter to the saddle-bow of a *chasseur* of the escort. During the battle he cut, naturally, a poor figure amidst the bullets and cannon-balls. He twisted in his saddle, turned his head, and leaned over the shoulders of his horse. At one time the Emperor said to him: "My friend, do not fidget so. A bullet can kill you as well from behind as in front and will make an uglier wound."

According to local traditions, Decoster, either through imbecility or ill-will, gave during the entire day false information. Another guide had been brought to the Emperor—a certain Joseph Bourgeois—from the hamlet of Odeghien. He stammered from fear and kept his eyes fixed obstinately upon the ground. Napoleon dismissed him. When asked how the Emperor looked, he said: "Had his face been the dial of a watch, one would not have dared to look for the hour."

The Emperor remained for some time in front of La Belle Alliance. After having ordered General Haxo to ascertain whether the English had constructed any entrenchments, he went to post himself, at nearly 1,500 yards in the rear, upon a hillock, which rises near the farm of Rossomme. There were brought from the farmhouse a chair and a small table, upon which were unfolded his maps. About two o'clock, when the action was seriously engaged, the Emperor established himself upon another eminence, nearer the line of battle, at some distance from the inn of Decoster. General Foy, who had recognized him from a distance by his gray great-coat, saw him walking to and fro, his hands crossed behind his back, halting, leaning over the table, and then resuming his walk.

At Caillou, Jérôme had acquainted his brother with the words heard the day before at Genappe in the inn of the *Roi d'Espagne*. The waiter who had served him with supper, after having served Wellington with dinner, related that an *aide-de-camp* of the Duke had spoken of a junction concerted between the English and Prussian armies in front of the Forest of Soignes. This Belgian, who appeared to be well informed, had even added that the Prussians would arrive by way of Wavre. The Emperor treated these words with incredulity. "After a battle like that of Fleurus," said he, " the junction of the English and Prussians is impossible before two days; besides, the Prussians have Grouchy on their traces."

Grouchy, always Grouchy! The Emperor had too much confidence in the information as well as the promise of his lieutenant. According to the letter of the Marshal, written from Gembloux at ten in the evening, and which had arrived at Caillou about two in the morning, the Prussian Army, reduced to nearly 30,000 men, had divided itself into two columns, one of which seemed to be directing itself towards Liège and the other on Wavre, perhaps to join Wellington.

Grouchy had added that if the reports of his cavalry apprised him that the main body of the Prussians was withdrawing on Wavre, he would follow it, "in order to separate it from Wellington."

All this was well calculated to reassure the Emperor. But had the Prussians but 30,000 men? had they not divided themselves to march? and would they not concentrate to fight? Would Grouchy, of whom they were greatly in advance, overtake them in time? Either Napoleon did not ask himself all these questions or he answered them in the manner most conformable with his desires. Blinded like Grouchy, he believed that the Prussians would halt at Wavre, or that, at all events, they would advance on Brussels, and not on Mont Saint-Jean.

From Rossomme the Emperor contented himself with writing to Grouchy to inform him that a Prussian column had passed through Saint-Géry, directing itself on Wavre, and to order him to march as swiftly as possible on that point, pushing the enemy in front of him.

A few minutes later the Emperor ordered Colonel Marbot to take position behind Frichermont with the 7th Hussars and to send detachments to Lasne, Couture, and the bridges of Mousty and Ottignies. Should we infer from this that Napoleon had suddenly an intuition of the movement that was about to be proposed to Grouchy by Gérard, and that he thought that before receiving his despatch the Marshal, instead of following the Prussians to Wavre, would pass the Dyle at Mousty to advance on their left flank? Or should we believe that, in the mind of the Emperor, these detachments were merely intended to reconnoitre the right of the army and to connect the communications with Grouchy's corps by assuring the passage of the couriers?

4

The troops began to take their positions for battle. Napoleon, on horseback, passed them in review as they formed on the ground. The entire plateau was furrowed with troops on the march. The corps of d'Erlon closed up on its right, in order to permit that of Reille to establish itself on its left. On the flanks and in the rear of these first lines of infantry—infantry of the Line, with blue coats, white pantaloons, and gaiters, light infantry clothed entirely in blue and gaitered in black—eight divisions of cavalry began to deploy, sabres and *cuirasses* glittering in the sun, and lance pennons fluttering in the wind. It was a *chatoyment* of bright colours and metallic flashes.

The *chasseurs*, wearing a dark green jacket with purple, gold-coloured, and scarlet trimmings, were succeeded by the hussars, whose dolmans, pelisses, Hungarian pantaloons, and plumes varied in colour in each regiment—maroon and blue, red and sky-blue, gray and blue, green and scarlet.

Then passed the dragoons, wearing copper helmets and tiger-skin turbans, white straps crossing over a green coat with red or yellow trimmings, and musketoon at saddle-bow striking against the rigid boot; the lancers, green like the *chasseurs* and having like them the sheep-skin *schabrack*, but distinguished from them by the crested helmet, the cut and colour of the plastron; the *cuirassiers*, who wore the short imperial blue coat with collar, facings, and sleeve-trimmings of red or yellow, according to the regiment, white pantaloons, tall boots, *cuirass* and helmet of steel, with copper crest and floating *crinière*; the *carabineers*, giants of six feet, clothed in white, wearing golden *cuirasses* and coifed, like antique heroes, with great helmets with red crests.

The Horse Guard deployed in the second line: dragoons with green coats with white facings and helmets with red plumes; grenadiers with blue coats and scarlet trimmings, leather pantaloons, orange-coloured epaulets and shoulder-knots, and great bear-skin caps with plume and *four-ragère*; lancers, who wore a red *kurka* with blue *plastron*, white and yellow epaulets and shoulder-knots, red pantaloons with a blue stripe, red *shapska* ornaments with a copper plate with the crowned N and surmounted by a snow-white plume eighteen inches high; finally, the *chasseurs* with green *dolmans* trimmed in orange-coloured braid, red *pelisses* edged with fur, *kolbachs* with scarlet pendant and a great green and red plume. The epaulets, braid, stripes, and *brandenburgs* of the officers scintillated with gold and silver.

Other troops debouched by the Brussels route. There arrived men and horses and cannon as far as the eye could reach; the numerous battalions of Lobau, the *chasseurs* of Domon, the lancers of Subervic; the foot artillery, in its simple dark blue uniform relieved by red; the horse artillery, the front, of the dolman covered with scarlet *brandenburgs*; the Young Guard, *tirailleurs* with red epaulets, *voltigeurs* with green ones; the foot cannoneers of the Guard, wearing great bear-skin caps and marching near those redoubtable 12-pounders, which the Emperor called his "most beautiful daughters."

Far in the rear advanced the sombre columns of the Old Guard. *Chasseurs* and grenadiers wore their campaign uniform—blue pantaloons, long blue coat with a row of buttons down the front, and bear-skin caps without plume or cordon. Their parade uniform for the triumphal entrance into Brussels was in their haversacks, which made for them, with their equipment and their fifty cartridges, a load of sixty-five pounds. The grenadiers were distinguished from the *chasseurs* only by their ' greater stature, the copper plate upon their bear-skin caps, and their epaulets, which were blood-red, while those of their comrades were green with red fringes. The one and the other wore their hair done up in a queue and powdered, and massive gold rings in their ears.

The drums beat, the trumpets sounded, and the bands played "Let us watch over the safety of the Empire." In passing before the Emperor, the standard-bearers inclined the flag—the flags of the Champ du Mai, the new flags, but baptized already at Ligny in fire and blood—the horsemen brandished their sabres, and the infantry waved their shakos on the point of their bayonets. The acclamations dominated and drowned the roll of the drums and the blare of the trumpets. Cheers of "Long live the Emperor!" followed one another with such vehemence and such rapidity that they prevented the commands from being heard.

"Never," says an officer of the 1st Corps, "had one cried 'Long live the Emperor!' with more enthusiasm; it bordered on frenzy. And that which rendered this scene more solemn and impressive was that in front of us, at a thousand steps, perhaps, the sombre red line of the English Army was seen."

The infantry of d'Erlon and Reille deployed in the first line, abreast of La Belle Alliance—the four divisions of d'Erlon, in two ranks, the right facing Papelotte and the left supported on the route of Brussels; the three divisions of Reille, in the same formation, the right resting on this route and the left not far from that of Nivelles. The light cavalry of Jacquinot and Piré, in line of battle in three ranks, flanked the right of d'Erlon and the left of Reille. In the second line, the infantry of Lobau established itself in double columns of divisions on the left of the route of Brussels, and the cavalry of Domon and Subervic placed itself in serried columns of squadrons along and to the right of this highway.

Prolonging the second line, the *cuirassiers* of Milhaud and Kellermann were in line of battle in two ranks, the former on the right, the latter on the left. The Imperial Guard remained in reserve near Rossomme—the infantry (Young Guard, Middle Guard, and Old Guard), in six lines, each of four battalions, deployed on both sides of the route of Brussels; the light cavalry of Lefebvre-Desnoëttes (lancers and *chasseurs*), in two lines, a hundred paces behind the *cuirassiers* of Milhaud; the reserve cavalry of Guyot (dragoons and grenadiers), likewise in two lines, the same distance behind the *cuirassiers* of Kellermann.

The artillery of d'Erlon was in the intervals between the brigades, that of Reille in front of his line of battle, and that of Lobau on the left flank. Each division of cavalry had near it its horse battery. The batteries of the Guard were entirely in the rear, between Rossomme and the Maison du Roi. The route of Brussels and the roads which cross it, left free intentionally, permitted the reinforcements of artillery to move rapidly on all points.

There were in position nearly 74,000 men and 246 guns. On the other side of the valley, at 1,300 yards, as the crow flies, were massed 67,000 Anglo-Dutch. Never in the wars of the Revolution and Empire had so great a number of combatants occupied so restricted a field. The distance from the farm of Mont Saint-Jean, position occupied by the last reserves of Wellington, to the farm of Caillou, where were the imperial treasure and the baggage under the protection of a battalion of *chasseurs* of the Old Guard, is 4,500 yards, and the front of each of the two armies was hardly more than three-quarters of a league in extent. On account of the serrated ridges of the plateau, the two armies, although in parallel order, were not square. The English right wing overlapped the centre and the left was refused. The French Army, having the right in advance, the left centre in the rear, and the extremity of the left wing *en flèche*, formed a concave and enveloping line.

It was nearly eleven o'clock, and all the troops had not yet reached the positions assigned them. The Emperor even thought that he would not be able to begin the attack before one in the afternoon. He returned to his observatory at Rossomme, where he dictated to Soult the following order:

> As soon as all the Army will have formed in line of battle, probably by one in the afternoon, the Emperor will give the order to Marshal Ney, and the attack will begin in order to obtain possession of the village of Mont Saint-Jean, at the intersection of the routes. For this purpose, the batteries of 12-pounders of the 2nd and 6th Corps will unite with those of the 1st. These twenty-four pieces of ordnance will fire on the troops at Mont Saint-Jean, and Count d'Erlon will begin the attack with his left division supporting it, according to circumstances, with the other divisions of the 1st Corps. The 2nd Corps will advance in such a manner as to keep abreast of Count d'Erlon. The companies of sappers belonging to the 1st Corps will hold

themselves in readiness to barricade themselves immediately in Mont Saint-Jean.

This order leaves no doubt as to the intention of the Emperor. His object was to pierce the centre of the English Army and to throw it back beyond Mont Saint-Jean. Once master of this position, which commands the plateau, he would act according to circumstances against the broken enemy—already he would have virtually gained the victory.

Thus Napoleon forgot or scorned the advice of Reille, that, by reason of the precision of fire and of the solidity of the English infantry, one could hope to conquer it only by manoeuvres. He disdained to manoeuvre.

No doubt an attack against Wellington's right, very numerous, covered by the village of Braine l'Alleud and the farm of Hougoumont, and having the village of Merbe Braine for *réduit*, would have exacted much time and great efforts; but the extremity of the enemy's left wing was very weak, entirely in the air, badly protected and easy to outflank. It was by Papelotte and La Haye Sainte that one should have operated at first. It appears that for a moment the Emperor had an idea of doing so. But what a fine result, for Napoleon, to inflict a half-defeat upon the English and to throw them back on Hal and Enghien! He desired the battle to be decisive.

As at Ligny, he sought to pierce the enemy's army in the centre in order to dislocate and exterminate it. He would employ his usual tactics—the parallel order, the direct attack, the assault by masses at the strongest point of the English front, without other preparation than a deluge of cannon-balls. The Emperor, it is true, could not well estimate the number of the English nor the strength of their position.

More than half of the Allied Army was masked by the undulations of the ground, and General Haxo, charged with ascertaining if there were any entrenchments in front of the enemy's position, had reported that he had discovered no trace of any fortifications.

Haxo's sight or judgment was at fault, for the sunken road of

Ohain, the sandpit, the barricade across the route of Brussels, the abattis closing the route of Nivelles, and the farms of Hougoumont, La Haye Sainte, and Papelotte, could well be classed as formidable entrenchments.

CHAPTER 3

The Battle of Waterloo - From Half-past Eleven to Three O'Clock

1

A few minutes after having dictated the order of attack, the Emperor thought of preparing for the assault of Mont Saint-Jean by a demonstration on the side of Hougoumont. By threatening Wellington's right he might cause him to weaken his centre. Appreciating, finally, the value of time, Napoleon resolved to make this movement without waiting until all his troops had reached their positions of battle. About a quarter-past eleven o'clock Reille received the order to occupy the approaches of Hougoumont.

Reille charged with this minor operation Prince Jérôme, whose four regiments formed his left. In order to protect the movement, a division battery of the 2nd Corps opened fire against the positions of the enemy. Three English batteries, established upon the edge of the plateau, to the east of the route of Nivelles, replied. At the first cannon-shot some English officers looked at their watches. It was thirty-five minutes past eleven.

During this artillery duel, in which soon took part other batteries of the English right, a part of Reille's artillery and the horse batteries of Kellermann (the latter by command of the Emperor), Bauduin's brigade of Jérôme's division, preceded by its skirmishers, descended into the valley in columns of *echelons*. At the same time the lancers of Piré made a demonstration along the route of Nivelles. The 1st Light, having at its head Jérôme and General Bauduin, the latter of whom was killed at the beginning of the combat, attacked the wood with the bayonet.

In spite of the obstinate defence of the 1st Nassau Battalion and of a company of Hanoverian *carabineers*, the French succeeded in establishing themselves on the outskirts of the wood. There still remained three hundred yards of very thick undergrowth to be conquered. The 3rd of the Line entered the wood behind the 1st Light. The enemy retired step by step, concealing himself behind each cluster of trees, delivering his fire at almost point-blank range, and incessantly resuming the offensive. One hour was required to clear the wood of the Nassauers and the companies of English Guards who had come to reinforce them.

On debouching from the wood, the French found themselves at thirty steps from the Chateau of Hougoumont, a vast stone building, and from the park wall, six feet in height. It was simply a question of Jérôme "remaining in the valley behind the wood and throwing out towards the front a strong line of skirmishers." But, either because the order had been badly understood or expressed, or because the brother of the Emperor was unwilling to limit himself to this passive *rôle*, or because the soldiers, who were very much animated, advanced spontaneously, the French rushed to the assault.

Wall and ramparts were pierced with loopholes, through which the English opened a sustained fire. Sheltered behind the walls, they aimed carefully; fired at point-blank range, every bullet found its billet. The soldiers of Jerome wasted their shots at an in- visible enemy. Some attempted to break down the great gate with the butt-ends of their muskets; but the gate being built in a re-entering angle, they were exposed to a fire in front and flank. Others, who endeavoured to scale the wall by climbing upon each other's shoulders, were spitted on the bayonets of the English. The dead and wounded accumulated in heaps at the foot of Hougoumont. The assailants sought shelter in the wood.

General Guilleminot, Jérôme's chief of staff, advised him to confine himself to this first attack, to break off the combat, and to simply occupy the wood. Reille, according to his relation of the battle, sent analogous orders. But Jérôme remained deaf to all entreaty. He was bent on carrying the position. He summoned his second brigade (General Soye) to relieve in the wood Bauduin's brigade, and with the survivors of this brigade he turned Hougoumont by the west. His column, which was no longer covered, marched under the fire of the English batteries, firing at a range of six hundred yards. It reached, however, the northern façade of Hougoumont and delivered the assault.

Whilst Colonel de Cubières falls, severely wounded, from his horse, a giant, surnamed The Crusher, Lieutenant Legros, seizes the axe of a sapper and breaks a panel of the gate. A handful of soldiers throw themselves with him into the court. Surrounded on all sides by the English, they are all shot, exterminated—not one escapes. At this moment the French column is assailed by four companies of Coldstreams, sole reinforcement which Wellington, who watches from a distance the combat, but who is not deceived as to the importance of the attack of Hougoumont, has judged necessary to send there. Taken between two fires, the decimated battalions of Jerome withdraw, part into the wood and part towards the route of Nivelles.

2

During this combat the Emperor prepared for his great attack. He reinforced with the 8-pounders of the 1st Corps and three batteries of the Guard the twenty-four 12-pounders which at first had been thought sufficient to cannonade the centre of the enemy's position. Thus there was formed, in front of and to the right of La Belle Alliance, a formidable battery of eighty guns. It was nearly one o'clock. Ney sent one of his *aides-de-camp* to Rossomme to inform the Emperor that everything was ready and that he awaited the order to attack. Before the smoke from all these guns had interposed a screen between the hills. Napoleon wished to take a last look at the field of battle.

At nearly two leagues to the northeast he saw, as it were, a dark cloud which seemed to issue from the wood of Chapelle Saint Lambert. Although his experienced eye left no doubt in his mind, he at first hesitated to admit that it was troops. He consulted his entourage. All the field-glasses of the staff were directed upon that point. As often happens in such cases, there was a difference of opinion. Some of the officers insisted that it was not troops, but a cluster of trees, or the shadow of a passing cloud; others saw a column on the march, and even claimed to be able to distinguish French and Prussian uniforms. Soult said that he recognized plainly a numerous corps stacking arms.

One was not long in being fully informed. As a detachment of cavalry started at a gallop to reconnoitre these troops, a subaltern of the 1st Silesian Hussars, whom the hussars of Colonel Marbot had just captured near Lasne, was brought to the Emperor. He was the bearer of a letter from Bülow to Wellington, announcing the arrival of the 4th Corps at Chapelle Saint-Lambert. This hussar, who spoke French, showed no hesitancy in telling all he knew. "The troops in the distance," said he, "are the advance guard of General Bülow. All our army passed the night around Wavre. We have seen no French troops, and supposed that they were on the march towards Plancenoit."

The presence of a Prussian corps at Chapelle Saint-Lambert, which would have perplexed the Emperor some minutes earlier, at the time when he treated as "chimerical" the words of Jérôme concerning the projected junction of the two Allied Armies, now occasioned very little surprise, for he had received in the meantime this letter from Grouchy, dated at Gembloux, at six in the morning: "Sire, all my reports and information confirm the supposition that the enemy is retiring towards Brussels in order to concentrate there or to deliver battle after having united with Wellington. The 1st and 2nd Corps of Blücher's army appear to be directing themselves, the 1st on Corbaix and the 2nd on Chaumont.

These troops, no doubt, started from Tourinnes yesterday at half-past eight in the evening, and have marched all night; fortunately, the weather has been so unfavourable that they cannot have made much progress. I am just starting for Sart-à-Walhain, from whence I shall proceed to Corbaix and Wavre." This despatch was less reassuring than that of the day before. Instead of the two Prussian corps retreating in two columns, one on Wavre and the other on Liege, Grouchy announced that these two columns were marching concentrically towards Brussels, with the probable design of uniting with Wellington. He no longer spoke of preventing their junction; and, if it might be conjectured that he would manoeuvre to this effect by advancing on Wavre, he seemed to be in no hurry, since at six in the morning he had not yet left Gembloux. Doubtless the Emperor had a right to hope that the Prussians would march straight on Brussels; but it was also very possible that they would join the English by a flank march:

In order to ward off this possible danger, the Emperor decided very late to send new instructions to Grouchy. It is almost certain that Grouchy's letter had reached the imperial headquarters between ten and eleven o'clock. It was only at one, a few minutes before discovering the Prussian masses upon the heights of Chapelle Saint-Lambert, that the Emperor caused Soult to write to Grouchy:

> Your movement on Corbaix and Wavre is in conformity with the dispositions of His Majesty. Nevertheless, the Emperor orders me to say to you that you should continue to manoeuvre in our direction and seek to draw near the Army (French), in order that you may be able to join us before any hostile corps can interpose itself between us. I do not indicate the direction for you to follow. It is for you to see the point where we are, in order that you may regulate your movements accordingly and connect our communications, as well as be always in position to fall upon any troops of the enemy who .may seek to threaten our right and crush them.

This despatch had not been forwarded when the Prussian

columns appeared in the distance. A few minutes after, the Emperor, having interrogated the captive hussar, caused this postscript to be added:

> A letter which has just been intercepted declares that General Bülow is to attack our right flank. We believe that we see now this corps upon the heights of Saint-Lambert. So you will not lose an instant in approaching and joining us, in order that you may crush Bülow, whom you will take in the very act.

The Emperor then was not greatly alarmed. Though judging that the situation was seriously modified, he did not regard it as compromised. The reinforcement on its way to join Wellington consisted, after all, of only a single Prussian corps, for the prisoner had not said that all the army was following Bülow. This army was probably yet at Wavre. Either Grouchy would overtake and attack it there and, consequently, prevent it from joining Bülow; or, renouncing the pursuit of Blücher, he was already on the march towards Plancenoit by way of Mousty, as the hussar supposed, and was bringing to the principal French Army a reinforcement of 33,000 bayonets.

The Emperor, who deceived himself easily, and who wished especially to deceive others, said to Soult: "We had this morning ninety chances out of a hundred in our favour. We still have sixty against forty. And if Grouchy repairs the horrible fault which he has committed in amusing himself at Gembloux and marches with rapidity, the victory will be more decisive, for the corps of Bülow will be entirely destroyed."

Nevertheless, as Grouchy might be late in arriving, and as the advance guard of Bülow was in sight, the Emperor took incontinently some measures to protect the flank of the army. The light cavalry divisions of Domon and Subervic were detached upon the right, in order to observe the enemy, occupy all the debouches, and connect with the heads of columns of Marshal Grouchy as soon as they should appear. Count Lobau received the order to establish the 6th Corps behind this cavalry, in a good intermediate position, where it could hold in check the Prussians.

3

It was nearly half-past one. The Emperor sent to Ney the order to attack. The battery of eighty guns opened with the noise of thunder a rapid fire, to which the English artillery replied. After a half-hour's cannonade the great battery suspended for an instant its fire, in order to permit the infantry of d'Erlon to pass. The four divisions marched in *echelons*, the left in advance, with an interval of four hundred yards between each *echelon*. The division of Allix formed the first *echelon*, that of Donzelot the second, that of Marcognet the third, and that of Durutte the fourth. Ney and d'Erlon conducted the assault.

Instead of forming these troops in columns of attack—that is to say, in columns of battalions, with regular intervals between each battalion; a tactical formation favourable to rapid deployments as well as formation in squares—each *echelon* was made up of a succession of deployed battalions, each following the other, at short intervals between.

The divisions of Allix, Donzelot, and Marcognet (Durutte had taken it on himself not to conform to this disposition) thus presented three compact phalanxes, with fronts varying from 160 to 200 files and a depth of 80 men. Who had prescribed such a formation, perilous under all circumstances, and doubly so upon this difficult ground? Ney, or rather d'Erlon, commanding the army corps. At all events, it was not the Emperor, for in his general order of eleven o'clock nothing similar had been specified; nothing had even been said of an attack in *echelons*. Upon the battlefield Napoleon rightly left all initiative pertaining to the execution to his lieutenants.

Irritated at not having fought the day before, the soldiers burned to grapple with the enemy. They rushed forward with cries of "Long live the Emperor!" and descended into the valley under the vault of iron formed by English and French cannonballs which passed over their heads. The French batteries had recommenced firing as soon as the columns had reached the dead angle. The advance of Allix's division (Quiot's brigade) moved, by a slight conversion to the left, against the orchard of La Haye Sainte, from whence came a heavy fire. Bourgeois' brigade, forming alone, henceforth, the left *echelon*, continued its march towards the plateau.

The soldiers of Quiot quickly dislodged from the orchard the German companies and assailed the farm. But, no more than at Hougoumont, no one had thought of making a breach in these buildings with a few cannon-balls. The French vainly attempted numerous assaults against the high and solid walls, from behind which the Germans of Major Baring kept up a murderous fire. One battalion turned the farm, escaladed the garden wall, and dislodged the defenders, who re-entered the buildings; but it could not demolish the walls with the butt-ends of their muskets.

Wellington stood on foot under a great elm planted to the west of the route of Brussels, at the intersection of this route with the road of Ohain. During almost the entire battle he remained on this spot with his staff and the Allied commissioners, Pozzo di Borgo, who received a slight contusion; Baron de Vincent, who was wounded; Müffling, and Generals Hugel and Alava. Seeing the French completely surrounding La Haye Sainte, Wellington directed Ompteda to send to the assistance of Baring a battalion of the German Legion. The Germans descended to the west of the main highway, recaptured the garden and, passing to the west of the farm, advanced towards the orchard. At this moment they were charged by the *cuirassiers* of General Travers, whom the Emperor had detached from Milhaud's corps to second the attack of the infantry. The *cuirassiers* rode them down and, with the same *élan*, came to sabre on the edge of the plateau the skirmishers of Kielmansegge's brigade.

To the east of the route the other columns of d'Erlon had climbed the ascent under the fire of the batteries, the bullets of the 95th English and the musketry of Bylandt's brigade, deployed in front of the road of Ohain. The charge beat, and the pace increased in spite of the tall wheat which impeded the march, and of the drenched and slippery ground through which the soldiers floundered. The cries of "Long live the Emperor!" drowned at intervals the noise of the detonations. Bourgeois' brigade (left *echelon*) repulsed the skirmishers, assailed the sand-pit, dislodged from it the *carabineers* of the 95th and thrust them back upon the plateau, beyond the hedges, which it attained in their pursuit.

Donzelot's division (second *echelon*) attacked the right of Bylandt, whilst Marcognet's division (third *echelon*) advanced towards the left of this brigade. The Dutch-Belgians fell back, repassed in disorder the hedges of the road of Ohain, and in their flight, broke the ranks of the 28th English. On his side, Durutte, who commanded the fourth *echelon*, dislodged from the farm of Papelotte the light companies of Nassau; he was already halfway up the incline, threatening the Hanoverians of Best.

In the Imperial Staff everyone thought that "the affair was getting on admirably." In fact, if the enemy was still in possession of his advance posts of Hougoumont and La Haye Sainte, these posts were outflanked, surrounded, and the left centre of his line of battle was seriously threatened. The *cuirassiers* of Travers and the skirmishers of d'Erlon seemed on the point of crowning the plateau, followed closely by the infantry. Let these troops make yet a few more steps, let them maintain themselves upon these positions long enough to permit the reserve cavalry "to deal the *coup de massue*," and victory is certain.

4

The vicious formation of d'Erlon's columns, which had already delayed their march and doubled their losses in the ascension of the plateau, was about to lead to a disaster. After the skirmishers had overthrown the Dutch of Bylandt, Donzelot's division advanced within thirty steps of the road. There Donzelot had halted his column to deploy it. During the ascension of the hill the battalions had still further contracted their intervals. They formed but one dense mass.

The deployment, or rather the attempt to deploy—for it

does not appear that the French succeeded in executing the manoeuvre—consumed a great deal of time. Each command increased the confusion. The enemy profited by this respite. When the French batteries had opened fire, Picton's division (brigades of Kempt and Pack) had retrograded, by order of Wellington, 150 yards from the road. The men were there, in line, but lying on the ground in order to avoid the projectiles. Picton saw the Dutch in rout and the French skirmishers pushing through the hedges and advancing boldly against a battery. He ordered his men to rise, and pushed Kempt's brigade as far as the road. It drove back the skirmishers, passed through the hedge, and then, discovering Donzelot's column, occupied in deploying, saluted this column with a file-fire at forty steps.

Fired upon unexpectedly, and surprised in the midst of their formation, the French made instinctively, involuntarily, a slight retrograde movement. Picton, seizing the moment, cried: "Charge! Charge! Hurrah!" The English passed through the second hedge and hurled themselves with fixed bayonets upon this disorderly mass, which resisted from its very weight. Though repeatedly repulsed, the English returned to the charge. The distance was so slight that the discharges set fire to the clothing of the combatants. During this hand-to-hand fight a French officer was killed in the act of capturing the flag of the 32nd English, and the intrepid Picton fell dead, struck by a ball in the temple.

The column of Marcognet (third *echelon*) had arrived almost on a line with that of Donzelot at the moment of the flight of the Dutch. Marcognet, not having believed it possible to deploy his division, had continued his march and had passed beyond Donzelot, who had halted. Already, with his leading regiment, crying victory, he had passed through the double hedge and was advancing against a Hanoverian battery, when, to the shrill sounds of the *pibroch*, the Scotch brigade of Pack advanced by battalions, deployed in four ranks. At less than twenty yards, the 92nd Highlanders opened fire; soon after the other Scotch fired. On account of their dense formation, the French could only reply from the front of a single battalion. They delivered one volley and rushed forward with the bayonet. The two lines clashed together; the first ranks were mingled in a furious *mêlée*.

"I pushed a soldier in front of me," relates an officer of the 45th Regiment. "I saw him fall at my feet from a sabre-blow. I raised my head. It was the English cavalry who were riding through our ranks and cutting us to pieces."

As the French were on the point of crowning the plateau, the *cuirassiers* of Travers on the west of the highway and the columns of d'Erlon on the east, Lord Uxbridge had ordered the *élite* of his cavalry to charge. Somerset's four regiments of Horse Guards (1st and 2nd Life Guards, Blues, and Dragoons of the King) started at a gallop in line. In a few strides of their horses they arrived within pistol-shot of the *cuirassiers*, separated from them by the road of Ohain. West of the route of Brussels this road extended for the distance of 400 yards between two steep banks, which disappeared farther on. The left of Travers and the right of Somerset charged each other at a gallop upon the level part of the road.

But the right companies of the *cuirassiers* encountered the trench. They resolutely descended the outer slope and gave the spur to their horses in order to mount the opposite bank when, thirty feet above them, they beheld the glittering sabres of the 2nd Life Guards, coming at full speed. In order to avoid being completely crushed, for time and space were lacking to deliver the charge, the *cuirassiers* threaded the hollow road in confusion, regained the highway near Wellington's elm, and rallied in a field near the sandpit. The Life Guards, who had pursued them in skirting the edge of the route, charged them before they had re-formed; and, after a hand-to-hand combat in which, said Lord Somerset, "the blows of the sabres on the *cuirasses* sounded like braziers at work," they overthrew some of the *cuirassiers* in the excavation of the sandpit. The main body of Travers' brigade was broken and forced back to the bottom of the valley by the other regiments of Somerset, who, better mounted than the *cuirassiers*, had also the superiority of numbers and the advantage of position on their side.

5

At the same time Ponsonby's brigade of dragoons (Royals, Inniskillings, and Scots-Greys) had launched itself against the columns of d'Erlon. The Royals debouched from the route of Brussels, jostled Bourgeois' brigade, which was fighting with the 95th, concealed behind the hedges, and repulsed it as far as the sand-pit. The Inniskillings crossed the road through the openings made in the double hedge to facilitate the artillery fire, and assailed the column of Donzelot.

The Scots-Greys, thus named on account of the colour of their horses, arrived in the rear of the battalions of Pack, which opened their ranks to let them pass. Highlanders and Scots-Greys saluted each other with the cry, "Scotland forever!" and the horsemen fell with impetuosity upon the division of Marcognet. Smitten in front by the fire of the infantry, charged on both flanks by the cavalry, and paralyzed by their dense formation, the unwieldy French columns could offer but slight resistance. The men recoiled one upon the other, and the press became so great that they lacked the space necessary for firing at, and even for striking with their side-arms, the horsemen who penetrated their disorganized ranks.

Muskets were discharged in the air, and the bayonet thrusts, badly directed, missed the mark. It was pitiful to behold the English cavalry, overthrowing and traversing these fine divisions like miserable flocks of sheep. Drunk with carnage, encouraging each other to slay, the enemy's horsemen pierced and hewed merrily in the throng. The columns were broken, truncated, dispersed, and rolled to the bottom of the valley under the sabres of the dragoons. Bourgeois' brigade, which had rallied at the sandpit, was thrown in disorder and drawn along helter-skelter with the fugitives and horsemen.

Quiot's brigade abandoned the attack of La Haye Sainte. Above Papelotte, the division of Durutte suffered on its right flank the charges of Vandeleur's dragoons (11th, 12th and 13th Regiments), seconded by the Dutch dragoons and Belgian hussars of Ghigny. Though broken at first, it withdrew without serious loss and repassed the ravine, still surrounded by the cavalry. There no longer remained a single Frenchman on the slopes of Mont Saint-Jean. Carried away by their horses, from which, it is said, they had received the order to remove the curb-chains, and excited by the pace, noise, combat, and victory, the English traversed the valley at a furious pace and began to mount the opposite hill. In vain Lord Uxbridge sounded the retreat. His horsemen heard or wished to hear nothing, and climbed at a rapid gallop the French positions.

They were powerless to make any impression on them. The Life Guards and dragoons were decimated by the fire of Bachelu's division, established near the hillock to the west of the highway. The Scots-Greys encountered half-way up the slope two division batteries, sabred the gunners and drivers, overturned the guns in a ravine, and then assailed the great battery. The lancers of Colonel Martigue charged them in flank and exterminated them, whilst those of Colonel Brô disengaged the division of Durutte from the murderous clutches of Vandeleur's dragoons. "Never," says Durutte, "had I seen so well the superiority of the lance over the sabre."

It was in this *mêlée* that the valiant General Ponsonby met his death. Unhorsed by a subaltern of the 4th Lancers, named Urban, he had surrendered, when some of his Scots-Greys returned to rescue him. Urban, fearing to lose his prisoner, had the sad courage to plunge his lance through the body of the general; after which he threw himself on the dragoons and killed three.

The magnificent charge of the lancers was soon supported by General Farine's brigade of *cuirassiers*. The Emperor, seeing the Scots-Greys on the point of attacking the great battery, had sent the order to General Delort, one of Milhaud's generals of division, to launch against them two regiments. Lancers and *cuirassiers* swept the acclivities of La Belle Alliance, the entire valley, and pursued the Horse Guards and dragoons as far as the first slopes of Mont Saint-Jean, beyond La Haye Sainte. The light cavalry brigades of Vivian and Van Merlen, which had followed the movement of Lord Uxbridge at a distance, deemed it prudent to take no part in this engagement.

There was a lull in the action. On both sides the soldiers regained their positions. The hillsides, an instant before covered with combatants, were abandoned to the dead and wounded. "The dead," says an English officer, "were in many spots as thick as the overturned pawns on a chessboard." The ground presented that desolate appearance of a stricken field on the morrow of a battle, and the battle had just begun!

During this lull in the combat a *cuirassier* detached himself from his regiment, which was re-forming at La Belle Alliance, and, at a gallop, descended the great route. He was seen to traverse all that mortuary valley, in which he was the sole living being. The Germans posted at La Haye Sainte supposed that he was a deserter, and refrained from firing on him.

When he had arrived opposite the orchard, at the foot of the hedge, he raised his gigantic body straight up in his stirrups, waved his sabre, and cried, "Long live the Emperor!" Then, under a hail of bullets, he returned into the French lines in a few strides of his vigorous horse.

At Hougoumont the battle had continued more and more ardent. Three companies of English Guards, a battalion of Brunswick, one of the German Legion of Duplat, and two regiments of Foy, had successively reinforced defenders and assailants. The French, once more in possession of the wood after having lost it, captured the orchard; but the English Guards held fast to the garden, which was surrounded by a slight wall with a natural *banquette*, and maintained themselves in the farm.

By order of the Emperor, a battery of howitzers bombarded the buildings. A fire started in a granary spread and devoured the *château*, the house of the farmer, the cattle-sheds, and stables. The English withdrew into the chapel, the granges, the house of the gardener, and the adjacent hollow road, and recommenced their fusillade. The conflagration itself was an obstacle to the French. In the burning cattle-sheds, from which the ambulances established by the English had not been removed, were heard vain appeals for help and cries of despair.

CHAPTER 4

The Battle of Waterloo - From Three O'Clock until Seven

1

Wellington's sole object was to. hold his positions until the entrance into line of the Prussian Army. This movement was delayed longer than he expected. He had hoped that Blücher would commence the attack at two o'clock; it was now half-past three, and the Prussians seemed to be in no hurry to unmask themselves. In the English Staff it was feared that it would be impossible to resist a second assault.

Napoleon had his anxieties. Major La Fresnaye had just delivered to him Grouchy's letter, written from Walhain, at half-past eleven. In this very unsatisfactory despatch two things especially struck the Emperor—one was that Grouchy had marched very slowly, since at half-past nine o'clock he was still three leagues from Wavre; the other, that the Marshal seemed to pay very little attention to what was passing on his left, and demanded orders to manoeuvre *the next day* in the eccentric direction of La Chyse.

It became evident that, unless Grouchy had conceived the idea at noon of marching to the sound of the cannon, he would be unable to attack in flank the corps of Bülow, already in position at Chapelle Saint-Lambert. At most the Marshal would be able to fall on the rear of this corps or detain far from the field of battle, by an attack pressed home, the other corps of the Prussian Army. Should we be astonished that the Emperor did not immediately send back La Fresnaye with new instructions for Grouchy? These instructions, which would have been none other "than to draw near the Army, in order to fall upon the hostile column which should attempt to molest the right wing," had already been sent by Napoleon to his lieutenant at a quarter-past one. He could have only reiterated them, and very tardily at that!

The presence of Bülow at Chapelle Saint-Lambert, the bloody check of Count d'Erlon, and the distance of Grouchy were perhaps sufficient reasons to cause the Emperor to break off the combat, as at Essling, and to take up a defensive position upon the plateau of La Belle Alliance. It does not seem that this expedient, which at most would have been good only for the day, ever occurred to him. The next day the French Army, even though reinforced by Grouchy, would have had to deliver battle almost in the proportion of 1 to 2 to the united armies of Wellington and Blücher. The Emperor preferred to profit by the expectancy in which Bülow appeared to remain, in order to overthrow the English before the entrance into line of the Prussians.

As soon as d'Erlon had rallied some of his battalions, about half-past three, the Emperor ordered Ney to attack La Haye Sainte again. He intended to use that position as a base for a combined movement with the corps of d'Erlon, that of Reille, which he thought would be soon in possession of Hougoumont, all the cavalry, and finally the Foot Guard. Ney led against La Haye Sainte Quiot's brigade, whilst one of Donzelot's brigades, deployed as skirmishers, scaled the hill to the east of the route of Brussels to attack in the rear the English concealed behind the hedges of the road of Ohain. The attack failed. The skirmishers of Donzelot were repulsed; and the soldiers of Quiot, decimated by the point-blank fire of the Germans of Major Baring, who had just received a reinforcement of two companies, withdrew into the orchard.

To second this assault, the great battery redoubled its fire against the left centre of the enemy's position, whilst the batteries of Reille, reinforced by a part of the 12-pounders of the Guard, cannonaded incessantly the right centre. It was at this period of the battle that the artillery fire was most intense.

"Never," says General Alten, "had the oldest soldiers heard such a cannonade." Some battalions of the first English line retrograded a hundred steps in order to shelter themselves behind the crest of the plateau. At the same time groups of wounded, convoys of prisoners, empty caissons, and crowds of fugitives streamed towards the Forest of Soignes. Ney, who saw with difficulty through the smoke, mistook these movements for the beginning of a retreat, and thought of establishing himself upon the plateau with the cavalry. He summoned immediately a brigade of *cuirassiers*.

The *aide-de-camp* addressed himself to General Farine, who put his two regiments on the march. But General Delort, commanding the division, arrested the movement. "We take orders only from Count Milhaud," said he. Ney, impatient, hastened to Delort. The Marshal was greatly irritated at this disobedience. He not only reiterated the orders concerning Farine's brigade, but he ordered the other six regiments of Milhaud's corps to advance.

Delort having again remonstrated against the imprudence of this manoeuvre upon such unfavourable ground, Ney invoked the instructions of the Emperor. "Forward!" cried he; "it is a question of the safety of France." Delort obeyed. The two divisions of *cuirassiers* started at a rapid trot, and behind them moved the red lancers and *chasseurs* of the Guard.

Did these regiments follow the movement by order of Lefebvre-Desnoëttes, to whom Milhaud had said when starting, "I am going to charge; support me," or did they advance spontaneously—seized, as it were, by an irresistible desire to charge at sight of their comrades hastening against the enemy, whose retreat had begun, and desirous of having their share of the English to sabre?

Since the beginning of the battle Ney had thought of a great cavalry action, of which he had spoken to the Emperor, who had for this purpose placed under his command the corps of *cuirassiers* and even the Horse Guard. The Prince of the Moskowa promised himself immense results from this charge. He who was classed, says Foy, among the first cavalry leaders of the army, was proud of having to lead it. He talked it over with Drouot, assuring him that he was certain of success. Ney at first, who was to engage the cavalry only after having received the Emperor's order, had only wished to establish himself upon the plateau with a brigade of *cuirassiers*. Then the idea had occurred to him to hasten the retreat of the English by launching against them all the *cuirassiers* of Milhaud. This is why he had ordered these two divisions to advance.

Perhaps, however, he would have hesitated to engage them without further orders from Napoleon; but when he saw descending into the valley of La Haye Sainte, with this multitude of mailed squadrons, the horse *chasseurs* and red lancers of the Guard, he did not doubt that it was in accordance with the instructions of the Emperor, who had judged the hour propitious for the grand attack. Otherwise, would the cavalry of the Guard have followed the *cuirassiers*? It appears almost certain, however, that Napoleon had seen nothing of this movement.

From the low ground where the divisions of Milhaud and Lefebvre-Desnoëttes were in position, it was possible for them to reach the route of Brussels, cross it close by La Belle Alliance, and descend into the valley without being seen by the Emperor, stationed near the Decoster house. But Marshal Ney was none the less justified in supposing that this glittering mass of 5,000 horsemen had not escaped the eye of Napoleon. He formed in haste these magnificent squadrons in the valley, to the left of the route of Brussels, and, placing himself at their head, launched them against the English Army.

2

Wellington thought so little of retreating that he had just reinforced his front of battle with many brigades from his second line and reserve. The Brunswickers advanced to the support of the Guards of Maitland, and the brigades of Mitchell and Adam crossed the route of Nivelles to establish themselves above Hougoumont, in front of the road of Ohain. One was not, however, without anxiety in the Allied Army. The staff watched anxiously the French positions, seeking to discover what movement was being prepared by Napoleon, when the cavalry descended towards La Haye Sainte.

The surprise of the English was great and many of their fears were dissipated. "We were astonished," says Kennedy, "that one should attack with cavalry an infantry as yet unshaken and which, thanks to the undulations of the ground behind which it was lying, had suffered little from the cannonade." In an instant the men were on their feet, formed in squares. The batteries remained in front of the line of battle, on the very edge of the plateau. The artillery horses were sent to the rear, and the cannoneers received the order to fire until the last moment, then to abandon their guns and seek refuge in the squares.

The French cavalry advanced in columns of squadrons in *echelons*, the *cuirassiers* on the right and the *chasseurs* and *chevau-legers* on the left. The direction was slightly oblique,, the first *echelons* manoeuvring to approach the level part of the road of Ohain, and the left *echelons* making a change of front towards the acclivities that rise above Hougoumont. In this movement they presented their flank to the fire of the enemy's artillery. As soon as the *cuirassiers* began to debouch from the low grounds where they had formed, the French batteries ceased firing and those of the English accelerated their fire. The guns were double-shotted with ball and cannister, or chain-shot—a whirlwind of iron.

Passing through the miry and rain-drenched bottoms, in which they sometimes sank up to their knees, and impeded by the tall rye which swept their chests, the horses mounted at a slow trot the steep slopes. By accelerating their fire, the batteries were able to make many discharges. A last salvo, at forty yards, from the batteries of Lloyd and Cleeves, established on the spot where rises today the Mound of the Lion, mowed down half of the leading squadrons. The survivors halted for some seconds, appearing to hesitate. The charge sounded more vibrant; and with cries of "Long live the Emperor!" the *cuirassiers* hurled themselves on the guns. One after the other, all the batteries were taken. A superb feat of arms, but an illusory capture. There were no teams to carry off the guns and no spikes to put them out of service. It would have been possible to have overturned them in the ravine and, in default of nails, to have forced into the touch-holes of the cannon the ramrods of pistols. But nothing of the kind was thought of; not an officer even thought of causing the sponge-staffs to be broken.

The cannon are silenced, but the musketry rolls and crepitates. Between the route of Nivelles and the highway of Brussels twenty English, Hanoverian, Brunswick, and German battalions form two lines of squares, arranged checker-wise. The bullets strike and ricochet against the *cuirasses* with the noise of hail upon a slate roof. *Cuirassiers* and lancers, their ranks already broken by the fire, the ascension of the hill, and even the passage of this hedge of the cannon, burst on the squares. But, from the edge of the plateau where they take the gallop to the first line of infantry, the field is insufficient. The charge lacks *élan* and consequently vigour.

The English are in squares in three ranks, the first rank kneeling, the butt-ends of the muskets supported against the ground, and the inclined bayonets forming *chevaux-de-frise*. In spite of their valour and rage, the horsemen are unable to pierce these walls of men. They oblique to the right and left and, under the cross-fires, charge the squares in the second line. Squadron succeeds squadron, like the waves of the sea. The sea of cavalry inundates all the plateau. *Cuirassiers, chasseurs*, and red lancers circle round the squares, assail them on their four faces, strike at the angles, beat down the bayonets with their sabres, discharge their pistols at close range, and in hand-to-hand combats open some partial breaches, which are closed as soon as made.

Lord Uxbridge saw this *mêlée*. Two-thirds of his cavalry had not been engaged. He launched against these disorganized masses the dragoons of Dörnberg, the hussars of Arenschild, the black lancers of Brunswick, the Dutch *carabineers* of Trip, and the two Dutch-Belgian brigades of Van Merlen and Ghigny—in all, 5,000 fresh horses. The enemy had numbers and cohesion in his favour. The French fell back under the shock, repassed through the intervals between the squares, and escaped the sabres only to fall under the bullets. They abandoned the plateau. The gunners hastened to their pieces; and along all the crest of the plateau the English batteries resumed their fire.

Hardly at the bottom of the valley, the valorous soldiers of Milhaud and Lefebvre-Desnoëttes resume the charge. Again they climb the miry slopes of Mont Saint-Jean under the iron hail, take possession of the guns, crown the plateau, burst on the infantry, and form a circle of glittering sabres around the squares.

More than one Englishman believed the battle lost. Many of the reserve batteries made ready to retreat at the first order. Colonel Gould, of the artillery, said to Mercer: "I am afraid that all is ended." From La Belle Alliance the Emperor and his staff had seen these magnificent charges; they saw the cannon abandoned, the horsemen galloping over the plateau, the enemy's lines pierced, and the squares surrounded; already the cry of victory was heard around Napoleon. Napoleon was surprised and vexed that his cavalry had been engaged without his order against infantry as yet unbroken. He said to Soult: "This is a premature movement, the results of which may prove disastrous."

The Major-General inveighed against Ney, "He is endangering us as at Jena!"

The Emperor looked long at the field of battle, reflected a moment, and then said: "It is too soon by an hour; but it is necessary to follow up what has already been done."

He sent one of his *aides-de-camp*, General Flahault, to carry to Kellermann the order to charge with the four brigades of *cuiras-*

siers and *carabineers*.

Like the Emperor, Kellermann thought the movement of Milhaud premature; he also believed it imprudent to engage his own cavalry. He was on the point of stating his reasons to Flahault when General Lhéritier, who commanded his first division (*cuirassiers* and dragoons), started at a rapid trot without awaiting orders. Kellermann was forced to follow with his second division, composed of the 2nd and 3rd Cuirassiers and the 1st and 2nd Carabineers; but not far from Hougoumont he halted the brigade of *carabineers* in a hollow of the ground, and gave positive instructions to General Blancard not to budge from there unless he received an order from him. This was a wise precaution, for these 800 *carabineers* were henceforth the only cavalry reserve left to the army. Flahault, according to the instructions of the Emperor, had transmitted the order to charge not only to Kellermann, but also to General Guyot, commanding the heavy cavalry of the Guard (dragoons and horse grenadiers).

The Emperor has said that he had been forced to support the divisions of Milhaud, as he feared that a check suffered by the latter, in presence of the entire army, would discourage the soldiers and lead to panic and rout. Did he not also hope to crush the English under a new mass of mailed cavalry? It was necessary to press the action, to gain at one point, to hold out at another, to conquer and impose by dint of audacity, for affairs had become terribly critical. The Emperor was fighting two battles at the same time, one parallel, the other oblique: in front, he attacked the English; on his right flank, he was attacked by the Prussian.

3

Towards one o'clock Blucher had rejoined, at Chapelle Saint-Lambert, the main body of Bülow's corps; but, though he was very anxious to take part in the battle, he judged it imprudent to engage himself in the defiles of the Lasne before being assured that he would not be taken *en flagrant délit* of march. Three-quarters of an hour later he learned from reconnaissances that, the French being a long way off, he was in no danger. He at once put his troops in motion in the direction of Plancenoit. His object was to outflank the right of the Imperial Army. The march was slow and laborious. When one follows the rough road that descends from Chapelle Saint-Lambert, crosses at Lasne the stream of this name, and ascends the no less precipitous side of the other hill, one wonders how the Prussian artillery ever managed to pass this defile.

All the energy of Blücher was necessary to accomplish the task. He was everywhere, reanimating his soldiers exhausted from fatigue and hunger (on the march since five in the morning, they had not eaten since the day before), lavishing upon them encouragements, appeals to duty, familiar and pleasant words. "Come, comrades," said he to some cannoneers, who were pushing at the wheels of a gun that had stuck fast in the mud, "you would not have me miss my word!"

About four o'clock his heads of column attained the wood of Paris (3,500 yards from Plancenoit) . The division of Losthin and Killer established themselves there without firing a shot; for instead of occupying the avenues of the wood, the cavalry of General Domon had confined itself to observing its *débouchés*. In this new position, the Prussians found themselves under cover. Before unmasking himself, Blücher would have preferred to await the other two divisions of Bülow, which were still in the defiles of Lasne.

But the messages from Wellington, urging him to take part in the battle, became more and more pressing; and he saw, it is said, the *cuirassiers* in motion upon the heights of La Belle Alliance. He decided to act with the force at hand. At half-past four the Prussians debouched: the infantry of Losthin on the right of the road of Plancenoit, the infantry of Hiller on the left, and the front covered by two regiments of cavalry and three light batteries. Blücher hastened to cannonade the squadrons of Domon; he wished, says Müffling, to warn and encourage Wellington and at the same time to prevent Napoleon from crushing the English.

Domon at first opposed offensive to offensive. He overthrew

the Prussian hussars and fell upon the batteries. Overwhelmed by their fire and by the musketry of Losthin's entire division, he fell back slowly; then passing in reserve, he unmasked Lobau's infantry, which had taken position astride of the road of Lasne, at nearly half a league to the east of the route of Brussels. The divisions of Simmer and Jannin, deployed one behind the other, were *en potence*, almost perpendicular to the line of battle.

In order to bring them in line with the front, the Emperor had ordered the Foot Guard to advance near La Belle Alliance, to the right of the route of Brussels, save the 1st Regiment of Grenadiers, which remained near Rossomme, and the 1st Battalion of the 1st Chasseurs, posted at Caillou. He had at the same time given the order to Durutte to assail Papelotte and La Haye Sainte, in order to second the grand attack of Ney and to sever the communications between Bülow's right and the English left.

Lobau, well knowing that all passive resistance is virtually condemned, pushed straight against the Prussians, who fell back. The divisions of Ryssel and Hacke debouched in turn from the wood. The Prussians resumed the offensive—30,000 against 10,000 Frenchmen. But Lobau's regiments were of ancient formation and as solid as rocks. The 5th of the Line, the first regiment to join Napoleon in the defile of Laffray, and the 10th of the Line, the only one that had fought for the Bourbons at the Bridge of Loriol, rivalled each other in enthusiasm and tenacity. With these fine troops, Lobau presented so bold a front that Blücher, instead of persisting in his parallel attack, manoeuvred to outflank the right of the 6th Corps.

The cavalry of Prince William of Prussia and the infantry of Hiller, supported by the division of Ryssel, advanced on Plancenoit. Lobau, fearing to be turned, recoiled until abreast of the village, which he caused to be occupied by a brigade. Assailed on three points, this brigade was unable to maintain its position. The enemy forced it out of Plancenoit, in which he established and entrenched himself. On his front, Blücher cannonaded the other three brigades of Lobau with eight batteries, whose balls fell upon the route of Brussels, in the midst of the battalions of the Guard and even in the Emperor's staff.

At the moment when his infantry attacked Plancenoit, Blücher had received an *aide-de-camp* from Thielmann. The commander of the 3rd Corps announced that he was attacked in Wavre by superior forces (they were the 30,000 men of Grouchy), and that he doubted his ability to resist them. "Let General Thielmann do the best he can," said Gneisenau. "It matters little if he is crushed at Wavre if we are victorious here."

With the enemy in possession of Plancenoit, Napoleon was outflanked and his line of retreat threatened. He ordered Duhesme, commanding the division of the Young Guard, to retake the village. The eight battalions, four of *voltigeurs* and four of *tirailleurs*, advanced at the charging step. The Prussians were dislodged from the houses and from the cemetery of which they had formed a *réduit*,

4

The English still held out. When the heavy cavalry of Kellermann and Guyot debouched into the valley, between five and half-past five o'clock, the *cuirassiers* of Milhaud had again been forced from the plateau by the English dragoons. Quickly re-formed, they followed to the charge these three fresh divisions of Kellermann and Guyot. *Cuirassiers* of Lhéritier, Delort, Wathier, and Roussel d'Hurbal, *chasseurs* and lancers of Lefebvre-Desnoëttes, dragoons and horse grenadiers of Guyot—more than sixty squadrons—scaled the plateau. The enemy was surprised to see 8,000 or 10,000 horsemen engaged upon a front where 1,000 at most would have been able to deploy. They covered the entire space between Hougoumont and La Haye Sainte. Their files were so contracted in the rush that many horses were raised off the ground by the pressure. This mass of *cuirasses*, helmets, and sabres rose and fell upon the rolling ground like billows on the ocean. To the English it appeared as if a sea of steel were mounting the plateau.

The enemy renewed the manoeuvre which twice already

had succeeded with him. After having scourged the cavalry with grape, the gunners abandoned their guns and sought refuge in the squares. The latter opened at thirty steps a file-fire, which mowed down entire ranks "like the sweep of a scythe," and then received the debris of the squadrons upon a triple rank of bayonets. Charge succeeded charge without intermission. Some squares suffered five, seven, ten, and even as many as thirteen assaults. Many were shaken and partially shattered, if not overthrown and broken.

A quartermaster of the 9th *Cuirassiers* took an English flag. Captain Klein de Kleinenberg, of the *chasseurs* of the Guard, had his horse killed while capturing the flag of a battalion of the German Legion. But the greater part of the squares remained impervious to assault. At moments they seemed submerged by the wave of cavalry, then they reappeared through the smoke, bristling with glittering bayonets, whilst the squadrons spread around them like waves of the sea that break themselves against a dike.

The *cuirassiers* of Lhéritier burst through a labyrinth of fire upon the squares of the second line, pass beyond them, and are overwhelmed by the reserve batteries. An entire regiment turns to the left, follows at a terrific pace the route of Nivelles, sabres the sharpshooters of Mitchell along the road of Braine l'Alleud, turns Hougoumont, and comes to re-form upon the plateau of La Belle Alliance The dragoons of the Guard engage the light cavalry of Grant, which, occupied all the afternoon in observing the lancers of Piré in front of Montplaisir and finally recognizing in the movements of the latter mere demonstrations, have turned back from the right wing on the centre.

Mercer's battery, the only one whose gunners have remained at their guns, notwithstanding the order of Wellington, is a little in the rear, its front sheltered by an embankment of the road, and its flank protected by two squares of Brunswick. The horse grenadiers—giants mounted on enormous horses and their stature still further increased by their tall bear skin caps—advance at a trot in line. One would have said that it was a wall on the march. Under the grape of Mercer and the cross-fire of the squares of Brunswick this wall crumbles, covering the ground with its blood stained *débris*.

At the second change there is a new butchery. Colonel Jamin, colonel of the grenadiers, falls mortally wounded across a gun-carriage. In front of the battery there rises a wall of dead men and disembowelled horses.

"You have a nice lot here," laughingly said Colonel Wood to Mercer. The last companies of grenadiers cross the hideous obstacle, pass between the guns, and, sabring the gunners, go to mingle their charges with those of the *cuirassiers*.

Too numerous for the extent of the ground, all these squadrons mutually hinder one another. They clash together, cross one another, break their charges, and mingle their ranks. The charges, still as ardent as ever, become less and less rapid, less and less vigorous, and less and less efficacious, in consequence of this confusion and the exhaustion of the horses, which, at each stride, sink into the heavy and rain-drenched soil. The atmosphere is as hot as the blast from the mouth of a furnace; and the combatants breathe only with the greatest difficulty. Generals Donop, Delort, Lhéritier, Guyot, and Roussel d'Hurbal are wounded. Edouard de Colbert charges with his arm in a sling. Wounded also are Generals Blancard, Dubois, Farino, Guiton, Picquet, Travers, and Wathier.

Marshal Ney, his third horse killed under him, stands alone near an abandoned battery, wrathfully striking with the flat of his sword the bronze muzzle of an English cannon. The entire field of battle is encumbered with non-combatants, dismounted *cuirassiers* staggering under the weight of their armour in the direction of the valley, wounded men dragging themselves out of the shambles, and riderless horses galloping wildly under the lash of the bullets which whistle by their ears. Wellington issues from the square of the 73rd, in which he had sought refuge during the hottest part of the action,, hastens to his cavalry, and throws it upon these exhausted squadrons, disunited and broken by their very charges. For the third time, the French abandon the plateau.

For the fourth time they re-ascended it, crying, "Long live the Emperor!" Ney led the charge at the head of the *carabineers*. He had seen at a distance their golden *cuirasses*, had hastened to them, and, in spite of the observations of General Blancard, who opposed the formal order of Kellermann, led them with him in this race with death.

The persistency of Ney and his heroic horsemen, like him drunk with rage, bordered on frenzy. This last charge with squadrons reduced to half of their effectives, with exhausted men and wind-broken horses, could only end in a new check. The ascendancy of cavalry over infantry consists solely of moral effect. What moral effect could one hope to produce with cavalry upon an infantry which had just learned in repulsing, with fire and bayonets, numerous charges, that the tempest of horse was only a scarecrow, and which, in these two rude hours, long as days, had become assured of its invincibility?

On the contrary, it was the horsemen who were demoralized by the failure of their attacks, the vanity of their efforts. They charged with the same intrepidity, but no longer with the same confidence. They crossed again the line of batteries; but, after having vainly pushed their harassed horses on the squares—or, more correctly speaking, on the ramparts of dead soldiers and slaughtered animals that protected the face of each square—they fell back of their own accord, discouraged, desperate, to the bottom of the valley, followed at a distance, rather than driven by the English cavalry, itself at the end of its strength.

5

These great charges might have succeeded, but on condition of being supported instantly by infantry. Whilst the enemy's batteries, passed by the *cuirassiers*, remained silent, the infantry could have climbed the slopes without danger of loss, taken position on the edge of the plateau and attacked the squares. The English would have been compelled either to sustain in a vicious formation the fire and assaults of the infantry, or to deploy, which would have placed them at the mercy of the horsemen. Bachelu's division and Jannin's brigade (Foy's division) had remained for many hours at 1,300 yards from the allied position, witnessing with grounded arms this furious combat. They awaited but an order to go to the assistance of the cavalry. Ney forgot them. It was only after the repulse of the fourth charge that he thought of utilizing these 6,000 bayonets. The six regiments marched by *echelons* in columns of divisions. It was too late. The batteries overwhelmed them, and the allied infantry, which had extended its front in a circle towards Hougoumont, riddled them with its convergent fire.

"It was a very hail of death," says Foy. In a few minutes 1,500 men were killed, wounded, or dispersed. In spite of all this, the French approached within pistol-shot of the enemy, but the fresh brigades of Duplat and William Halkett, having executed an offensive movement (Duplat was killed at this moment), the columns, truncated by the cannon-balls, retreated. It was in vain that Marshal Ney caused them to be supported by a few skeleton squadrons, notably the *carabineers*. In these partial charges, which succeeded one another until the end of the battle, the horsemen pierced no more the line of English batteries.

During all the charges of the cavalry Ney, in the fire of this tumultuous action, had lost sight of his first objective—the capture of La Haye Sainte. There, as at Hougoumont, but with less intensity, the fight had continued without result. And yet the intrepid defenders, supplied with only sixty cartridges per man, began to decrease their fire. Major Baring had asked for more ammunition. Wellington gave him none; but sent a new reinforcement of two companies.

About six o'clock, at the moment when the divisions of Foy and Bachelu were advancing towards the plateau, the Emperor traversed the line of battle under a rain of shells and cannon-balls. General Desvaux de Saint-Maurice, commander-in-chief of the artillery of the Guard, General Lallemand, commanding the foot batteries, and Bailly de Monthyon, chief of the general staff, were struck down at his side. Napoleon sent the order to

Ney to take possession of La Haye Sainte, regardless of the cost. It was a new prey pointed out to the Marshal, a new occasion to meet death.

Ney hurried to the 13th Light (Donzelot's division) and threw it, with a detachment from the 1st Regiment of Engineers, against the farm. The bullets, fired at point-blank range, thinned the ranks of the assailants. Some of the soldiers sought to disarm the Germans by attempting to draw the muskets through the loopholes. In an instant seventy French fell at the foot of the east wall. Their comrades mounted upon their bodies to climb on top of the wall, from which they fired upon the *chasseurs* of Baring in the court; others climbed upon the roof of the grange.

Lieutenant Vieux, of the engineers, who fell later, with the rank of colonel, in the breach of Constantine, struck with heavy blows of the axe upon the gate. He received one ball in the wrist and another in the shoulder. The axe passed from hand to hand, the gate finally yielded, and the wave inundated the court. Driven back into the buildings, and without ammunition, the Germans defended themselves with their side-arms. Major Baring, with forty-two men—all that remained of his nine companies—broke through the mass of assailants, and regained Mont Saint-Jean.

Ney immediately established a horse battery on a hillock near La Haye Saint, and pushed a regiment against the sand-pit, which was abandoned by the 95th English. From these two positions the cannoneers fired at a range of less than 300 yards, and the sharpshooters at less than 80, upon the very centre of the enemy's line. Supported by this fire, which opened a breach, the *débris* of the divisions of Allix, Donzelot, and Marcognet ascended from both sides of the farm as far as the road of Chain. French and Allies fired at each other through the hedges, over the banks, and then rushed on each other with the bayonet. Ompteda, with the 5th and 8th Battalions of the German Legion, executed on the great route a counter-attack, which was at first successful. A ball hurled him mortally wounded from his horse. The 5th Battalion retired; the 8th, which was further advanced, was exterminated by a squadron of *cuirassiers*. Its flag was captured; its commander, Colonel Schrader, was killed; and only thirty men escaped the sabres of the *cuirassiers*.

The enemy's left centre (brigades of Kempt, Pack, Lambert, Best, and Wincke) stood firm; but, on the extreme left, the Nassauers of Prince Bernard of Saxe-Weimar permitted themselves, for the second time, to be dislodged from Papelotte by the division of Durutte, and at the right centre the Allies were shaken and incapable of further resistance. The ammunition was exhausted, some of the guns dismounted, and others without gunners. The Prince of Orange and General Alten, both wounded, quitted the field of battle. Colonels Gordon and De Lancey Evans, *aides-de-camp* of Wellington, were killed. The cavalry brigades of Somerset and Ponsonby were reduced to two squadrons between the two brigades; the brigade of Ompteda had but a handful of men in line; that of Kielmansegge withdrew behind the village of Mont Saint-Jean, and that of Kruse recoiled.

In the rear the fugitives multiplied. The hussar regiment of Cumberland turned bridle and scampered away in the direction of Brussels with its colonel at its head. Everywhere the ranks grew thinner. The wounded were numerous, and numerous also were the men who left the ranks to carry them to the ambulances. There was some disorder even in the intrepid brigade of Colin Halkett, in which a battalion was commanded by a simple lieutenant. The flags of the 30th and 73rd Regiments were prudently sent to the rear.

"The centre of the line was open," says an *aide-de-camp* of General Alten. "We were in peril. At no moment was the issue of the battle more doubtful." In spite of his accustomed assurance, Wellington became anxious. He saw, indeed, the black masses of Blücher outflanking the French Army, but he himself remained without support. He was heard to murmur: "Night or Blücher!" Already he had despatched towards Ohain many *aides-de-camp* to hasten the march of Ziethen's corps. But his resolution remained as firm as ever. Officers arrived from all sides to inform him of their desperate situation and to demand new orders. He coldly replied: "There is no other order than to hold out to the last man."

The slight recoil of the enemy's line had not escaped the eye of Marshal Ney. But his soldiers were as exhausted as those of Wellington. He felt that a few fresh troops would suffice to reanimate them and overcome the resistance of the English. He sent Colonel Heymès to ask of the Emperor a small force of infantry. "Troops!" cried Napoleon. "Where do you think I can get them? Do you think I can make them?"

The Emperor had still eight battalions of the Old Guard and six of the Middle Guard. If, at this moment, he had given half of them to Marshal Ney, we may believe, even from the avowal of the best informed and most judicious English historian, that this reinforcement would have overthrown the enemy's centre. But Napoleon, without a cavalry reserve, did not believe that he had too many men, with all his bear-skin caps, to maintain his own position. The moment was no less critical for him than for Wellington.

Under a third surge of Bülow's entire corps, Lobau fell back, and the Young Guard, after an obstinate resistance, yielded Plancenoit. Once more the balls from the Prussian batteries laboured the ground near La Belle Alliance. Napoleon, already outflanked, was threatened by an irruption of the Prussians in the rear of his line of battle. He formed eleven battalions of the Guard in as many squares and stationed them in front of Plancenoit, along the route of Brussels, from La Belle Alliance to Rossomme. The 1st Battalion of the 1st Chasseurs was maintained at Caillou. Generals Morand and Pelet received the order to retake Plancenoit with the 1st Battalion of the 2nd Grenadiers and the 1st of the 2nd Chasseurs.

With drums beating, these old soldiers marched at the double-quick, in serried columns of companies. They passed the Young Guard, which was being rallied by Duhesme, attacked Plancenoit at two points, penetrated into the village without deigning to fire a shot, overturned, ground to pieces, and drove out the Prussians. The attack was so impetuous that in twenty minutes the village was cleared. The grumblers, with their bayonets dripping blood, debouched at the backs of the fugitives, pursued them 600 yards, and drove them back upon the opposite hill, even behind the batteries of Hiller, which were for an instant abandoned. The Young Guard seconded this movement; it occupied Plancenoit once more, and Lobau, fighting with the divisions of Losthin and Hacke, recovered the ground that he had lost.

CHAPTER 5

The Battle of Waterloo - From Seven to Nine O'clock

1

With a single blow of his Old Guard, Napoleon had arrested the Prussians. His right flank disengaged, he again became free to act on the front of battle. It was more than seven o'clock; but there still remained two hours of daylight; for the sky was clear and the sun shone above Braine l'Alleud. The cannonade of Grouchy increased in violence, drew nearer, and roared in the direction of Limale. It was supposed that the Marshal had finally overtaken the Prussian Army, was fighting it, and, victorious or vanquished, would detain it long enough to prevent its junction with the English.

Blücher, it seemed, had only been able to detach the single corps of Bülow, which Lobau, Duhesme, and two battalions of the Old Guard would suffice henceforth to hold in check. The Emperor levelled his glass on the side of the English. The points from which came the fire of artillery and musketry and the direction of this fire served him as landmarks. On the extreme right the division of Durutte, in possession of Papelotte and La Haye, was climbing the plateau. On the left, the fight continued around Hougoumont in flames; a brigade of Jérôme outflanked this position, and the French sharpshooters, supported by the lancers of Piré, had crossed the route of Nivelles.

At the centre, above La Haye Sainte, from whence the enemy

had finally been dislodged, the soldiers of Donzelot, Allix, and Marcognet had crowned the crests, and were pressing the enemy vigorously along the road of Ohain. In the valley, the regiments of Bachelu and Foy, as well as the *débris* of the cavalry, were rallying. The enemy's line appeared to be shaken. The Emperor presumed that Wellington had engaged all his troops, while he had still his Old Guard—his Invincibles.

It was the hour when victory decided in favour of the most stubborn. He commanded Drouot to order to advance in the formation in squares which they had previously taken nine battalions of the Guard (of the other five, two were to remain in Plancenoit and three upon the plateau as a last reserve). He put himself at the head of the first square and descended towards La Haye Sainte to the bottom of the furnace.

From the testimony of the enemy, this attack might have succeeded a half-hour earlier, at the time when Ney had called for a reinforcement. The moment had passed. Whilst Morand had retaken Plancenoit, and even during the short time it had taken the Guard to form and put itself in motion, Wellington had strengthened his position. To reinforce his wavering and almost broken centre he had recalled from his left the brigade of Wincke and from his right four battalions of Brunswick, of which he himself had taken the command.

Seconded by these fresh troops, the brigades of Kempt, Pack, and Best, on the east side of the route of Brussels, and the brigades of Kruse and Halkett, to the west of this route, had made a vigorous counter-attack, and had driven back the infantry of Donzelot, Allix, and Marcognet. Whilst the soldiers were withdrawing to the bottom of the hill, the Anglo-Germans reoccupied the brow of the plateau, and their batteries, delivered from the fusillade at short range, silenced the fire of the guns established at La Haye Sainte. At the same time the Dutch-Belgian division of Chassé arrived from Braine l'Alleud, and the six cavalry regiments of Vandeleur and Vivian, which, informed of the imminent arrival of the Prussian corps of Ziethen, had quitted their post as flankers above Papelotte, hastened up at a rapid trot.

The Prussian reinforcements, which had become so necessary, and the first result of whose approach had been to render available the 2,600 fresh cavalry of Vivian and Vandeleur, had been on the point of failing Wellington. Starting from Bierges at noon, constrained to halt for more than two hours upon the heights northeast of the Dyle, in order to permit the corps of Pirch I. to defile, then retarded in his march by the scarped paths of the wood of Rixenart, through which the men advanced sometimes in Indian file and forced to cut a passage for the guns, Ziethen had arrived at Ohain about six o'clock with his advance guard. He was joined there by Colonel Freemantle, Wellington's *aide-de-camp*, who explained to him the critical situation of the English Army, and asked for a reinforcement, "should it only consist of 3,000 men, but at once."

Ziethen was unwilling to run the risk of having his army corps beaten in detail; he replied that he would hasten to the support of the English as soon as the main body of his troops would have closed up on the advance guard. Meanwhile he sent a staff officer towards Mont Saint-Jean in order to see exactly the state of affairs. The latter, deceived by the great number of wounded and fugitives who were fleeing to the rear, returned to report that the English were in full retreat. Fearing to be drawn into a rout without any advantage for the Allied Army, Ziethen immediately turned the head of his column to the left, in order to rally Bülow between Frichermont and the wood of Paris. Müffling, in observation above Papelotte, saw this movement. He set his horse at a gallop, overtook Ziethen, informed him more exactly, and entreated him to join the left of the English. "The battle is lost," he cried vehemently, "if the 1st Corps does not support the Duke!"

After hesitating a long time, Ziethen yielded to the reasons advanced by Müffling, and resumed his first direction.

Ziethen's head of column debouched from Smohain when the Guard descended towards La Haye Sainte. Already some of the troops were falling back at sight of the Prussians. The Emperor hastened to them and harangued them; they resumed their advance. A new enemy's corps, making an irruption upon the angle of the square formed by our two lines of battle, was the *coup de grace*. But it is very doubtful if the Emperor could have then broken off the combat. By reason of the disorder in which the troops already found themselves, of their extreme dissemination, and of the advanced position of Bülow's corps upon their flank, a retreat would have been terribly hazardous.

Even if it had been effected without too great loss or confusion, protected by a dike formed incontinently at the summit of the plateau of La Belle Alliance with all the battalions of the Guard, what tomorrows it would have prepared for Napoleon! The army reduced by half (for the corps of Grouchy, left isolated, cut off from its line of retreat, appeared devoted to certain destruction); the frontier open; France discouraged; patriotism abased; the Chamber passing from secret hostility to open war; and everywhere intrigue, desertion, treason. Rather than to live again the agony of 1814, it were better to attempt a supreme and desperate effort to violate rebellious Fortune.

2

The approach of the 1st Prussian Corps had no other effect on the Emperor than to cause him to hasten his attack. Six battalions of the Guard had alone arrived in the lowlands of La Haye Sainte. The Emperor posted one of them (the 2nd of the 3rd Grenadiers) upon a little hillock, half-way between the farm and Hougoumont; and, seeing Ney, who was always to be found wherever death was to be affronted, gave him the command of the others to deliver the assault against the enemy's right centre. At the same time he ordered the batteries to increase their fire, and d'Erlon, Reille, and the commanders of the cavalry corps to second on their respective fronts the movement of the Guard. It was possible that the report of the arrival of the Prussians by way of Ohain might spread.

The Emperor wished to prevent this alarm. He directed La Bédoyère and his orderly officers to traverse the line of battle, and to announce everywhere the arrival of Marshal Grouchy. Ney has said that he was indignant at this stratagem. As if Napoleon had the choice of means! It is certain that, at this false news, confidence returned and enthusiasm kindled up again. The troops re-formed their ranks crying, "Long live the Emperor!" Some of the wounded drew themselves up in order to acclaim the passage of the columns on the march. One soldier with three chevrons, a veteran of Marengo, seated, his legs broken by a cannon-ball, against the side of the road, repeated in a loud and firm voice: "It is nothing, comrades; forward! and long live the Emperor!"

Had Wellington, in spite of the smoke which became more and more thick, seen the preparatory movements for this final assault? At all events, he was warned of them by a traitor. At the moment when Drouot assembled the Guard, a captain of *carabineers* traversed the valley at full speed, defying the cannon-balls and a hail of bullets, and approached, sabre in its scabbard and right hand raised, the advanced skirmishers of the 52nd English. Conducted before the major of this regiment, who was talking with Colonel Fraser, commanding the light artillery, he cried, "Long live the King! Prepare yourself! That rascal Napoleon will be on you with the Guard before a half-hour.'"

Colonel Fraser rejoined Wellington and transmitted to him this information. The Duke traversed the line of battle from the route of Brussels to that of Nivelles, giving his last orders. The brigade of Adam and the Guards of Maitland, which had retreated into a hollow in order to shelter themselves from the balls, resumed their positions. The Hanoverian brigade of William Halkett and the German brigade of Duplat prolonged the right of Adam, towards Hougoumont. The Dutch-Belgian division of Chassé established itself: the brigade of d'Aubremé behind the Guards of Maitland, having behind it the cavalry of Vivian; the brigade of Ditmer in the rear of the three battalions of Brunswick, posted on the left of the English brigade of Colin Halkett.

The cavalry of Vandeleur deployed to the west of the route of

Brussels in support of the decimated battalions of Ompteda and Kruse and another battalion of Brunswick. The three batteries left until then in reserve advanced to the front. The cannoneers were ordered to reply no longer to the French artillery, but to concentrate their fire on the assaulting columns. They were to fire until they had exhausted the last cartridges.

It seems that Ney gave a bad formation as well as a bad direction to the Guard. Instead of forming a single column, powerful enough to pierce the enemy's line, the Marshal left the battalions divided. And instead of ascending from the lowlands of La Haye Sainte straight to the plateau by the route of Brussels, by which the column would have had hardly 400 yards to traverse, and where the embankments of the road would have protected it from the enfilading fire of the artillery, it marched diagonally, by the unprotected slopes which had been scaled by the *cuirassiers* in their first charge.

The five battalions of the Middle Guard, formed in as many squares, advanced in *echelons*, the right in advance. Between each *echelon* the horse cannoneers of the Guard conducted two 8-pounders, a total of one battery, under the orders of Colonel Duchand. In this oblique march, almost analogous to the movement "towards the left, *en avant en battaile*," all the *echelons* did not maintain their intervals. The fourth approached the third. Soon the five battalions formed but four: on the right, the 1st Battalion of the 3rd Grenadiers; in the centre, the sole battalion of the 4th Grenadiers; further to the left, the 1st and 2nd Battalions of the 3rd Chasseurs: and on the extreme left, the 4th Chasseurs, reduced to a single battalion.

All the troops had received the order to second this attack. Already the divisions of Donzelot, Allix, and Marcognet had begun to climb the plateau, the first along and to the left of the route of Genappe, the other two to the right of this route. But the infantry of Reille and the *débris* of the cavalry had hardly begun to advance. Between La Haye Sainte and Hougoumont the five battalions of the Guard advanced alone against the English Army. They marched at a shoulder arms, aligned as if for a review at the Tuileries, superb and impassive.

All their officers were in front, the first in the midst of the balls. Generals Friant and Porret de Morvan commanded the battalion of the 3rd Grenadiers; General Harlet, the battalion of the 4th Grenadiers; General Michel, the 1st Battalion of the 3rd Chasseurs; Colonel Mallet, a faithful of the Island of Elba, the 2nd Battalion; and General Henrion, the battalion of the 4th Chasseurs. Ney rolled upon the ground with his horse, the fifth one killed under him. He disengaged himself, arose, and marched on foot, sword in hand, by the side of Friant.

The English artillery, disposed in a semi-circle from the route of Brussels to the neighbouring heights of Hougoumont, for from convex the front of the enemy's right had become concave, fired double charges of grape at a range of 200 yards. The Guard was battered in front and flank. Each volley made a breach. The grenadiers closed up the files, contracted the squares, and continued to ascend with the same step, crying, "Long live the Emperor!"

The 1st Battalion of the 3rd Grenadiers (right *echelon*) overthrew a corps of Brunswick, took possession of the batteries of Cleeves and Lloyd, which were abandoned by the cannoneers: and, by a slight conversion, directed itself towards the left of the brigade of Halkett. The 30th and 73rd English recoiled in disorder. Friant, wounded by a gunshot, quitted the field of battle, believing the victory assured. But the Belgian General Chassé, one of the heroes of Arcis sur Aube (he served then in the French ranks!), caused to advance on the right of the 30th and 73rd Regiments the battery of Van der Smissen, whose fire enfiladed the assailants. Then he deliberately sent to the left of the two English regiments the brigade of Ditmer, 3,000 strong, launched it with fixed bayonets against the feeble square, broke, dislocated, and crushed it under the weight of numbers, and threw back the survivors to the foot of the slopes.

During this time the battalion of the 4th Grenadiers (second *echelon*) had engaged the right of Halkett's brigade. Under the iron hail of the two guns of Duchand and the fusillade of the grenadiers, the *débris* of the 33rd and 69th Regiments gave ground. General Halkett seized the flag of the 33rd and, by his example, succeeded in checking the disorder.

"See the General!" cried the men. "He is between two fires! He cannot escape!" In fact, he fell, severely wounded. But the English had rallied and held their ground.

An old soldier said, in biting off his cartridge: "It is who will kill the longest."

The 1st and 2nd Battalions of the 3rd Chasseurs (third *echelon*) almost attained the crest of the plateau without meeting with any infantry. They marched towards the road of Ohain, distant from them hardly a pistol-shot. Suddenly, at twenty steps, arose a red wall. It was the 2,000 Guards of Maitland, drawn up in four lines. They had been waiting, lying down in the rye. At the command of Wellington, "Up, Guards, and be ready!" they had risen as if moved by springs. They aimed, fired. Their first volley mowed down 300 men, nearly half of the two battalions already decimated by the fire of the artillery. General Michel fell, mortally wounded.

The French halted; their ranks broken, their march obstructed by the dead. Instead of ordering them to advance instantaneously with fixed bayonets, without disquieting themselves at the disorder in which they found themselves, the officers attempted to form them in line in order to reply to the fire of the enemy. The confusion increased. The deployment was effected with great difficulty and loss of time. For ten minutes the *chasseurs* remained exposed to the fire of the Guards of Maitland and the batteries of Bolton and Ramsay, which enfiladed them. Wellington saw the Guard on the point of giving way; he ordered the charge.

"Forward, my lads!" cried Colonel Saltoun; "now is the time!" The 2,000 English rushed headlong upon this handful of soldiers, overthrew them, and descended intermingled with them in a furious hand-to-hand combat, even near the orchard of Hougoumont.

"The combatants were so mingled," says an officer of Bolton's battery, "that we were compelled to cease firing."

At the sudden commands of their officers the English halted abruptly. The battalion of the 4th Chasseurs (left *echelon*) approached to disengage the survivors of the 3rd Chasseurs, as well as those of the 4th Grenadiers, who had likewise begun to retreat. Without awaiting the shock, the soldiers of Maitland fell back in disorder and re-ascended to their positions as swiftly as they had descended. *Chasseurs* and grenadiers followed them up closely, scaling the hillside under the volleys of grape. They crossed the road of Ohain, when the brigade of Adam (52nd, 71st, and 95th Regiments), which had quickly formed *en potence* on their left flank, raked them with a fire from four ranks.

The guards of Maitland faced about and, re-forming as well as possible, recommenced to fire in concert with the brigade of Colin Halkett, whilst the Hanoverians of William Halkett debouched from the hedges of Hougoumont, and opened fire upon the French from the rear. From all sides the bullets arrived in clusters. Mallet was severely wounded. One battalion deployed in front of Maitland; and what remained of the other two marched by the left against the brigade of Adam. Colonel Colborn, whom the soldiers called in Spain "the fire-eater," charged with the 52nd. All the brigade followed with fixed bayonets. Considerably shaken already by the formidable fire to which they had been exposed, *chasseurs* and grenadiers yielded under the weight of numbers, and retired in confusion.

3

The cry, "The Guard recoils!" sounded the death-knell of the Grand Army. Everyone felt that all was ended. The infantry of Reille, the *cuirassiers*, and the squadrons of the Guard, who had finally put themselves on the march to second Ney's attack, halted, paralyzed. The soldiers of Donzelot and Allix, fighting upon the crests above La Haye Sainte, with the brigades of Kruse, Lambert, Kempt, and Pack, saw the Guard falling back. They also yielded the conquered ground, and again descended to the foot of the hill, drawing in their retreat the division of

Marcognet, which had attacked upon the prolongation of their right the positions of the enemy.

The backward movement gained the entire line of battle, from left to right. At the same time the infantry of Durutte was attacked in Papelotte and La Haye by the Prussian heads of column, debouching by the road of Ohain. The cry, "*Sauve qui peut*! We are betrayed!" arose on all sides. This panic can be readily explained, if one thinks of the state of mind of the soldiers, troubled and possessed for three months by the fear of treason. Everything appeared to justify their suspicions. They had seen passing over to the enemy a general, a colonel, and officers of every grade.

Among their cartridges they had found some filled with bran instead of powder. They were astonished at so many disconnected movements; they were disheartened by so many unsuccessful assaults. Finally, they had expected the corps of Grouchy, whose arrival had been announced, and it was the corps of Ziethen that arrived to crush them. Confusion set in, increased. The Prussians hurled themselves to the assault, dislodged from the farms the few handfuls of brave men who still held out in spite of the panic, and threw them into the ravines. The debris of the four divisions of d'Erlon ran foul of, jostled, and mutually broke one another. East of the great highway, in the depths of the valley over which crossed the English shrapnel and Prussian cannonballs, there was the most lamentable confusion.

Wellington wishes to finish this mortally wounded army. He urges his horse to the brow of the plateau, uncovers, and waves his hat in the air. His men understand this signal. All the troops put themselves instantaneously on the march in the order in which they find themselves. Without taking time to re-form, the battalions, batteries, and squadrons of the different divisions advance side by side, passing over the dead and crushing the wounded under the feet of the horses and the wheels of the cannon.

There alone remain upon the positions the brigades of Pack, Ompteda, and Kielmansegge, and two or three batteries which are literally prevented from moving by the carcasses of horses and the bodies accumulated along their front. From right, to left,. English, Hanoverians, Belgians, Brunswickers, cavalry, infantry, and artillery, forty thousand men, descend in torrents to the sound of drums, bugles, and pibrochs, in the first shadows of twilight.

At this sight, frightful even for brave men, the last *echelons* of infantry turn and re-ascend precipitately, with most of the cavalry, the hills to the west of La Belle Alliance; the leading battalions, more immediately threatened with being overwhelmed by the avalanche, disband and flee. La Haye Sainte, the orchard of Hougoumont, and the wood are abandoned. The hussars of Vivian and the dragoons of Vandeleur, who open the way for the English masses, sabre the fugitives, with the ferocious cry, "No quarter! No quarter!"

4

Whilst the Middle Guard attacked the English positions, the 2nd Battalions of the 1st Chasseurs, the 2nd Grenadiers, and the 2nd Chasseurs, with Generals Cambronne, Roguet, and Christiani, had arrived near the Emperor at the foot of La Haye Sainte. Napoleon occupied himself with forming them in column of attack, one battalion deployed and two upon the flanks in serried column, to lead them himself upon the plateau, where "all was going well," according to the words of Friant, who returned from there wounded, when he saw the sudden collapse of his line of battle. He also felt then that he was irremediably defeated. But he preserved the hope of being able to organize the retreat. Without losing any of his presence of mind, he broke the column of the Old Guard and placed the three battalions, in as many squares, at nearly a hundred yards below La Haye Sainte, the right square on the route of Brussels. Protected by this dike, he thought the army would be able to rally and retire in good order.

The hussars of Vivian, powerless to make any impression on these squares, turned them and continued to trace red furrows in the throng of fugitives. Drunk with blood, they were intent on slaughter. A subaltern of the 18th said to Vivian: "We will follow you to hell, if you will lead us." Behind the hussars rushed other horsemen of the enemy. The Emperor launched the four squadrons of his escort against this new wave of cavalry, which submerged them.

Not far from the road, Ney, on foot, bare-headed, unrecognizable, his face black with powder, his uniform in rags, one epaulet cut in two by a sabre-stroke, and a broken sword in his hand, cries with rage to Count d'Erlon, who is borne along in an eddy of the rout: "D'Erlon, if we escape, we shall be hung!" The Marshal "is less like a man than a furious beast." His efforts during this entire day have exceeded human energy and strength. Never in any battle had any chief, any soldier, exposed himself as much. Ney has surpassed Ney. He has led twice to the attack the infantry of d'Erlon; he has charged four times upon the plateau with the *cuirassiers*; he has led the desperate assault of the grenadiers of the Guard.

He hastens now to Brue's brigade (Durutte's division), sole troops of the Line retiring in good order, and which is reduced, moreover, to the effective of two battalions. He stops the soldiers and throws them once more against the enemy, crying: "Come and see how a marshal of France can die!" The brigade quickly broken and dispersed, Ney clings to this fatal field of battle. Since he cannot find death there, he wishes, at least, to be the last to quit it. He enters into a square of the Guard with Major Rullière, who has taken the eagle of the 95th from the dying hands of Lieutenant Puthod. Durutte, his right hand severed at the wrist, his forehead laid open by a sabre-blow, and all covered with blood, is borne along by his horse in a charge of the enemy's cavalry; he gallops in the midst of the English as far as La Belle Alliance.

The three battalions of the Guard repulsed the cavalry without difficulty. But their formation in squares, which, however, they were forced to preserve in order to resist new charges, put them in a state of tactical inferiority with the English infantry, in line in four ranks. Its more extended and denser fire battered the squares in front and flank. With the musketry was mingled the grape from the batteries of Rogers, Whyniates, and Gardiner, which fired at a range of sixty yards.

The masses of the enemy increased around the grenadiers: the brigades of Adam and William Halkett, which were especially persistent in their attack, and those of Kempt, Lambert, Kruse, Wincke, and Colin Halkett.

The Emperor gave the order to quit this untenable position. As for himself, reflecting, too late perhaps, that to check a rout one should not remain upon the broken front of troops who are falling back, but should betake himself to the rear, in order to rally them in a new position, gained at a gallop, with a few chasseurs of his escort, the heights of La Belle Alliance.

The three battalions—as well as that of the 3rd Grenadiers, posted on their left and assailed in turn by the English dragoons, the Black Lancers of Brunswick, the infantry of Maitland and Mitchell—retrograded step by step. Reduced to too few men to remain in squares in three ranks, they formed in two ranks, in triangles and, with fixed bayonets, pierced slowly through the crowd of fugitives and the English. At each step men stumbled over the dead or dropped under the balls. Every fifty yards it was necessary to halt to re-form the ranks and to repulse a new charge of cavalry or a new attack of infantry.

In this heroic retreat, the Guard marched literally surrounded by enemies, like a wild boar among a pack of dogs. The distance separating the combatants was so slight that, in spite of the multiple noises of the battle, one was within speaking distance. In the midst of the musketry the English officers cried to these old soldiers to surrender. Cambronne was on horse-back in the square of the 2nd Battalion of the 1st Chasseurs. Despair in his heart, choking with rage, and exasperated by the incessant summons of the enemy, he cried wrathfully: "M.——!" A few instants after, as he was on the point of attaining with his battalion the summits of La Belle Alliance, a ball full in his face overturned him bloody, and inanimate.

5

During the last assault of Mont Saint-Jean half of the corps of Pirch (divisions of Tippelskirch and Krafft and the cavalry of Jurgass) had rejoined Bülow, who had just met with a bloody repulse. Blücher immediately ordered a general attack against all our right flank. In Plancenoit the Young Guard of Duhesme and the two battalions of the Old Guard of Morand and Pelet remained inexpugnable. But on the prolongation of this village, the infantry of Lobau and the cavalry of Domon and Subervic fell back before the 15,000 men of Hacke, Losthin, and Prince William; they were overthrown when the division of Steinmetz and the cavalry of Roder, debouching from Smohain in pursuit of Durutte, attacked them in flank.

The French masses, stationed a quarter of an hour before from the route of Nivelles to the ravines of Papelotte and Plancenoit, inundated the plateau around La Belle Alliance. Behind them, sabring, shooting, and cheering, hastened on one side the English, on the other the Prussians. The two jaws of the vice closed upon the panic-stricken and defenceless crowd that had been the Imperial Army.

In this terror-stricken mob everyone pushed and scrambled in order to flee more swiftly. There were *cuirassiers* who threw aside their *cuirasses*, drivers who cut the traces of the teams, and men who were trampled underfoot. One stumbled among the dead horses, the overturned caissons, the abandoned cannon. The shadows of night, which began to grow thicker (it was nearly nine o'clock), added to the fright and increased the confusion. The 12th and 16th English Dragoons were charged by the 1st Hussars of the German Legion. The brigade of Adam received the fire of a Prussian battery. The Highlanders of the 71st turned some French guns against the fleeing columns.

The four battalions of the Guard, which had just regained the plateau, were the only infantry still in order. English and Prussians enclosed each of these squares in a circle of grape, sabres, and bayonets. Charged simultaneously by the cavalry and infantry, they were broken, demolished, crushed. Their *débris* were swallowed up in the *débacle*.

Five hundred yards in the rear, near the Decoster house, await, formed in squares, on the left and right of the route, the two battalions of the 1st Grenadiers, commanded by General Petit. These men are the *élite* of the *élite*. Almost all of them wear two *chevrons*, and four out of six are legionaries. The Emperor is on horseback in the square of the 1st Battalion. With these living redoubts, he still hopes to cover the retreat. He orders to be established, upon the prolongation of the squares, the battery of 12-pounders which had for a long time cannonaded the Prussians above Plancenoit, and causes the *grenadière* to be beaten in order to rally all the detachments of the Guard.

A crowd of fugitives pass along the route on both sides of the squares, followed closely by the enemy. The battery of the Guard has only one shot for each piece. Its last discharge, at close range, overwhelms a column of cavalry. The gunners, henceforth, without ammunition, remain stoically by their guns, in order to impose still upon the assailants. Other squadrons approach at a gallop. "Do not fire," cries a grenadier; "they are French hussars."

They are English hussars; they burst upon the battery and sabre the disarmed cannoneers. But upon the squares these incessant charges break and scatter like whirlwinds of sand upon blocks of granite. Before each battalion of grenadiers rises a wall of dead men and horses.

In Plancenoit, where the Prussian batteries had started a conflagration, one fought by the light of the flames. The Young Guard, recruited almost entirely from among the volunteers of Paris and Lyons, and the 1st Battalions of the 2nd Chasseurs and 2nd Grenadiers, fought one against five. The combined attacks of the divisions of Hiller, Ryssel, and Tippelskirch failed. Gneisenau reanimated his soldiers; they rushed again to the assault and penetrated into the village. There French and Prussians engaged in a murderous death-grapple, in which they killed one another with thrusts of the bayonet and blows of the butts of their muskets.

Drum-Major Stubert, of the 2nd Grenadiers, a giant, brained

the Prussians with the head of his baton. A battalion of the Young Guard caused itself to be exterminated in the cemetery, which served as a *réduit*. The Prussians captured the houses one by one. The combatants massacred one another in the chambers, in the attics; and during these fights, in which no mercy was shown by either side, the thatched roofs, which the fire had gained, crumbled over the heads of the combatants.

"It was necessary to annihilate the French," says Major Von Damitz, "in order to obtain possession of Plancenoit." On the outskirts of the village the remains of these heroic battalions were charged and driven fighting as far as the plateau. There the English cavalry finished them.

General Pelet found himself for an instant alone in the midst of the enemy, with a few men and the eagle-bearer of the *chasseurs* of the Old Guard. "Help! help! *chasseurs!*" he cried in a piercing voice. "Let us save the eagle or die near it!" All those who heard this desperate appeal turned back and cut their way through the mass of horse; they rallied around the eagle and formed for it an impenetrable rampart of bayonets.

From Plancenoit French and Prussians debouched upon the route of Brussels, near the squares of the 1st Grenadiers. The fugitives crowded around to seek a refuge within these squares, but they were pitilessly repulsed by steel and fire. The safety of the squares demanded it. General Roguet came near being killed by a grenadier. "We fired," said General Petit, "on all that which presented itself, friends as well as enemies, for fear of permitting to enter the one with the other. It was an evil for a good." The squares were outflanked on the right and left; the English and Prussians became more and more numerous, more and more compact. The grenadiers repulsed every charge. Two battalions against two armies!

Finally, the Emperor ordered the position to be abandoned. The grenadiers put themselves slowly in retreat, the 1st Battalion on the left of the route and the 2nd on the route itself. Every few minutes they halted to dress the squares and to delay the pursuit of the enemy by a rolling file-fire.

The Emperor marched at some distance in front of the squares with Soult, Drouot, Bertrand, Lobau, and five or six horse chasseurs of the Old Guard. At the farm of Caillou he rejoined the 1st Battalion of the foot chasseurs of the Old Guard. This battalion, charged with the safety of the Imperial treasure and baggage, was commanded by Major Duuring, a Dutchman by birth. About seven in the evening, two Prussian columns having advanced through the wood of Chantelet with the manifest intention of intercepting the retreat of the army by occupying the main highway, Duuring had at once ordered the wagons to retire on Genappe, in accord with General Radet, provost-general of the army, who had succeeded in rallying two or three hundred dismounted cavalry and infantry. He had then deployed his battalion in front of the enemy.

The Prussians (25th Regiment), received with a heavy fire and then charged with the bayonet, retired towards Maransart. The Emperor stopped for a few minutes to question Duuring under the last cannon-balls from the Prussian batteries of Plancenoit; he praised him for the firmness and spirit of initiative of which he had given proof, and ordered him to follow him, "I count upon you," said he. The battalion having closed up in mass, the Emperor gave the reins to his horse and marched at a walk upon the flank of the column.

Chapter 6

The Rout

1

About a quarter-past nine, at the time when the divisions of Hiller, Ryssel, and Tippelskirch wrested Plancenoit from the Young Guard, and the squares of the 1st Grenadiers still held out near the Decoster house, Blücher and Wellington met in front of the inn of La Belle Alliance. Blücher followed the troops of Bülow, who had driven back Lobau, and Wellington arrived from La Haye Sainte with the last *echelons* of his army. The two generals met and, according to the words of Gneisenau, "they congratulated each other upon the victory." The bands of the Prussian cavalry played in passing, "God Save the King"; in the distance the noise of the firing decreased. The infantry of Bülow, who had halted to re-form their ranks, intoned the hymn of Luther: "Lord God, we praise Thee! Lord God, we thank Thee!"

Blücher, impressed with the fact that his meeting with Wellington had taken place precisely in front of La Belle Alliance, wished to give this name to the battle, in which the alliance of the English and Prussians had produced such great results. But Wellington desired that the victory—his victory—should bear the name of the village which had had the honour the preceding night of serving him as headquarters.

It was decided that in spite of the night it was necessary to pursue *à outrance* the wrecks of the Imperial Army. The English were worn out with ten hours' fighting, "tired to death," says Wellington. The Prussians had made five leagues on an average over the worst kind of roads, and they had fought between Frischermont and Plancenoit with no less obstinacy than had the soldiers of Wellington at Mont Saint-Jean. Nevertheless, Blücher proposed to charge his troops with the pursuit. The offer being accepted without shame, he called together his corps commanders and ordered them "to pursue the enemy as long as they would have a man and horse in condition to stand up." Gneisenau put himself at the head of the squadrons of Count Roder. All the army followed. Towards Rossomme they caught up with a part of the Prussian divisions, which had debouched from Plancenoit, and the furthest advanced of the columns of the English cavalry and infantry.

The army of Wellington halted. The soldiers saluted with a triple "Hip, hip, hurrah!" the Prussians who passed them, and established themselves in bivouac in the midst of the shambles. From the plateau of Mont Saint-Jean to the heights of Rossomme, from Hougoumont to Plancenoit, and even towards Smohain, the entire ground was covered with dead men and horses. More than 25,000 French and 20,000 English, Belgians, Germans, and Prussians lay upon the ground, here scattered like uprooted trees, there in long lines like rows of grain which had fallen under the reaper's scythe.

The moon, which had risen, lighted up distinctly their livid and bloody faces, their uniforms soiled with mud and spotted with blood; the arms which had fallen from their hands scintillated in the moonbeams. At times great sombre clouds, drifting across the sky, concealed this vision, from which the least sensitive among the oldest soldiers turned away their eyes; but it soon reappeared under the glacial light of the moon. Amidst the death-rattle of the dying and the groans of the wounded, one heard at short intervals a raucous cry similar to that uttered by someone being strangled by horror and fright. It was some officer being finished by a robber of the dead, in order to steal from him his purse or his cross of the Legion of Honour.

The Prussians conducted the pursuit with vigour. The fugitives of the right wing (corps of Lobau and d'Erlon, Young

Guard, and cavalry of Domon, Subervic, and Jacquinot) who, pursued too closely, or cut off from their line of retreat, had not been able to overtake and pass the squares of the 1st Grenadiers forming the rear guard, were sabred or made prisoners. On the right wing a certain number of *cuirassiers*, whose horses were still in condition to travel, and the lancers of Piré, who had only skirmished during the battle, gained Quatre-Bras, without being molested, by way of Neuve-Court, Malplaquet, and Vieux-Genappe. They passed the Sambre at Marchienne.

Five or six thousand infantry of Reille's corps, rallied at nightfall, directed themselves on Genappe across the fields, parallel with and at nearly a half-league from the highway. A few Prussian squadrons were sufficient to disperse them. Save three companies of the 93rd Regiment, which turned at bay and repulsed the charges, all this mass dispersed. Some of the soldiers threw away their haversacks and guns in order to flee more rapidly, justifying only too well the old adage: *Frenchmen are more than men in attack, and less than women in retreat.* They no longer listened to their officers, and panic reigned supreme.

The Old Guard alone remained worthy of itself. The *chasseurs* and lancers of Lefebvre-Desnoëttes, who had quitted the field at walk and with so bold a front that the English cavalry had not dared to attack them, retired in good order on the west of the highway, and reached Quatre-Bras without suffering any new losses. On the highway itself the Prussians were held in check by the two squares of the 1st Grenadiers, which were preceded by the 1st Battalion of the 1st Chasseurs. The grenadiers continued to march at the ordinary step, defying all attacks. Not being able to bite, the Prussian pack desisted from further attacks and confined itself to following out of musket-range. Half a league from Genappe, General Petit, no longer deeming it necessary to preserve the order of combat, ordered the squares to break up and to march in column by sections. It was at this moment that the Emperor separated from the 1st Battalion of *chasseurs* to gain Genappe, where he hoped to check the enemy and to rally the wrecks of the army.

2

Genappe consisted of only one long street, steep and winding, which abutted upon a bridge over the Dyle. It would have been possible to have held for many hours this defile, although it is commanded on the north by heights upon which the Prussian batteries could have been established. But there were in this village so much obstruction and confusion that one could not think of organizing a methodical defence especially with soldiers who never ceased to cry, "We are betrayed! Let us save ourselves!"

Overturned wagons, carriages, limbers, guns, and *caissons* abandoned by the auxiliary drivers obstructed for a considerable distance the approaches to the bridge, which was, in 1815, no more than seven feet wide, owing to the crowding of the fugitives into the street, from which they could issue only three or four abreast, there arose a frightful disorder. Mad from fear, some of the men sought to open a passage by striking everything in front. General Radet, provost-general of the army, was terribly beaten with the butt-ends of muskets. Some of the cavalry used their sabres, and the infantry replied with bayonet-thrusts, sometimes even with gunshots.

They killed each other without being able to advance, the living entangled with the dead. The rear of the column accumulated at the entrance of Genappe. The Prussians approached. The three battalions of the Old Guard, threatened with being crushed between the masses of the enemy and the crowd of fugitives, broke column and gained Charleroi by turning the village on the east. The Prussians did not pursue them, but turned upon the crowds of unarmed men in front of Genappe. These unfortunates were literally under the lances of the *Uhlans* before they thought of escaping by the right and left of the village and of passing the Dyle by fording. This little river, which at this spot was not thirty feet wide, and whose depth did not attain three, was an obstacle only for the carriages, on account of the steepness of its banks.

Genappe was still crowded with French. A handful of men,

who alone in this panic had preserved their resolution and courage, attempted to arrest the enemy. They rapidly erected with overturned wagons a barricade from behind which they opened fire. A few cannon-balls gave only too quickly an account of this feeble work and its defenders.

The horsemen of Roder descended the sloping street, crushing the inert multitude, and striking with sabre and lance without more risk than butchers in an *abattoir*. The Emperor, who had taken, it is said, more than an hour to clear for himself a passage through this long street, was still on the north side of the bridge. He had just entered his carriage, which had been found by chance in the midst of the abandoned train. The horses had not yet been hitched to it. Hearing the hurrahs, he hastily abandoned it, mounted his horse, and succeeded in escaping with a few horsemen. The Prussians pillaged the carriage, which contained a dressing case, a sword, an iron bed and a uniform, in the lining of which were sewed some uncut diamonds, valued at a million *francs*.

Blücher had pushed as far as Genappe with the corps of Bülow. He halted to pass the night in the inn of the Roi d'Espagne. Almost immediately there was brought to the inn upon a stretcher General Duhesme. In the last hour of the battle Duhesme had fallen grievously wounded between Plancenoit and Rossomme; a few devoted soldiers had picked him up and carried him till near Genappe, where he had been made prisoner by the Prussians. The Field Marshal went to visit him and recommended him to the surgeon of his staff. But the wound was mortal, and Duhesme died during the following night. Although worn out, Blücher did not wish to retire before writing to his wife:

> "I have kept my promise," he wrote. "On the 16th I was forced to recoil before numbers; but on the 18th, in concert with my friend Wellington, I have exterminated the Army of Napoleon."

He sent also this letter to his old comrade Knesebeck:

> My friend, the finest battle is fought, the most brilliant vic-

tory is won. The details will follow. I can write no more, for I tremble in all my members. The effort has been too great.

3

Beyond Genappe the pursuit became more rapid. As there was no longer an organized body of troops forming the rear guard, the Prussians sabred with impunity the panic-stricken mob. "It was a regular chase," says Gneisenau; "a chase by the light of the moon." The great highway, the country roads, the lanes and fields, as far as the eye could see, were covered with soldiers of every arm, dismounted *cuirassiers*, lancers upon foundered horses, infantrymen who had thrown away guns and haversacks, wounded men losing their blood, and soldiers who had suffered amputation and had escaped from the ambulances ten minutes after the operation.

Without authority over these men and, besides, no less demoralized and thinking like them only of their own safety, captains, colonels, and generals marched intermingled with the mass of fugitives. Durutte on horseback, but blinded by the blood that flowed from his open forehead, was guided by a sergeant of *cuirassiers*. A corporal of the Old Guard supported Ney by the arm until the moment when Major Schmidt, of the red lancers, dismounted from his horse to give it to the Marshal. Surgeon-in-Chief Larrey, wounded by two sabre-blows, was struck again by the *Uhlans*, robbed, stripped of his clothing, and carried, almost naked, with his hands tied, to a general, who ordered him to be shot. Just as this order was on the point of being carried out, a Prussian surgeon recognized him, threw himself in front of him, and saved him.

Each one marched, ran, dragged himself along as best he could, went wherever he pleased, no one thinking to give orders, which would not have been obeyed. And when the sound of the Prussian trumpets, the galloping of the horses, and the savage clamours of the pursuers drew nigh, from this terror-stricken mob arose the cry: "Here they are! Here they are! . . . Let us save ourselves!" And, under the lash of fear, cavalry and infantry, officers and soldiers, wounded and unwounded, again found strength to run.

Bands of fugitives, who, falling from fatigue, halted in the woods, hollows of the ground, farmhouses, and hamlets, were quickly set running again by the cavalry. The Prussians broke up no less than nine bivouacs. Some of the wounded killed themselves to avoid falling alive into the hands of the enemy. An officer of *cuirassiers*, seeing himself surrounded by *Uhlans*, cried: "They shall have neither my horse nor myself!" And coolly he dropped his horse with a ball in the ear and then blew out his own brains with a second pistol.

Most of Bülow's infantry having halted at Genappe and Ziethen and Pirch's corps having gone no further than Caillou, Gneisenau had with him only the dragoons and *Uhlans* of General Roder, one battalion of the 1st Pomeranian, and one of the 15th Regiment. It is truly incredible that thirty or forty thousand Frenchmen should have fled before four thousand Prussians! If a few hundred soldiers had overcome their terror and had re-formed to make a stand, their resistance would have put an end to this lamentable pursuit.

The Prussians, who sabred especially the defenceless fugitives, allowed themselves, as it seems, to be easily imposed upon, since a handful of resolute men marching grouped around the eagle of each regiment sufficed to defend the flags. The enemy picked up on the battlefield and along the highway more than two hundred abandoned cannon and more than a thousand wagons; during the retreat, he did not capture one flag.

Hardened and insensible as is the soldier, by habit and the very nature of his profession, to spectacles of death, the fugitives in passing through Quatre-Bras were seized with horror. The men killed in the battle of June 16th had not been interred. Three to four thousand bodies, entirely naked, for the peasants had even removed their shirts, covered all the ground between the main road and the wood of Bossu. The scene presented the aspect of an immense morgue.

By turns lighted up by the moon and drowned in shadow

by the veil of clouds, the dead, in the fleeting movements of the light, seemed to move their stiffened bodies and to contract their livid faces. "We thought," said a grenadier of the Guard, "to see some spectres who demanded burial of us." Lower down the soldiers quenched their thirst in the stream of Gemioncourt, which, swollen by the storm of the day before, was filled with floating bodies.

Less and less numerous, more and more fatigued, but as ardent as ever, the Prussians continued the pursuit. Gneisenau had knocked up *en route* half of his force. There alone marched with him a few squadrons and a small detachment of the 15th Infantry, whose drummer beat the charge, perched upon a horse taken from the imperial carriages. They passed Frasnes. Gneisenau judged that the fatigue of the men and horses would not permit of the chase being pushed further. He gave the order to halt in front of an inn, which, supreme irony, bore the name "*A l'Empereur.*"

4

From Genappe Napoleon had gained on horseback Quatre-Bras, with Soult, Drouot, Bertrand, a few officers, and ten red lancers and chasseurs of the Guard. He arrived there about one in the morning. He expected to find there the division of Girard, left on June 17th at Fleurus, to protect the passage of the convoys, and to which, during the evening of the 18th, had been despatched the order to advance to Quatre-Bras and to take position there. These instructions had not been carried out. Colonel Matis, who commanded temporarily the remains of this division, received, indeed, the order of Soult; but, either because he judged, in view of the lateness of the hour, that the prescribed movement could not be effected in time, or for some other cause, he broke camp in the night and went to pass the Sambre at Charleroi.

Meanwhile the Emperor awaited the arrival of these troops at Quatre-Bras. He dismounted from his horse in a clearing in the wood of Bossu, near a camp-fire which had been started by some grenadiers of the Guard. A wounded officer, who was fleeing along the highway, recognized the Emperor by the light of the fire He stood, his arms crossed over his chest, motionless as a statue, eyes fixed, turned towards Waterloo.

There was no news from Grouchy, who, it was thought, was in great danger. The Emperor directed Soult to send him a despatch to inform him of the retreat of the army and to direct him to withdraw upon the lower Sambre. Soldiers of every arm passed, running along the route and through the fields. Commandant Baudus, who marched on horseback in the midst of the fugitives, discovered the little group composing the Imperial Staff. He approached. The Emperor asked him if he had not met with some corps that was not entirely disorganized. Not far from Quatre-Bras, Baudus had passed the 5th Lancers, commanded by Colonel Jacquiminot, which still marched in order. He informed the Emperor of the fact. "Go quickly," said Napoleon, "and tell him to halt at Quatre-Bras. It is already late, and the enemy, finding this point occupied, will probably halt."

Baudus set out at a gallop, but, received with shots at the first houses of Quatre-Bras, he returned and begged the Emperor to retire, "since he was no longer covered by anyone." While uttering these words he looked closely at the Emperor. Napoleon wept silently his lost Army. The tears which trickled down his cheeks were the only sign of life upon his mournful face, pallid as with the look of death.

Amidst the confusion resulting from this great overthrow the Emperor never lost his presence of mind. Seeing no signs of Girard's corps, he concluded that it had not received the order of the major-general. Ignorant of the defeat, it was in danger of being surprised in its bivouacs and enveloped by the enemy. He commanded Baudus to hasten to Fleurus, to cause the troops to take up arms, and to lead them upon the right bank of the Sambre. Then, yielding to necessity, he remounted his horse, and put himself *en route* for Charleroi by way of Gosselies and Lodelinsart.

At Charleroi, where the Emperor arrived about five in the

morning, there was the same tumultuous mob, the same disorder, as at Genappe. Since June 15th the ammunition wagons, the bridge equipage, and the carriages containing food and baggage encumbered the squares and avenues. On the 17th there had been evacuated on Charleroi the wounded of Ligny, the prisoners, the twenty-seven pieces of artillery, and the baggage captured from the Prussians.

Doubtless, on the evening of the 18th, at the moment when all the troops began to give way, a commissary of war had been sent from Rossomme with orders to cause all the wagons to pass the Sambre immediately. But arrived at Charleroi, between one and two in the morning, he had found the commandant of the place sick, say some; dead drunk, say others; incapable, at any rate, of being of any assistance to him. The commissary of war had been compelled to seek one by one the different heads of the departments. All employed themselves with the greatest zeal, but much time had been lost. Already the first convoys of wounded began to debouch by the route of Brussels, and bands of fugitives traversed the town, spreading the alarm, and saying that the enemy was in close pursuit.

The sole bridge of Charleroi was 125 feet long and 25 feet wide. It formed a shelving ridge; the parapets were of wood. Some *cuirassiers*, descending at full speed the sloping street which abuts on the bridge, charged so violently against one of the parapets that it broke and fell. Many horsemen were drowned in the Sabre. The turret of the bridge was overthrown, a wagon overturned; the carriages, which were immediately in the rear, started at a rapid trot down the slant of the Rue de la Montague, were unable to stop in time, and upset over the first obstacle.

Many soldiers were crushed to death. Sacks of flour and rice, casks of wine and brandy, and hundreds of loaves of bread, rolled upon the pavement. The bridge thus obstructed, all the convoy halted, whilst the fugitives climbed over this barricade of overturned wagons and fallen horses. Each soldier in passing stuck his bayonet in a loaf of bread. The contents of the casks were still more tempting; some of the soldiers pierced them with bullet-holes and drank through the openings the wine and brandy. When these casks were half emptied, they pierced in the same manner those loaded on the wagons.

All along the street red streams flowed towards the Sambre. The wagon containing the Imperial treasure, which Provost-General Radet had caused to set out from Caillou the day before at seven o'clock in the evening, was caught with its six horses in the jam at some hundred yards from the bridge. Despairing of being able to open a passage, the paymaster, who was responsible for this precious cargo, thought of opening the wagon and confiding to his employees and the soldiers composing the escort as many sacks of gold as each one could carry. All these men were ordered to report at a certain point on the other side of the Sambre. The paymaster entered in a notebook the names of the depositaries and the number of sacks of 20,000 *francs* that were confided to them.

But, precisely at the moment when he was proceeding with this operation, there resounded from the foot of the street the shots fired into the casks of wine. An alarm followed which degenerated into a panic, with cries of "The Prussians are coming!" uttered designedly by the inhabitants and even by some of the soldiers. These wretches hurled themselves on the wagon. They ripped open the sacks of gold with sabres and bayonets. Everything was pillaged. The stopping of the head of the convoy arrested the carriages as far as the entrance to the upper town. The berlin containing the Portfolio remained stationary on the route in the midst of the artillery train. The Duke of Bassano, hearing the fusillade in the distance, caused the most important papers to be torn up and scattered to the winds.

The evacuation of Charleroi, however, might have been effected without disorder, for on June 19th the Prussians had slackened their pursuit. With the exception of a few cavalry reconnaissances, they did not approach the town before noon; it was rather late in the day when they seized the bridges of Marchienne, Charleroi, and Châtelet. During the evening, whilst Pirch, who had been sent the preceding night towards Gembloux with the 2nd Corps to intercept the retreat of Grouchy, occupied Mellery the corps of Ziethen and Bülow bivouacked; their front covered by the Sambre. It was not until the next day that the Prussian Army passed the river in three columns, and directed itself on Beaumont and Avèsnes. The English, less ardent or not as good marchers, were still between Nivelles and Binche.

5

The Emperor had vainly attempted to organize resistance in the bottoms of La Haye Sainte, at Rossomme. Genappe, and Quatre-Bras. He understood that, with an army in dissolution and yielding obedience only to fear, the best thing to do was to retreat as quickly as possible. He traversed Charleroi and halted in a meadow on the right bank of the Sambre. He gave some orders, which were not obeyed, for rallying the fugitives and reassembling the train. At the end of an hour he remounted his horse and proceeded towards Philippeville, where he arrived at nine in the morning. The gates of the place being closed, he was forced to make himself known to the officer of the guard.

Napoleon had with him Bertrand, Drouot, Dejean, Flahault, and Bussy. He was rejoined at Philippeville by the Duke of Bassano, accompanied by Fleury de Chaboulon, then by Marshal Soult. Of all his preoccupations, the most pressing was the rallying of the army. Instructions were sent to the commandants of Givet, Avèsnes, Maubeuge, Beaumont, and Landrecies. They were to provide for the wants of the detachments and isolated soldiers that might present themselves before these places, and then to direct them on the points of concentration: Laon for the 1st, 2nd, and 6th Infantry Corps; La Fère for the artillery; Marie, Saint- Quentin, Réthel, Vervins, and Rheinis for the cavalry; and Soissons for the Guard.

Of all the corps commanders, Reille alone had rejoined the Emperor at Philippeville; he was entrusted with the work of reorganizing the troops who might arrive upon the glacis of that fortress. A new despatch, directing Marshal Grouchy to retreat towards Philippeville or Givet, had been forwarded by a spy named Cousin. The commandants of the fortresses of the 2nd and 16th Military Divisions were warned to be on the lookout for the enemy.

The Emperor had not only to think of his army—there was public opinion, the enemies in the interior, and, finally, the Chamber. He wrote two letters to his brother Joseph. One, destined to be read in the Council of Ministers, related only, with certain reticences, the outcome of the battle; in the other, entirely personal, Napoleon concealed nothing of the great disaster, and announced his immediate return to Paris. Fleury de Chaboulon, to whom these letters were dictated, assures us that the second terminated as follows:

> ... All is not lost. By uniting my forces, the depôts, and the National Guards, I shall have 300,000 men to oppose to the enemy. But it is necessary that I be assisted and not interfered with. ... I believe the Deputies will realize the fact that their duty is to unite with me in order to save France.

The Emperor then set about preparing the bulletin of the battles of Ligny and Mont Saint-Jean, which was to appear in the *Moniteur*. Then, leaving Soult at Philippeville to watch over the rallying of the army, he entered all alone, as it seems, one of the *calèches* of the Major-General. Bassano, Bertrand, Drouot, and the *aides-de-camp* followed in two other carriages.

From Philippeville to Paris, the most direct route was by way of Barbancon, Avèsnes, La Capelle, Marle, and Laon. But the Emperor did not wish to run the risk of being captured by some party of Prussian cavalry which might have passed the Sambre at Marchienne: he took a longer route, which passed through Marienbourg, Rocroi, Maubert-Fontaine, La Capelle, Marle, and Laon. At sunset the party stopped for some time in sight of Rocroi.

The inhabitants knew nothing of the great defeat; they flocked in crowds upon the ramparts with the hope of seeing the Emperor. Their acclamations awakened him from a deep sleep. Events had succeeded one another with such rapidity that, for a moment, he imagined that he had just awakened from a frightful dream.

As it was feared that it would be impossible to find relays of horses at Maubert-Fontaine (a great number of horses had been requisitioned eight days before for the auxiliary services of Vandamme's corps), a *détour* was made as far as Mézières. There also horses were lacking. One was compelled to go the distance of a league in search of them. From half-past ten until midnight the *calèches* remained upon the Place des Fontaines in front of the post-house. General Dumonceau, Governor of Mézières, Traullé, commandant of the place, and the officers of their staffs surrounded the carriages. They remained motionless, and conversed in a low tone, "as on a day of mourning."

None of the travellers dismounted save Bertrand, whom Napoleon summoned to the door of his *calèche* by a superior officer of hussars, who constituted the entire Imperial escort. Finally, the journey was resumed. As the carriages approached the Porte de Pierre the soldiers of the post cried, "Long live the Emperor!" and repeated this cry—"very poignant under the circumstances," says Commandant Traullé—until the last carriage had crossed the glacis.

The Imperial party did not arrived until the next day, June 20th, between six and seven in the evening, at the foot of the mountain of Laon, in the *faubourg* of Vaux. The Emperor dismounted from the *calèche* in the court of the post-house.

Through the great gate, which remained open, he was seen from the street walking to and fro, his head bowed and his arms folded over his chest. There was a great deal of straw scattered over the courtyard, upon which opened the granaries and stables. One of the spectators said in a low voice: "It is Job upon his dung-hill." Napoleon appeared so crushed and so sad, the scene was so impressive, even for rustic souls, that one dared not acclaim him. A few cries of "Long live the Emperor!" very weak, timid, and suppressed, issued, however, from the crowd.

The Emperor stopped and raised his hat. The Emperor's arrival had been reported in the town. A detachment of the National Guard descended to form the guard of honour. Soon after came General Langeron, commanding the department, the prefect, and some of the municipal councillors.

General Radet, provost-general, and General Neigre conferred also with the Emperor. He ordered the prefect, with whom he associated his *aide-de-camp* Bussy, who was from that part of the country, to collect great supplies of provisions, as the Army was to concentrate under Laon. He sent Neigre to La Fère to organize the field batteries, Dejean to Guise to examine the condition of the fortifications, and Flahault to Avèsnes to gather information upon the march of the enemy. Night came. The Emperor did not wait for Marshal Soult; besides, he had given him his instructions at Philippeville. About ten or eleven o'clock he started for Paris.

Since Philippeville, and doubtless even since the halt in the meadows of the Sambre, Napoleon had resolved to hasten to Paris. He remembered the grievous lesson of 1814—that vote of deposition, which had paralyzed him at the head of his army. He felt that, unless he returned in haste to his capital to impose on Fouché, the conspirators of all parties, and the hostile or deluded Deputies, it was all over with his crown and the last resistance of the country. From a military as well as from a political standpoint, his true place, for some days at least, was in Paris. Without soldiers and without cannon, he could not think of stopping the enemy on the frontier.

As to rallying at Laon the wrecks of the army, Soult and the generals could do that as well as he. There was no need of genius for that! During this time, in Paris, the Emperor would take, in conjunction with Davoût and Carnot, the measures necessary' for assuring the public safety. He would allay the political crisis; would push forward the preparations in every branch of the service; would direct on Laon all the available men in the depôts, the mobilized battalions, the field batteries, and the convoys of arms and ammunition; would decree, in concert with the Chambers, new levies of soldiers and National Guards, and would go, after four or five days, to resume the command.

It has been said that Napoleon "deserted" his army, as in Egypt and Russia. Alas! Napoleon no longer had an army. Of Grouchy he knew nothing; it was presumed that he was in great peril with the corps of Vandamme and Gérard. Of the 74,000 combatants at Waterloo, 40,000 had perhaps retired safe and sound and had repassed the Sambre; but more than three-fourths of these men were still dispersed from Cambrai to Rocroi, marching along the roads singly or in small squads, camping in the woods and stopping at the homes of the peasants. On June 20th, at the hour when Napoleon quitted Laon to go to Paris, there were 2,600 soldiers assembled at Philippeville and nearly 6,000 at Avèsnes. These soldiers constituted the entire army.

CHAPTER 7

The Combats of Wavre and the Retreat of Grouchy.

1

We have seen that, on June 18th, about noon, Marshal Grouchy, in the course of his discussion with Gérard at Walhain, had received an *aide-de-camp* from Exelmans, who informed him of the Prussian rear guard before Wavre.

Between nine and ten o'clock Exelmans' two divisions of dragoons had arrived at La Baraque, at five kilometres from that little town. Some scouts who had pushed beyond the defile of La Huzelle reported a body of Prussian troops, consisting of cavalry, infantry, and artillery, in position upon the heights of Wavre. It was the entire corps of Pirch, still on the right bank of the Dyle, and two cavalry regiments of the *landwehr*, composing the rear guard of Bülow. Although he had orders to pursue the enemy closely, Exelmans feared to engage these masses with only his cavalry in a region so wooded. He knew, moreover, from new information or indications, that the Prussian Army would manoeuvre to join the English. He thought that Grouchy would interrupt the march on Wavre, henceforth without object, in order to pass the Dyle at the nearest point.

With the design of preparing for this movement, he directed towards that river the brigade of Vincent; it took position at the farm of La Plaquerie, at the distance of a cannon-shot from Ottignies. Exelmans sent towards Neuf Sart the brigade of Berton to reconnoitre the right, left at La Baraque an advance guard of two squadrons, and fell back with the bulk of the division of Chastel nearly a league in the rear, near Corbaix. It was during this halt that he sent an *aide-de-camp* to Grouchy to inform him of the presence of the Prussians before Wavre and of the dispositions that he had made.

The corps of Vandamme was then halted at Nil Saint-Vincent, in conformity with the orders of Grouchy of the day before. On the evening of June 17th, the Marshal, in spite of all his information concerning the march of the Prussians towards Wavre, was still so undecided touching the direction to take that he had directed Vandamme to advance only as far as Walhain. A little later, about eleven or twelve at night, he had written to him as follows:

"I have forgotten to tell you to push beyond Walhain, in order that General Gérard may take position in the rear. I think we will go farther than Walhain; it will then be rather a halt than a definite position."

On the morning of the 18th, on breaking camp, Grouchy, fully decided from that time to march on Wavre, would have had plenty of time to rectify these instructions and to order Vandamme to follow as rapidly as possible the cavalry of Exelmans. He did not think of this. Vandamme, after having passed Walhain, halted at Nil Saint-Vincent, pending new orders.

About one o'clock. Grouchy warned by Exelmans' *aide-de-camp*, Commandant d'Estourmel, that the Prussian rear guard was in sight, arrived at Nil Saint-Vincent. He gave to Vandamme and sent to Exelmans the order to put the troops on the march. A little before two o'clock, as the advance of the dragoons approached La Baraque, the two squadrons that had been left there as an advance guard were attacked by the 10th Prussian Hussars, debouching on their left flank. This regiment, with two battalions and two guns, formed the detachment of Colonel Ledebur, posted in observation at Mont Saint-Guilbert.

Until one o'clock Ledebur had not budged. Badly informed by his patrols and *videttes*, he was completely ignorant of the approach of the French Army, as well as the *pointe* pushed in the morning to La Baraque by the two divisions of Exelmans, and the occupation of the farm of La Plaquerie by the brigade of Vincent. Although surrounded by enemies, he did not know it. Warned, finally, of the presence of the French at Nil Saint Vincent and on the route of Wavre, Ledebur saw that his direct line of retreat was in danger of being intercepted. He pushed rapidly his hussars through the fields to La Baraque, whilst his two battalions gained at a run, by way of Bruyères and Bloc-Ry, the wood of La Huzelle, which bordered the road on both sides, to the north of La Baraque, and made of it a kind of defile.

The hussars drove back the two French squadrons to the east of the road, kept up for some minutes the combat, and then, on the approach of the bulk of the dragoons, they withdrew through the defile, which had just been occupied by the sharpshooters of Ledebur. Infantry was required to dislodge the latter. The dragoons made way for the head of Vandamme's column; it attacked without delay. Two battalions of Brause's division, which were still with Langen's division (both belonging to Pirch's corps), on the right bank of the Dyle, had been sent to the support of Ledebur.

The defence was obstinate. Grouchy, unknown to Exelmans, had recalled from the banks of the Dyle the brigade of Vincent, All the dragoons were assembled. He ordered Exelmans to turn the position towards Dion-le-Mont with these three thousand horsemen. The manoeuvre, well conceived, but effected too late or two slowly, did not give the expected results. Before the French cavalry had finished its movement, the Prussians had fallen back on Wavre. Vandamme passed the defile. He had orders from Grouchy to pursue the enemy even upon the heights which dominate this town, and to take position there pending new instructions.

In spite of the assurance with which .he had spoken to Gérard, Grouchy was none the less troubled by the cannonade heard on his left. He advanced at a gallop towards Limelette, "in order," says he, "to form a better opinion as to the causes of this cannonade." He finally acquired the conviction that a great battle was being waged upon the edge of the Forest of Soignes. On regaining the route of Wavre, between half-past three and four o'clock, he received the Emperor's (or rather Soult's) letter, written from Caillou, at ten in the morning. It was addressed to "*Marshal Grouchy, at Gembloux, or somewhere in front of this town.*" The courier, Adjutant-Commandant Zenowicz, had been forced to pass through Genappe, Sombreffe, and Gembloux. This made a journey of ten leagues. Zenowicz, however, might have effected it in less time than it took him to do so. Besides, had this despatch, which directed Grouchy to march on Wavre while connecting the communications with the Imperial Army, reached him sooner, it would have led to no change in his essential dispositions.

After having read it, he even remarked to his *aide-de-camp* Bella "that he congratulated himself on having so well carried out the Emperor's instructions in marching on Wavre, instead of listening to the advice of General Gérard"; and he replied to Berthezène, who had sent one of his *aides-de-camp* to inform him of the march of the Prussian columns in the direction of the fire: "Let the General be tranquil; we are on the right road. I have just heard from the Emperor, and he orders me to march on Wavre."

The Emperor also ordered him, as subsidiary, it is true, to connect the communications with the main body of the Army. Grouchy took some tardy measures to execute these instructions. Pajol had just informed him, through an *aide-de-camp*, that the right column, in its march from Grand Leez to Tourinnes, had discovered no trace of the enemy. Grouchy sent back the *aide-de-camp* with the order for Pajol to advance immediately with the 2nd Cavalry Corps and the division of Teste to Limale and to pass the Dyle by main force. Grouchy was ignorant of the value of time, otherwise he would have selected to capture the bridge of Limale, not Pajol, who, at Tourinnes, was distant three leagues and a half from it; but the cavalry of General Vallin, which was a league from the Dyle, and the division of Hulot, of the corps of Gérard, which had arrived at La Baraque;

The despatch sent to Pajol, Grouchy galloped towards Wavre, against which he intended to direct the attack in person. The impetuous Vandamme had not waited for him. Despite the orders of the Marshal, without reconnoitring the position, and without preparing the way with his artillery, he had launched *à la française* the entire division of Habert against the town in columns of assault.

The second *echelon* of the corps of Ziethen (divisions of Brause and Langen and the cavalry of Sohr) had passed the Dyle after the combat at the defile of La Huzelle and had marched towards Chapelle Saint-Lambert. But there still remained to defend Wavre and its approaches almost all of the corps of Thielmann. Believing at first that the deployment of the cavalry of Exelmans between Sainte-Anne and Dion-le-Mont was only a demonstration, Thielmann had set his troops in motion in the direction of Couture Saint-Germain; two battalions alone were to remain to guard Wavre.

Then, at sight of Vandamme, who debouched in front of the town, he had caused the positions which he had just evacuated to be reoccupied. The divisions of Kempher and Luck, three battalions of the division of Borcke and the cavalry of Hobe, established themselves in Wavre, Basse-Wavre, and upon the heights of the left bank, of the Dyle. The division of Stulpnagel came to occupy Bierges; the detachment from the corps of Ziethen (three battalions and three squadrons, under Von Stengel), detached to guard the bridge of Limale, was maintained at that post.

The infantry of Habert quickly dislodged the Prussians from the *faubourg* of Wavre; but their furious charge was arrested at the Dyle, which separated the town from the *faubourg*. The two bridges were strongly barricaded and enfiladed by batteries established upon the different heights in the inclined streets abutting on the river; finally, more than a thousand sharpshooters were concealed in the houses of the left bank. General Habert, Colonel Dubalen, of the 64th, and 600 men were put *hors de combat* in a few minutes. Powerless to carry the bridge, the soldiers hesitated to retire, for fear of being exposed to the terrible fire of the Prussian batteries, which swept the approaches of the faubourg and the steep acclivities of the right bank. They sheltered themselves in the streets parallel with the Dyle. "They were engulfed," says Grouchy, "in a kind of *cul-de-sac.*"

2

After having examined attentively the position, Grouchy resolved to second the attack on Wavre by two other attacks above and below the town. Some reinforcements entered the faubourg; one of Lefol's battalions was detached to pass the Dyle at the mill bridge of Bierges; and Exelmans advanced with his dragoons in front of Basse-Wavre. As the Marshal finished taking these dispositions, he received, about five o'clock, the dispatch which Soult had sent him from the battlefield at half-past one, and which terminated as follows:

> At this moment the battle is engaged along the line of Waterloo in front of the Forest of Soignes. So you will manoeuvre to join our right. We believe that we see now the corps of Bülow upon the heights of Saint-Lambert. So you will not lose an instant in approaching and joining us, in order that you may crush Bülow, whom you will take in the very act.

The despatch, written with a pencil, was partly effaced, and almost illegible. Grouchy and many officers of his staff read this letter as follows:

> "*La battaile est gagnée*" ("The battle is gained"), instead of "*La battaile est engage*" ("Battle is engaged").

They wished to interrogate the courier. But Grouchy pretends that this officer was too drunk to answer. At any rate, the Marshal had only to reflect. It was evident that a despatch written at one o'clock could not call gained an action which the noise of the cannon, more and more violent, indicated only too well still lasted at five.

However, whether the battle was engaged or gained, the order of the Emperor existed none the less, formal and imperative: it was necessary to march on Saint-Lambert in order to crush Bülow. Grouchy understood it; but he displayed neither resolution nor method in his dispositions. Two of Vandamme's divisions were sufficient to occupy the Prussians before Wavre. It seems then that the Marshal ought to have directed immediately towards Limale Vandamme's third division as well as Exelmans' eight regiments of dragoons, whose diversion upon Basse-Wavre was no longer useful.

But Grouchy, by the strangest of strategical conceptions, wished at the same time to capture Wavre with half of his army and to direct the other half on Saint-Lambert by the bridge of Limale. He left then before the Prussian positions all of the 3rd Corps and Exelmans' cavalry, and sent his *aide-de-camp* Pont-Bellanger to carry the verbal order to Pajol, who had left Tourinnes, to hasten his march on Limale. "Never has the Emperor been so great!" said Pont-Bellanger, on approaching Pajol. "The battle is gained, and only the cavalry is awaited to finish the rout."

At the same time that he despatched this order to Pajol, Grouchy came at a gallop with Gérard to La Baraque to direct from thence on Limale the 4th Corps, whose leading division (General Hulot) had alone arrived upon the heights of Wavre. Is it true, as Grouchy says, that the other two divisions of the 4th Corps (Vichery and Pécheux) had not yet attained La Baraque at six in the evening; that, tired of waiting for them, the Marshal returned in front of Wavre, leaving the order for these two divisions to march directly on Limale; finally, that, this order having been badly interpreted, Vichery and Pécheux continued their movement on Wavre?

Or should we rather believe that Grouchy found these divisions at La Baraque; that he gave them the order to march on Limale, but that the head of column got lost *en route* for want of a guide, and resumed its march towards Wavre? It appears impossible to get at the truth in the midst of the contradictory testimonies of Gérard, General Hulot, and of Grouchy himself, whose own assertions do not agree with each other. It is certain, however, that Grouchy went to La Baraque and then returned to Wavre.

The combat continued to rage fiercely on both sides of the Dyle. The attack on the bridge of Bierges by the battalion of Lefol had been repulsed. Grouchy, bent on passing the Dyle at this point, ordered Gérard to renew the attack with a battalion of Hulot's division. Gérard having remarked to him that it would be better to cause the detachment of Lefol to be supported by other troops of the same corps, he received badly this very apposite observation. Gérard then transmitted the order to Hulot, who conducted in person to the assault a battalion of the 9th Light. To reach the bridge, it had to cross some very marshy ground intersected parallel with the Dyle by ditches, very deep and wide.

Hulot directed the men to throw themselves into these ditches, if they could not leap them. They found themselves in water from four to six feet in depth, and the skirmishers were on the point of being drowned; the assistance of their comrades was necessary to extricate them from their dangerous position. During this time the bullets fell as thick as hail. Rebuffed, the soldiers fell back. Grouchy and Gérard, the latter at the head of another battalion, arrived about this time on the edge of the meadow. Gérard, little accustomed to spare himself, exposed himself all the more, as he had reasons to be in a very bad humour. He was shot through the body and carried to the rear. Grouchy then ordered General Baltus, commanding the artillery, to replace Gérard at the head of the assaulting column.

The latter having positively refused to do so, Grouchy leaped from his horse, crying: "If one can no longer command the obedience of his subordinates, he should at least know how to die." This third assault failed, like the preceding ones. Grouchy left the division of Hulot before Bierges, as if he had wished, says Hulot, to make new dispositions for attacking the mill; then, suddenly changing his mind, he rejoined the other two divisions of Gérard and advanced with them towards Limale.

During these vain assaults, one continued to skirmish in front of Basse-Wavre, and at Wavre the fight was pursued with terrible ferocity. Vandamme made as many as thirteen attacks without being able to wrest from the Prussians this little town, which had been transformed into a veritable fortress. At eleven in the evening the combat still raged.

When Marshal Grouchy arrived at Limale, at nightfall, the bridge over the Dyle was free. Renewing the audacious manoeuvre of the preceding year at Montereau, Pajol had launched at full speed the hussars of General Vallin upon this bridge, which, however, was accessible to only four horses arriving abreast, and which was defended by an entire battalion. The Prussians overthrown and sabred, the infantry of Teste and the rest of the cavalry passed the bridge behind the hussars and took position on the left bank. Von Stengel yielded Limale after a combat of some duration, and took up a position on the height which dominates this village.

In spite of the gathering darkness, the assault was vigorously conducted by Teste, when Grouchy debouched by the bridge of Limale with the divisions of Vichery and Pécheux. These reinforcements were necessary, for Thielmann, hearing the cannonade, had sent to the support of Stengel, by the left bank of the Dyle, the division of Stulpnagel and the cavalry of Hobe. The combat continued until eleven in the evening for the possession of the crest of the plateau, which, finally, remained in possession of the French. The road to Mont Saint-Jean was open: but for a long time the cannon of the Emperor had been silent.

3

The French bivouacked in squares, almost intermingled with the enemy, who occupied the wood of Rixensart. The advance posts were so close to each other that the bullets exchanged throughout the night fell in the rear of the first lines. At half-past eleven in the evening Grouchy wrote to Vandamme to rejoin him at once at Limale with the 3rd Corps. He intended to recommence the combat early in the morning, in order to join the Imperial Army at Brussels, for the report was circulated—we know not upon what grounds—that the Emperor had defeated the English.

The Prussian Staff was better informed. An officer of Marwitz's cavalry, sent on a reconnaissance, had reported that the French Army was in flight. Thenceforth reassured, Thielmann directed most of his troops upon the plateau of Limale, in order to resume the offensive at dawn. At three in the morning the cavalry of Hobe debouched from the wood of Rixensart with two horse batteries, which, in a few minutes, riddled with balls the French bivouacs. Grouchy, hastening upon the firing-line, ordered his batteries to reply; then, having formed all his force in line of battle, the cavalry of Pajol on the extreme left, the divisions of Pécheux and Vichery in the centre and in reserve, and the division of Teste on the right, he marched against the enemy.

After a stubborn defence, the Prussians yielded the wood of Rixensart. It was nearly eight o'clock. Thielmann received from Pirch positive information of the defeat of the French. The despatch added that the 2nd Corps was about to manoeuvre to intercept the retreat of Marshal Grouchy. The news of this great victory, which was immediately announced to the troops, reanimated them. Thielmann, pivoting upon his left wing, which still occupied the wood of Bierges, executed a change of front. By this movement the Prussian right found itself deployed parallel with the route from Wavre to Brussels.

The combat was resumed, not without advantage for the Prussians, till the division of Teste had carried the village and the mill of Bierges. In this assault General Penne, one of Teste's brigadiers, who was wounded himself, had his head carried away by a cannon-ball. Berthezène, posted on the right bank of the Dyle, had seconded the attack of Teste; the two divisions united. Thielmann, seeing his left outflanked and his right on the point of being turned by the cavalry of Pajol, which was manoeuvring towards Rosieren in order to get possession of the route of Brussels, put himself in retreat in the direction of Louvain.

The four battalions left in Wavre evacuated that position, and proceeded at first to La Bavette, from whence they were quickly dislodged by the advance guard of Vandamme. Notwithstanding the order of Grouchy to come to rejoin him at Limale with the 3rd Corps, Vandamme had remained all the morning before Wavre. He had only sent to the Marshal the dragoons of Exelmans and the division of Hulot, which he had caused to be relieved in front of Bierges by the division of Berthezène.

Master of the field of battle, upon which the Prussians had abandoned five pieces of artillery and numerous wounded, Grouchy had his right at La Bavette and his left beyond Rosieren. He was making his preparations to march on Brussels when, about half-past ten, an officer of the Major-General arrived. His haggard face, his eyes big with fright, and his enfeebled body appearing, like his horse, broken by fatigue, he seemed the living image of defeat.

Hardly able to collect his ideas and to find his speech, he related in so incoherent a manner the disaster of Mont Saint-Jean that the Marshal thought at first that he had an affair with a fool or a drunken man. To the questions asked him by Grouchy—if he was the bearer of an order; upon what point the retreat was to be effected; and if the Army had repassed the Sambre—the officer, instead of replying, recommenced the confused recital of the battle. Some precise details, seized in the midst of divagations, finally convinced Grouchy. It was not the moment to yield to grief; it was necessary to save what remained of the army.

Grouchy united his general officers in a sort of council of war. He announced to them the terrible news. While speaking he had, it has been said, tears in his eyes. The officers knew of the discussion that he had had the day before with Gérard at Walhain. The Marshal thought that the circumstances made it necessary for him to justify himself for not having listened to the counsel of his lieutenant.

"My honour," said he, "demands that I explain my dispositions of yesterday. The instructions which I had received from the Emperor forbade me to manoeuvre in any other direction than Wavre. I have been forced to reject the advice that Count Gérard believed he had a right to give me. I render justice to the talents and the brilliant valour of General Gérard; but, no doubt, you were as much astonished as myself that a general officer, ignorant of the Emperor's orders and of the information upon which the Marshal of France under whom he was placed acted, should permit himself to trace publicly for him his conduct.

"The advanced hour of the day, the distance at which we were from the point where the cannon was heard, and the state of the roads, rendered it impossible to arrive in time to take part in the action that was being fought. Besides, whatever may be the events that have taken place, the orders of the Emperor, of which I have just communicated to you the contents, did not permit of my acting otherwise than I have done."

After having pronounced these words, which were merely an apology for his conduct, the Marshal unfolded his plan of retreat. He had at first thought of advancing upon the rear of the Anglo-Prussians, in order to delay by this diversion their pursuit of the Imperial Army; but he quickly renounced this idea, whose sole result would have been the total destruction of his 30,000 men submerged, crushed by 150,000. For the same reason he wisely rejected the bold project of Vandamme, which consisted in marching on Brussels, where they would set free numerous prisoners, and in regaining the frontier towards Valenciennes or Lille by way of Enghien and Ath.

Vandamme supposed that on this side only a few detachments of the Allied Army would be encountered. Grouchy rightly preferred to take his line of retreat on Namur, Dinant, and Givet. It was necessary to make haste, for it was not only to be feared that the army would be harassed by Thielmann, who, no doubt, would resume the offensive at the first retrograde movement of the French, but that it would be attacked in flank by one of Blücher's army corps. Perhaps this detachment would even arrive in time to take position at Gembloux and bar the retreat.

This was, in fact, the object of the Prussians; and at eleven o'clock, when Grouchy still had his army beyond the Dyle, its front between Rosieren and La Bavette, Pirch, who had been detached from Rossomme in the night with the 2nd Corps, already occupied Mellery. He had nearly two hours the start of Grouchy, for the distance from Mellery to Gembloux is ten kilometres, as the crow flies, and from La Bavette to Gembloux, twenty.

The retreat began between eleven o'clock and noon. The dragoons of Exelmans, with the exception of the 20th Regiment placed under the orders of Vandamme, advanced very rapidly on Namur to seize the bridges over the Sambre; their advance guard reached there about four o'clock. The 4th Corps and the cavalry of Vallin repassed the Dyle at Limale and took the direct route to Gembloux; they bivouacked at night at two leagues beyond that village on the road leading from Nivelles to Namur, between Le Mazy and Temploux. Grouchy, who marched with this *echelon* of the army, established his headquarters in Temploux.

From La Bavette the corps of Vandamme withdrew to Wavre, remained in position there until late, and then marched by way of Dion-le-Mont, Tourinnes, and Grand Leez. It halted about eleven in the evening on the road from Gembloux to Namur, on a line with Temploux. Pajol, charged with forming the rear guard with the cavalry of General Soult and the indefatigable division of Teste, imposed on Thielmann by following him even near Saint-Achtenrode, where the latter took position. Then, when the entire corps of Vandamme had repassed the bridges of Wavre, Pajol put himself in retreat, gained Gembloux by way of Sauvenierre, and there established himself in bivouac in the night.

This hazardous retreat was not effected without some disorder; but not a shot was fired. Thielmann, whose corps was reduced to 12,500 men by the losses of the day before and of the morning, did not learn until very late of the retreat of the French. As to the 2nd Prussian Corps, though it had reached Mellery at noon, it had arrived there in the worst state of fatigue, for it had, so to speak, been on the march for twenty-four hours without intermission. Besides, it seems that Pirch did not feel strong enough to act alone. He was without news of Thielmann, whose cooperation he expected. He was unwilling or did not think it possible to lead further on this day his harassed soldiers.

4

The next day, June 20th, Pajol and Teste quitted Gembloux early in the morning, in accordance with the orders of Grouchy, and marched by way of Saint-Denis and Saint-Marc on Namur. About nine o'clock Grouchy likewise directed on Namur the 4th Corps, which convoyed all the wounded and the reserve park. The Marshal intended to traverse the town with this army corps, whilst that of Vandamme remained in position across the route of Gembloux until past noon to cover the movement.

But things did not pass exactly as the Marshal had planned. At the moment when the advance of the 4th Corps quitted Temploux a brisk cannonade was heard in front towards the left. Instead of bivouacking in the midst of his troops, Vandamme had gone to pass the night in Namur. He had not received the order, sent by Grouchy, to hold the position; and in the morning Generals Lefol, Berthezène, and Habert, left without instructions, had put themselves on the march for Namur and, by this movement, uncovered the flank of the 4th Corps. They were attacked near La Falise by more than thirty squadrons of Hobe, which Thielmann had caused to set out from Saint-Achtenrode at five in the morning with a horse battery, and which had made ten leagues in pursuit of the French.

At the same time Grouchy was informed that a considerable body of the enemy was debouching from Mazy. It was the advance guard of Pirch on the march from Mellery.

Grouchy found himself in grave peril, for if the infantry of Vandamme should withdraw too quickly beyond the Sambre, Hobe would bar to him the route of Namur while he was fighting Pirch. The troops, also understanding the danger, showed some uneasiness; the numerous wounded who had been brought from Limale and Wavre expressed by murmurs, groans, and cries of rage their fear of falling alive into the hands of the Prussians.

Grouchy rode among the wagons with General Vichery. He said in a loud voice: "Be tranquil! We swear not to abandon you. But I am confident that our dispositions will save us."

Then, with the cavalry of General Vallin, he charged the Prussian squadrons which, having turned the divisions of Vandamme, flanked his line of retreat, and drove them back on the left. Continuing his march, he went to the support of Vandamme. In the meantime the 4th Corps, which thenceforth found the road free, gained Namur with the wounded and the park; the rear guard, commanded by Vichery in person, arrested for some time at Boquet the Prussians of Pirch; it then withdrew, disputing the ground foot by foot.

Surprised by the sudden attack of the Prussian cavalry, the 3rd Corps found itself in a critical situation. A square of Lefol was broken; the men escaped the lances of the *Uhlans* only by seeking refuge in the woods. Two pieces of artillery were lost. The arrival of Grouchy arrested the enemy. The cavalry of Vallin charged at a gallop. Colonel Briqueville, who charged at the head of the 20th Dragoons, overthrew the furthest advanced of the Prussian squadrons, retook the two guns, and even captured a cannon. All of Hobe's cavalry fell back upon Pirch's corps, which debouched from Temploux.

On hearing the noise of the combat, Vandamme had hastened from Namur. Grouchy reiterated to him the order to cover the retreat of the 4th Corps. Vandamme re-formed his battalions, took position in front of the *faubourgs*, and succeeded in checking the Prussians. The cavalry, the 4th Corps, and the convoys entered Namur, where the Prussians were detested. The French brought with them the terrible hazards of war. They were none the less received as friends. The municipality distributed 100,000 rations of bread and the same number of brandy. The brave Namurois loaned their boats for the transportation of the wounded by the Meuse, and themselves aided in embarking them. The women brought, even under the cannon-balls of the enemy, food to the soldiers and assistance to the wounded.

The army passed through Namur without halting. First

Grouchy, with the 4th Corps, and then Vandamme, wounded slightly, with the 3rd, passed the Sambre and plunged into the long defile formed by the Meuse and the Forest of Morlagne. The division of Teste was ordered to hold the town until night. To defend Namur, whose dilapidated fortifications were not proof against an escalade, Teste had eight field-pieces and 2,000 men at most. He distributed them upon the ramparts and at the three eastern gates—Louvain, Iron, and Saint-Nicholas.

Hardly were his men in position when Pirch launched his columns to the assault. Received by a discharge of grape and a rolling fire of musketry, the Prussians retreated, leaving upon the glacis a pile of dead and wounded. A second attack, in which Colonels Zastrow and Bismarck were mortally wounded, failed like the preceding. On account of the scarcity of cartridges, each Frenchman aimed carefully and brought down his Prussian. It was eight in the evening. Pirch, having lost 1,500 men, and despairing of capturing the place by main force, broke off the combat. But General Teste, almost out of ammunition, had already begun his retreat.

The Prussians, having discovered this, penetrated into the town through the windows and door of the custom-house, and pushed rapidly as far as the bridge of the Sambre. There, a detachment of engineers, posted in some houses which the sappers had had time to pierce with loopholes, checked them a long time by a sustained and well-aimed fire. This rear guard then withdrew by the gate of France, where a great quantity of fascines, bundles of straw, and pieces of wood soaked in tar had been accumulated. The sappers set fire to the pile. The gate and neighbouring houses burst into flames, closing the street to the Prussians.

During this combat the bulk of Grouchy's army had attained Dinant. On the next day, June 21st, all the army was assembled under the cannon of Givet.

If this march from Wavre to the frontier is not "one of the most astonishing retreats of modem military history," for the carelessness of Thielmann and the timidity of Pirch singularly facilitated it, it, nevertheless, does great honour to Grouchy. He did not despair when all hope seemed lost. He knew how to act with precision and rapidity. By the direction which he chose and by the dispositions which he took, he saved his army. We may ask ourselves, What would have happened if the unfortunate Marshal had shown on June 17th and 18th as much resolution, activity, military talent, and the same understanding of the exigencies of the situation?

CHAPTER 8

The Campaign of 1815

1

The initial plan of the Campaign of 1815, and even the movements requisite for its development, are among the finest strategical conceptions of Napoleon. All failed from errors of execution, of which some are attributable to the Emperor, a great number to his lieutenants,

On the first day Drouet d'Erlon put himself on the march an hour and a half too late; Gérard interpreted for his greater convenience the instructions of the Emperor; Vandamme broke camp three hours after the time specified, halted his troops before the end of the combat, and refused to second Grouchy; and Ney, become suddenly circumspect even to timidity, dared not execute the manoeuvre with which he was charged. The service of the staff was poor; the transmission of orders was slow and uncertain. The chiefs were irresolute, apathetic, without zeal, initiative, or enthusiasm. It seemed that they no longer had faith in the Napoleonic Fortune; that they wished to advance very slowly beyond the frontier; and that they felt already the inevitable embrace of the two great Allied Armies. The powerful machine of war constructed by Napoleon appeared to be worn out or out of gear.

Thus the day of June 15th did not give the results that Napoleon had a right to expect. Had the orders of the Emperor been carried out, before noon all the army would have been across the Sambre; at three o'clock the Prussians of Pirch II. would have been driven from Gilly; and in the evening Grouchy would have occupied Sombreffe and Ney Quatre-Bras.

The next day Blücher and Wellington, separated by this double manoeuvre, and neither the one nor the other wishing to risk alone a combat against the entire French Army, would have fallen back upon their respective base of operations, the first to the northeast of Sombreffe and the second to the west of Brussels. This divergent retreat would have separated the English from the Prussians twenty leagues, as the crow flies. Many days would have been required for them to concert together and effect a new junction. In the meantime Napoleon would have occupied Brussels without firing a shot, and combined some overwhelming movement against one or the other of the two Allied Armies.

On the morning of June 16th, however, in spite of the fault of Ney and the delays at the right wing, nothing was yet compromised. The Emperor even thought that the English and the Prussians were in full retreat, and that he would be able to reach Brussels without meeting with any resistance. The probabilities led him to reason thus; for, according to the remark of Kennedy, Blücher and Wellington committed a grave fault, in view of the dispersion of their troops and the separation of their armies, in delivering battle on June 16th. The Emperor then gave his orders for a march on Brussels, and at nine o'clock left Charleroi. The criticism, that he lost time in the morning, does not appear to be justified.

The Emperor not expecting a battle on this day, which, in fact, was very improbable, he thought this day would be sufficient for his diversion on Gembloux and the night march on Brussels. At six in the morning he dictated his orders, in view of a concentration of all the right wing at Fleurus. He cannot be held responsible for the delay of Gérard, who did not arrive until after one o'clock. If the Emperor did not reiterate early in the morning to Ney the order to take position at Quatre-Bras, it was because, deceived by the report of the latter, he believed this post feebly occupied, or even evacuated, and judged that the left wing would be able to establish itself there without difficulty. In fact, the Prince of Orange having received reinforcements only at three o'clock, it would have been as easy for Ney to have dislodged from Quatre-Bras the division of Perponcher at eleven—the moment when the instructions of the Emperor reached him—as in the first hours of the morning.

In the meantime Fortune intervenes in favour of Napoleon. Blücher knows that the French number 120,000 men; he has, on account of Bülow's delay, but 80,000 soldiers. But faithful to his promise to protect the English left, impatient to fight, and confiding, moreover, in the very uncertain support of Wellington, be rashly offers battle to Napoleon in the position of Ligny. When the Emperor sees the deployment of the Prussian Army, he congratulates himself that it places itself within reach of his sword. This battle which he has not foreseen gives him the opportunity to close in a single day with a thunderbolt the campaign commenced the day before. He is on the point of exterminating the Prussian Army. He at once decides upon his plan, marshals his troops, and sends some orders to Ney. While he will attack, the Marshal will advance upon the rear of the Prussians, and at the end of the battle, when the final assault is delivered, the army of Blücher, overthrown at the centre, outflanked on the right, and assailed in reverse, will be caught almost entirely in a net of steel and fire.

Müffling, Rogniat, and others pretend that Napoleon ought to have confined himself to mere demonstrations towards Ligny and directed all his efforts against Saint-Amand, where the Prussian right, which was in an exposed position, would have made only a feeble resistance. This is ignoring one of the finest tactical inspirations of Napoleon. Most assuredly the attack by Saint-Amand would have brought about in less time and with less loss the retreat of the Prussians. But, on June 16th, the Emperor had in view a more decisive object than that of separating Blücher from Wellington by throwing back the former towards the Meuse—he aimed at the destruction of the Prussian Army. For this it was necessary to pierce its centre and envelop its right wing. Only the left wing would escape a disaster.

We have seen by what concatenation of faults and mistakes this well-conceived plan miscarried, and how each contributed to this result. Flahault, the bearer of the first instructions of the Emperor, took two hours to go four leagues. Reille delayed a movement which he had been ordered to make, under pretence that a little lost time would be of no importance; he judged, according to the strange explanation of Jomini, that it was better "to obey the laws of *la grande tactique*" than the orders of the general-in-chief. Forbin-Janson did not understand a word of the despatch entrusted to him; he was unable to explain it, and, after having transmitted it to General d'Erlon, he omitted to communicate it to Marshal Ney.

D'Erlon engaged himself in a false direction; he had no inspiration to rectify it; he determined, after having made three-fourths of the way, to retrace his steps in obedience to the injunction of Ney, who recalled him, notwithstanding the formal order of Napoleon; and he did not stop to think that, by this counter-march, he would deprive the Emperor of a very efficacious support, and would not reach Ney in time to take part in the action. In short, during this entire afternoon d'Erlon neutralized his troops, promenading them with shouldered arms from the left wing to the right and then back again, without seconding either the one or the other. Vandamme, who first discovered the corps of d'Erlon, caused it to be imperfectly reconnoitred and reported it to the Emperor as being an enemy.

Napoleon, perplexed by the information of Vandamme and the direction of this column, lost his presence of mind. He did not think nor could he admit that the column which threatened his flank might be the 1st Corps, which, however, he had himself called upon the field of battle; he neglected to prescribe eventually to the officer whom he had sent to reconnoitre again the supposed hostile column to direct it on Brye if, contrary to his expectations, it proved to be the corps of d'Erlon.

Marshal Ney, finally, must bear the principal responsibility for the incomplete results of the day. In recalling d'Erlon in spite of the formal order of the Emperor, he committed an act of disobedience which rendered him liable to a council of war, and which can be explained only by the spirit of indiscipline that existed at that time throughout the entire Army. But this act of desperation had no influence on the results of the day; for already Count d'Erlon, by taking Saint-Amand instead of Brye for his objective, had compromised the fine manoeuvre conceived and ordered by the Emperor.

That for which Ney should be especially held accountable is the initial fault that led to all the delays, all the mistakes, all the false movements, and all the *contretemps* of this double action Had he acted as both the circumstances and the principles of war dictated, by eight or nine o'clock he would have had the 2nd Corps massed at Frasnes and the 1st concentrated at Gosselies. Thus, at eleven o'clock, on receipt of the order borne by Flahault, he would have attacked Quatre-Bras with the four divisions of Reille and the cavalry of Lefebvre-Desnoëttes, and he would have summoned to Frasnes the four divisions of d'Erlon and the four brigades of *cuirassiers* of Kellermann.

Long before two o'clock he would have wrested the position from the 7,500 Dutch, who alone occupied it at that time. At three, with his 43,000 men, he would have driven back without difficulty upon the route of Brussels—admitting that Wellington would have dared to take the offensive—the 7,500 English of Picton and the 6,000 Brunswickers of Duke Frederick William. At four—at the moment when the despatch of the Emperor directing him to turn back on Brye arrived—he would have been able to detach, by the Roman way, more than half of his forces upon the rear of the Prussian Army to change into disaster the defeat of Blücher.

Jomini admits that the battle of Ligny would have produced decisive results if Ney had sent to Brye a part of his troops. But he objects that the Marshal would not have been able to effect this movement, even if he had had in hand the corps of Reille and that of d'Erlon, for he would have found himself engaged with the 40,000 Anglo-Dutch of Wellington. This reasoning is based upon a material error.

At four o'clock Wellington had as yet only the division of Perponcher, the cavalry of Van Merlen, the corps of Brunswick, and the division of Picton, or 21,000 men. Furthermore, upon the hypothesis of the capture of Quatre-Bras by Ney, between noon and two o'clock, the 7,500 soldiers of Perponcher, who would have been crushed, would have been almost incapable of further resistance on the arrival of the English reinforcements. The division of Alten (4,000 muskets) did not debouch until half-past five, and the divisions of Cooke and Kruse (7,000 men) until seven.

Now, either Wellington would have attacked at three with Perponcher, Picton, and Van Merlen, in which case these 15,000 men fighting against 43,000 would have been exterminated; or rather, not wishing to expose his divisions to being destroyed in detail, he would have awaited, to take the offensive, not only Brunswick, but Alten, and consequently he would have engaged battle only about six o'clock. At this hour half of Ney's troops would have been already in the rear of the Prussians, and there would have remained 20,000 men with the Marshal to resist until night, in a good position, first 28,000 and then 30,000 assailants. Had he even been forced to withdraw to Frasnes, this retreat, in the gathering darkness, would have been without strategical importance.

It is very probable, however, that if Wellington, on his return from the mill of Bussy, about three o'clock, had found Quatre-Bras occupied in force by the French, he would have prudently concentrated his troops at Genappe, pending the issue of the battle then being fought in front of Ligny. At least this is what may be inferred from his customary prudence and his Britannic egotism.

Clausewitz, after having argued long and confusedly, concludes that "10,000 men in the rear of the Prussian Army would have only rendered the battle more doubtful by obliging Blücher to withdraw sooner."

The proof of the weakness of his case is that he wittingly

gives us false figures. Clausewitz knew very well that it would not have been 10,000, but 20,000, horse and foot, that would have attacked the Prussians in reverse. Now, if this attack could have no other effect than to hasten the retreat of Blücher, by what miracle, two days later at Waterloo, had the attack of Bülow been able to produce an entirely different result?

According to Clausewitz, one would believe in truth that an army is free to quit a battlefield like a field of manoeuvres, and that a sudden retreat in the midst of an action can be effected without disorder and without peril. Charras has a wholly personal way of looking at things. "The generals," he cries, "were admirable. They did not fail the general-in-chief; the general-in-chief failed them."

He extols the conduct of Ney, "who accomplished the impossible in arresting Wellington with 20,060 men." Charras seems to ignore the fact that Wellington, until the arrival of the divisions of Cooke and Kruse (at half-past six) had scarcely 26,000 men to oppose to the French, who numbered more than 23,000. And he voluntarily forgets to say that if Ney had but one army corps to oppose to the English, it was because he had neglected in the morning to concentrate the 2nd and 1st Corps between Gosselies and Frasnes. This was—we cannot too often repeat it—the initial fault from which all the others proceeded—those of Ney, those of Reille, those of d'Erlon, and those of the Emperor.

The facts and written orders, the hours and figures, contradict the conclusions of Clausewitz and Charras. There is also the testimony of Kellermann:

> Napoleon did not attain his object through the fault of Marshal Ney;

of Reille:

> A far greater success would have been obtained by taking in reverse the right of the Prussian Army;

of General Delort:

> Ney could have, with 44,000 men, contained the English

and turned the army of Blücher.

There is the judgment of Ropes:

> If Ney had executed the orders of the Emperor, the issue of the campaign would have been modified.

There is the judgment of Marshal Wolseley:

> If everything had passed as Napoleon had planned, we are justified in saying that the corps of Ziethen and Pirch would have been annihilated, and that, according to all probabilities, Blücher and Gneisenau would have been made prisoners.

There is finally—and it is worth all the rest—the admission of Gneisenau, chief of staff of the Prussian Army, who wrote, June 12, 1817, to the King of Prussia:

> If General Perponcher had not made so vigorous a resistance, Marshal Ney, arriving at Quatre-Bras, would have been able to turn to the right and fall upon the rear of the army that was fighting at Ligny and cause its total destruction.

2

The battle to be gained—to be gained even to the crushing arid annihilation of the enemy—was the battle of Ligny. A complete victory gained on June 16th over the Prussian Army could have closed at a single blow the Campaign of the Low Countries. Through the fault of Ney the battle was indecisive. On the next day another occasion of terminating the campaign by destroying the English Army presented itself. This occasion was allowed to escape through the fault of Napoleon.

The Emperor had separated Blücher from Wellington, and, in spite of the lull in the action and the beginning of a panic caused by the approach of d'Erlon's corps, he had beaten in six hours 87,000 Prussians with 65,000 Frenchmen, thus demonstrating, as he had so often done, the inanity of his axiom, that victory is always on the side of the heaviest battalions. There remained the English Army in position at Quatre-Bras, where it had resisted with advantage Marshal Ney. On June 17th the Emperor was free to exterminate it. This battle, decisive and gained in advance, and of which he had the intuition in useful time, he, unfortunately, did not prepare to deliver till after having lost four long hours in inaction and irresolution. This was leaving too much respite to the enemy. Wellington decamped.

Doubtless at daybreak the Emperor was ignorant of the Prussian line of retreat and the result of the battle of Quatre-Bras. But, between seven and eight o'clock, he was informed by a despatch from Pajol that Blücher's army was retiring towards the Meuse, and by the verbal report of Flahault that the English were still at Quatre-Bras. If he had taken at that time the course upon which he resolved only between eleven o'clock and noon—that is to say, if he had marched towards Quatre-Bras with Lobau's corps, the Guard, and Milhaud's *cuirassiers*, these troops would have debouched between ten and half-past ten on the flank of the English Army, precisely at the moment when it was preparing to break camp.

Wellington's forces, after deducting the losses of the day before, and adding the five brigades of Uxbridge's cavalry, which had arrived during the night and in the morning, amounted at most to 35,000 muskets and sabres. Caught in the act of marching, and attacked at the same time on its left by the 30,000 soldiers of Napoleon and in front by the 40,000 soldiers of Ney, the English Army, which would have either made head against this attack, or would have attempted a very hazardous retreat on Genappe or Nivelles, would have been unable to avoid a disaster.

Instead of this. Napoleon purposed at first to leave his army in bivouac during this entire day. Then he changed his mind, matured a new plan, despatched his orders, and put himself on the march. It was too late. The Emperor did not reach Quatre-Bras till two o'clock. The Anglo-Dutch divisions had repassed the Dyle at Genappe. He could only give chase to the cavalry of Lord Uxbridge. When be overtook the English Army in position at Mont Saint-Jean, night approached. "Would that I had the power of Joshua," said he, "to retard the course of the sun!" But for fourteen hours the sun had lighted up the earth and Napoleon had not profited by it.

We may add that the information received by Napoleon at seven in the morning did not appear to be either precise or definite enough to determine him to act immediately. Was it, indeed, towards the Meuse that the Prussians were retiring, and could he engage himself in their pursuit without being assured of the direction that they had taken? On the other hand, could he, in this uncertainty, march with his army towards Brussels without exposing himself to an offensive return of Blücher, either against his right flank, or upon his lines of communication?

As for Wellington, was it possible that, informed of the defeat of the Prussians, he had not already evacuated his position at Quatre-Bras? In that which regarded the retreat of the Prussians and the march on Brussels, the hesitation of the Emperor is perfectly explicable. But he had not as good reasons for deferring the movement against Wellington This movement was pregnant with such immense results that it was necessary to undertake it at the earliest possible moment with the corps of Lobau and the Guard, even at the risk of a useless march.

Either Wellington would have still been at Quatre-Bras, and Napoleon would have attacked him, in concert with Ney, under the most favourable conditions: or the English would have already decamped, in which event the Guard and the 6th Corps would have effected their junction with the corps of Reille and d'Erlon. At any rate, the march on Quatre-Bras, which might have led to the extermination of the English Army, would have compromised nothing, for, in view of the short distance from that point to Brye, it would have caused the Emperor no more inconvenience to have concentrated his reserve on his left wing than to have left it with his right.

One has further alleged the necessity of giving repose to the troops and of re-supplying them in munitions. Repose? The horsemen of Exelmans and Pajol, who had combated the day before until nightfall, marched none the less at sunrise. With greater reason, the Guard, which had been engaged only a short time, and the 6th Corps, which had fired hardly a shot, would have been able to set out at seven in the morning. Munitions? The corps of Gérard and Vandamme alone had need of being re-supplied, and this operation was certainly completed before noon. As for the 30,000 men of the Guard and the 6th Corps who would have marched on Quatre-Bras, their cartridge-boxes and ammunition-chests were still well supplied.

There were then other reasons for the inaction of the Emperor on the morning of June 17th. Charras, General Berthaut, Ropes, and Marshal Wolseley attribute it to the state of his health. (Neither Wolseley nor Ropes state the malady from which he suffered; Charras assures us that he was afflicted with all the ills that flesh is heir to.) It is possible, in fact, that Napoleon did suffer, in the night following the battle of Ligny, one of those attacks of ischury to which he had been subject for three years, and which had become rather frequent in April and May, 1815.

Grouchy relates incidentally that the Emperor was fatigued on quitting the Château of Fleurus on the morning of the 17th. According to General Le Senecal and Colonel de Blocqueville, chief of staff and first *aide-de-camp*, respectively, of Grouchy, Napoleon had been ill during the night. We repeat, it is possible. But, as Thiers has said, "Whatever may have been the state of Napoleon's health in 1815, his activity was not affected by it."

Let us review these memorable days during which, if Marshal Wolseley is to be believed, Napoleon was "under a veil of lethargy." On June 15th the Emperor rises at three o'clock, goes as far as Jamignon, remounts his horse, captures Charleroi, prescribes the movement of the left wing, directs at the right wing the combat of Gilly, and returns to Charleroi at ten in the evening. On the 16th we find him busy sending off *aides-de-camp* and writing orders at four in the morning.

At nine he goes on horseback to the mill of Fleurus, delivers the battle of Ligny, and, in the final assault at twilight, he advances in person with the Guard beyond the first Prussian lines. If he is ill during the night, we find him none the less the next day, at ten in the morning, at Brye, passing his troops in review and superintending the removal of the wounded. Then he marches on Quatre-Bras at the head of the troops, whom he outstrips in his impatience. He attacks the English cavalry and pursues it with the advance guard for three leagues at the pace of a steeple-chase and under a torrential rain.

At Caillou, where, all streaming with water and as wet as if he had just issued from a bath, he takes his quarters for the night after sunset, dictates some orders for the Army, and becomes absorbed in the reading of letters from Paris. He throws himself upon his bed for a few minutes; then, at one in the morning, he rises again, and makes on foot, under the rain which continues to fall, the entire round of his advance posts. Returned about three, he listens to the reports of the reconnaissances and spies, and dictates new orders.

From nine he is upon the battlefield; he quits it only after dark, with the last squares of the Guard; and, still on horseback, he goes to pass the Sambre at Charleroi, at eight leagues from La Belle Alliance. Out of ninety-six hours, this man, who is represented as being prostrated and depressed by sickness, without energy, without resistance to sleep, and incapable of remaining on horseback, takes scarcely twenty hours' rest; and, supposing that he re- mains on the ground three-fourths of the time of the two great battles, he is in the saddle thirty-seven hours.

In 1815 Napoleon's health was still such as to support the fatigues of war, and his brain had lost nothing of its puissance. But in him his moral nature no longer equalled his genius.

While in his dictations at Saint Helena he attempts to demonstrate that he had committed no fault in the course of his last campaign, in his familiar conversations he permits the secret of these faults to escape him: "I no longer had in me the sentiment of final success. It was no longer my first confidence. ... I felt Fortune abandoning me. I no longer obtained an advantage that was not followed by a reverse.... None of these blows surprised me, for I had a presentiment that the result would be unfavourable."

This state of mind explains the hours lost by the Emperor during the campaign, his sometimes troubled views, the respite left the enemy. He no longer believes in success; and his boldness declines with his confidence. He no longer dares to seize, to seek the occasion. While his faith in his destiny lasted, he had always been an audacious player. Now that he feels Fortune deserting him, he becomes a timid one. He hesitates to begin the game, no longer yields to inspiration, temporizes, weighs the chances, sees the pros and cons, and wishes to take no risks.

3

In order to be able to act freely against the English, it was necessary that the Emperor should be protected against an offensive return of Blucher. Where were the Prussians? in retreat towards the Meuse, or on the march to unite with Wellington to the south of Brussels? The Emperor ordered Grouchy to discover their traces and to pursue them. It has been said that, in the uncertainty in which he found himself concerning the direction taken by the Prussians in their retreat, Napoleon ought, by all means, at ten or eleven o'clock on June 17th, to have ordered Grouchy to march laterally by the left bank of the Dyle.

The Emperor himself has refuted this criticism: "If Grouchy," says he, "had marched at noon on the 17th by the left bank of the Dyle, without knowing in what direction the Prussians were retiring, he would have assuredly covered the flank of the principal column, but he would have also left without protection our lines of communication." In fact, the Prussians, if they had retired on Namur, would have been able to return towards Charleroi to cut the Imperial Army from its base of operations.

It has also been said that in detaching upon his right only two corps of cavalry, a few guns, and a division of infantry—forces sufficient to observe the Prussians—the Emperor would have kept with him 20,000 men more, who would have been very useful to him at Waterloo. Doubtless, in 1814, after Arcis-sur-Aube, Winzingerode, with 10,000 horse, had imposed for two days upon the French Army. There are, however, some objections to this criticism.

In spite of the absence of the corps of Vandamme and Gérard, and the cavalry of Pajol and Exelmans, the French at Waterloo were superior in numbers to the English; and, if a part of the Army had not been paralyzed by the approach of the Prussians, it is very probable that the plateau of Mont Saint-Jean would have been carried towards five o'clock. Now Napoleon had detached 35,000 men with Grouchy precisely to contain the Prussians. It was far more important to keep Blücher from the field of battle than to have there 20,000 men more.

This division of the army into two masses, so much blamed by the historians of the Campaign of 1815, was the usual tactics of Napoleon. It was thus he manoeuvred at Marengo, Jena, Friedland, and in all the Campaign of France, which has been so justly admired. When one has to fight two armies, it is necessary to contain one whilst one directs all his effort upon the other.

But was it possible for Grouchy to oppose the movements of the Prussians, and, at first, were the orders of the Emperor precise and explicit enough in order that he might make no mistake and know that the principal thing was to guard against an offensive return of Blucher upon the flank or the rear of the Army? It is presumable that in his verbal instructions Napoleon had explained them to the Marshal; but upon the words of the Emperor the testimony is so interested and contradictory that it is necessary, as a good critic, to confine oneself solely to the written order. I have given this order integrally. I will recall only its essential dispositions:

> Go to Gembloux; reconnoitre in the direction of Namur and Maëstricht; pursue the enemy. It is important to find out if Blucher wishes to unite with Wellington in order to deliver battle in front of Brussels.

If, indeed, the Emperor, in this letter does not explicitly direct Grouchy to cover the Army, it appears to me that he implicitly does so. "To find out if Blucher wishes to unite with

Wellington"—this is the important thing Now, as Grouchy had with him not a few squadrons sufficient to reconnoitre the enemy, but an army capable of serious resistance, his manifest duty was not only to keep the Emperor posted, but also to protect him against an offensive return by manoeuvring so as to interpose himself between the Prussians and the Imperial Army. A man who had made war for twenty years could not mistake the object of the operation with which he was charged. And, in fact, these words of Grouchy's letter, written on the evening of June 17th,

> ... I shall follow the Prussians in the direction of Wavre, in order to separate them from Wellington,

prove that he thoroughly understood the implicit instructions of the Emperor.

Unfortunately, Grouchy did not know how to manoeuvre with sufficient rapidity, intelligence, or resolution. On June 17th his troops marched with incredible slowness. At the time when Napoleon reached La Belle Alliance at seven in the evening, after having made nearly six leagues fighting, Grouchy only arrived at the same hour at Gembloux, fourteen kilometres from Saint-Amand. And, though in these long days it was still possible to march two hours longer, he ordered his army to bivouac.

On the next day it was yet possible for him to regain the time lost. Informed as he was, there was no doubt for him—the Prussians were marching to join Wellington. Though the Emperor, being ignorant of the direction of Blucher's retreat, had not prescribed the march by the left bank of the Dyle, Grouchy, who was henceforth acquainted with this direction, ought not to have hesitated to undertake it. He risked nothing at all events in doing so; for either the Prussians would still be at Wavre and he would turn them by the left bank—a more advantageous manoeuvre than to attack them by the right bank; or they would be already on the march either for Brussels or for Mont Saint-Jean, in which event he would make a flank pursuit, or would come to prolong the right of the Emperor.

Grouchy ought then, on June 18th, to have marched on Wavre, not at seven in the morning, in a single column and by way of Walhain and Corbaix, as he did, but at sunrise, in two columns, and by way of Vilroux, Mont Saint-Guibert, and Ottignies. *En route* at four in the morning, the two columns would have arrived upon the banks of the Dyle, at the bridges of Mousty and Ottignies (seventeen and eighteen kilometres, respectively, from Gembloux), between nine and ten o'clock. Allowing an hour and a half for the passage of the two bridges, Grouchy would have found himself at eleven upon the left bank of the Dyle with all his army.

Doubtless before this time (about eight o'clock) Colonel Ledebur, in observation at Mont Saint-Guibert with the 10th Hussars and two battalions, would have discovered Grouchy's heads of columns. His detachment being too weak to offer any resistance, he would have first sent a courier to Gneisenau to inform him of the approach of the French. The despatch would have arrived at Wavre about nine o'clock, at the time when the single corps of Bülow was on the march. It is presumable that Blücher, or rather Gneisenau, who was invested with all the authority, would not have modified the orders directing Bülow and Pirch I. to march on Chapelle Saint-Lambert, but that he would have taken some measures to defend the approach to Wavre with the corps of Ziethen and Thielmann.

Pending the development of the manoeuvre of the French, would he have confined himself to leaving these two corps in position at Bierges and Wavre? or, informed that Grouchy had passed the left bank of the Dyle, would he have ordered Ziethen and Thielmann to advance to encounter the French Army by way of Bierges and Limelette? Upon the first hypothesis, it would have been easy for Grouchy, hearing the cannon of the Emperor, to march by his left on Ayviers or Maransart, a movement which would have brought him near the battlefield at half-past two, or two long hours before Blücher took the offensive. Upon the second hypothesis—the most probable, I admit—Grouchy, in a good position upon the plateau of Mousty-Ceroux, would have resisted without difficulty with 33,000 men the 40,000 Prussians of Ziethen and Thielmann. But would he have been able, between eleven and four o'clock, to inflict upon them a defeat sufficiently decisive to put them out of action and to become free again to march on Maransart? It is doubtful.

By this battle Grouchy would have at any rate detained far from Mont Saint-Jean the corps of Ziethen and Thielmann, which would not have been without importance. First, it would have prevented the panic which took place at the end of the battle of Waterloo, when Ziethen debouched on Papelotte. It would have done more. We have seen that at half-past six, at the moment when, according to the avowal of Colonel Kennedy, Alten's *aide-de-camp*, "the centre of the English line was open," the approach of Ziethen's corps permitted Generals Vandeleur and Vivian to move from the extreme left to the centre with their 2,600 fresh horsemen and to reaffirm the confidence of Wellington.

If this support—support effective and moral—had failed him, it is probable that he would have been unable to re-establish his position before the assault of the Middle Guard, and that, under this supreme push, the English line would have yielded. Wellington has admitted that on June 18th he was in dire peril. "Twice," said he, "did I save the day by my obstinacy; but I hope that I shall never have to fight another such battle." We may also believe that if Blücher had heard at noon, at two leagues on his left flank, the cannonade of a great battle, and that if couriers had come from hour to hour to announce to him the successive checks of his lieutenants, he would have attacked Plancenoit with less resolution.

We should not forget, finally, that if the Emperor had been informed between eight and nine o'clock, by a despatch from Gembloux, that Grouchy was on the point of passing the Dyle at Ottignies, he would have been able, long before noon, to send him new orders and to remain all day in close communication with him. What consequences!

Grouchy would have been able to repair the grave strategical fault which he had committed in the morning by servilely following the traces of the Prussians, by marching at half-past eleven towards the sound of the cannon, according to the counsel of Gérard. At that hour Exelmans had three brigades of dragoons between Corbaix and La Baraque and one brigade at the farm of La Plaquerie (1,500 yards from Ottignies); the corps of Vandamme was halted at Nil Saint-Vincent; that of Gérard had arrived at Walhain; and Pajol with his cavalry and the division of Teste was on the march from Grand Leez to Tourinnes.

It was only necessary to push Exelmans as far as the wood of La Huzelle—or further towards Wavre, if it could be done without compromising him—so as to disquiet the enemy and to mask from him the movement of the French Army; to direct Vandamme on Ottignies by way of Mont Saint-Guibert, and Gérard on Mousty by way of Cour Saint-Etienne; and, finally, to recall Pajol, who would come to form the rear guard. Put *en route* at noon, the head of Vandamme's column would have attained the bridge at Ottignies (ten kilometres from Nil Saint-Vincent) towards a quarter-past three, whilst that of Gérard, starting a quarter of an hour earlier, would have arrived at the bridge of Mousty (thirteen kilometres from Walhain) about four.

After having passed the Dyle, the troops having to march henceforth upon a single route, Vandamme would have taken the lead and his first division would have reached Maransart (two leagues from Ottignies, by way of Ceroux) towards six o'clock. For this, doubtless, it would have been necessary to march, during this journey of eighteen kilometres, at the rate of three kilometres per hour. Notwithstanding the bad roads, all of which, moreover, as far as the Dyle shelved downwards towards this river, and in spite of the time required for crossing the bridges, this pace was possible, especially if we remember that at each step the soldiers would have heard the cannon thundering nearer and more intense. Whilst a moral factor for soldiers of 1815 to go to the support of the Emperor and to combat under his eye!

Let us now see if, as Charras and others have pretended, the

Prussians would have been able to interfere with this movement. At noon Bülow was at Chapelle Saint-Lambert with his cavalry and two divisions; his other two were on the march to rejoin him at this point. The corps of Pirch I., which had bivouacked at Aisemont, had hardly commenced to pass the bridge of Wavre; and the corps of Ziethen, which had camped at Bierges, was just taking up its line of march for Ohain by way of Fromont. The corps of Thielmann, destined to remain last in position on the banks of the Dyle, was massed between Wavre and La Bavette. Finally, Ledebur with his detachment occupied Mont Saint-Guibert, where he remained tranquilly, little suspecting that he was outflanked on his left.

If Grouchy had marched on Ottignies and Maransart instead of Wavre, things on the side of the Prussians would have passed, at least until three o'clock, exactly as they did. Between one and two Ledebur would have cut his way through the cavalry of Exelmans; at two the divisions of Brause and Langen (corps of Pirch), hearing the combat in the wood of La Huzelle between the skirmishers of Ledebur and the dragoons of Exelmans, who had two batteries, would have marched in the direction of this wood, and Thielmann would have deferred his departure until the end of the combat.

About three, it is true, the enemy would have discovered that the attack of Exelmans, unsupported by infantry, was only a feint. The Prussians would have then resumed the prescribed movement. The second *echelon* of Pirch (divisions of Brause and Langen) would have passed the bridge of Wavre and would have proceeded towards Chapelle Saint-Lambert. Thielmann would have left only a few battalions in Wavre, and would have prepared to march on Couture with the bulk of his troops. But in order to advance from La Bavette in the direction of Couture he would have been forced to await the defile of the divisions of Brause and Langen and the cavalry of Sohr (of Pirch's corps), which, as we have seen, were compelled to await the passage of the entire corps of Ziethen, which itself had been forced to permit the rear of Bülow's corps and the leading divisions of Pirch to precede it.

The Prussian Staff had so badly conceived the disposition of the march that the crossing of the different columns was inevitable. The principal column (Bülow and Pirch I.), on the march from Dion-le-Mont and Aisemont by way of Wavre to Chapelle Saint-Lambert, was bound to cross the route of Ziethen's corps advancing from Bierges to Ohain by way of Fromont, and Thielmann's corps, which had orders to "direct itself from La Bavette on Couture.

Under these conditions, Thielmann would not have set himself in motion until four o'clock at the earliest. The distance from La Bavette to Maransart by way of Couture is nearly nine miles. The 3rd Prussian Corps would have then been unable to reach Maransart before a quarter to nine, much too late, consequently, to arrest Grouchy. At that moment, Bülow, attacked in flank by the troops of Grouchy, whilst he was fighting against Lobau and the Young Guard, would have been for more than an hour driven back beyond the wood of Paris, if not perhaps exterminated in the valley of the Lasne.

Grouchy acted like a blind man, but Napoleon did nothing to enlighten him. Though informed on the evening of June 17th, by Milhaud, of the retreat of a hostile column towards the Dyle; though advised in the night, by a despatch from Grouchy, of the march of at least one Prussian corps towards Wavre; and though warned on the morning of June 18th, by Prince Jérôme, against a possible junction of the two hostile armies in front of the Forest of Soignes, it was only at one in the afternoon, when the battle was engaged, that the Emperor despatched to Grouchy the formal and precise order to cover his right.

Doubtless he had believed until then—he even yet believed—that the Marshal would manoeuvre to fulfil this great object; and doubtless the letter of Grouchy in which he had said: "I shall follow the Prussians, in order to separate them from Wellington," had strengthened this opinion. But ought he to have put so much confidence in Grouchy? Was it not very hazardous to rely, for the safety of his right flank, with an adversary as bold as

Blücher, upon the strategical intelligence, the initiative, and resolution of a commander who had never exercised so important a command? The Emperor, at any rate, ought to have renewed his instructions much sooner, and should have explained them more fully than he had at first done

4

At Waterloo, Napoleon wished to begin the action early in the morning—his orders show it. If the battle had begun about six or seven o'clock, the great strategical fault of Grouchy and the negligence of the Emperor in reiterating to him his orders would have had no consequences, for the English Army would have been overthrown before the arrival of the Prussians. The corps of Lobau, the Young Guard, the cavalry of Domon and Subervic, which the Emperor employed against Bülow, and the Old Guard itself, which, being uneasy for his right, he had held in reserve until the last moment, would have certainly, by supporting the other troops, determined towards noon or one o'clock—perhaps earlier— the retreat of Wellington.

The condition of the ground, or, if one wishes to quibble, the false appreciation of the condition of the ground, by ' Drouot and the artillery officers, obliged the Emperor to modify his orders. The attack was put off from six or seven o'clock until nine and then again delayed, as the troops had not yet reached their positions. This delay saved the English Army.

It is certain that an attack against the left of the enemy, very weak and in the air, or even against his right, which would have permitted of a vast deployment, would have been more easy and less murderous than the assault against the centre. But Napoleon, manoeuvring between two armies, found himself between the chops of a vice. It was not sufficient to get rid of one of the Allied Armies for a day or two, as he had done at Ligny; it was necessary to crush it. For this, the Emperor must pierce the centre of the English Army and crush the broken wings.

"Napoleon," said Wellington, "attacked me in the old manner, and I repulsed him in the old manner." Under the circumstances, and in spite of the compact position of the enemy, "the old manner" was for the Emperor the best to employ.

But how many mistakes, how much negligence, and how many faults in the execution! We have seen that the demonstration against Hougoumont, ordered by the Emperor, had developed through the ardour of Jérôme, the impetuosity of the soldiers, the lack of vigilance and firmness of Reille, into a real attack, in which half of the 2nd Corps had been uselessly sacrificed. We have also seen that the heavy formation of the four divisions of General d'Erlon was the virtual cause of the confusion in which they found themselves on attaining the crest of the plateau and of the lamentable rout in which they were thrown by the English cavalry.

Why was it that Reille, who, according to the order of the Emperor, was "to advance so as to keep abreast of the corps of Count d'Erlon," did not operate this movement? One of his divisions (that of Jérôme) was, it is true, engaged at Hougoumont, but Bachelu and Foy remained available for marching against the right centre of the enemy.

Why was it that Ney, who had under his immediate command all the first line, consisting of the corps of d'Erlon and Reille—more than 30,000 bayonets—delivered vainly two assaults against La Haye Sainte, defended by five companies? Why did he not demolish its walls with cannon-balls? Why, having failed twice in the attack of this farm, did he not renew the assaults? Why did he not obey the orders of the Emperor? Why did he not understand that the possession of La Haye Sainte—"the key to the English position," says the *aide-de-camp* of Alten, Kennedy—was his first objective?

Ney found it shorter to begin at the end. Too circumspect at Quatre-Bras, he was too audacious at Mont Saint-Jean. He risked before the hour, without orders, without preparation, and without support, the great cavalry movement planned by the Emperor. He thought to overthrow with cavalry an infantry as yet unshaken and occupying a commanding position. He launched rashly to the assault the two corps of *cuirassiers*, the

Horse Guard, and even the brigade of *carabineers*—the last cavalry reserve of the army—which Kellermann had halted with the formal order not to budge

In spite of their temerity, these heroic charges would have succeeded, however, if they had been supported by infantry. There was near La Belle Alliance, within short cannon-range of the English position, half of Reille's corps. These twelve battalions had not yet been engaged; they waited with grounded arms the order to take part in the action. Ney, who, according to the words of Napoleon, "forgot in the heat of the action the troops who were not under his eye," did not think to summon them upon the plateau. It was only when the last charges had been repulsed, and when the intervention of the infantry was no longer opportune, that he launched these 6,000 men against the slope of Mont Saint-Jean, where they were decimated without advantage.

It was nearly six o'clock. La Haye Sainte, of which Ney had attempted to take possession at two, then at four, was still held by the enemy. It was necessary, however, for the Emperor to renew the order to capture it at any price. This time Ney carried the position, and it was only then that Wellington deemed himself in peril. Unfortunately, it was too late to profit by this point of support. Men and horses were harassed. Napoleon gave to the Marshal the Middle Guard for a supreme effort; but instead of making a breach in the English line with these five battalions of heroes formed in a single column, Ney arranged them in *echelons*, so that each one found itself outnumbered by the enemy at every point.

It would seem that on the right there were also some negligence and faults. The cavalry of Domon and Subervic advanced upon the skirts of the wood of Paris when it ought to have watched its approaches. The defence of Lobau was valorous, but badly conceived and prepared. It was not at 1,200 yards to the east of La Belle Alliance and upon open ground that he should have established himself to arrest the Prussians.

At half-past one, when the corps of Bülow was inactive at

Chapelle Saint-Lambert, Lobau had received from the Emperor the order to move in that direction "and to choose a good intermediate position in which he could, with 10,000 men, arrest 30,000." This "good intermediate position" Lobau did not seek. It was the rugged heights which command the valley of the Lasne in front of the only bridge over this river.

There, his communications with the main body of the army being assured by the numerous squadrons of Domon and Subervic, Lobau would have been able to make a longer and more efficacious resistance than in front of Plancenoit. Perhaps this position would have even been impregnable. Clausewitz admits that Blücher would have been obliged to turn it by way of Couture. This would have been much time gained for the Emperor! Even in case Lobau had felt some hesitancy in advancing so far *en flèche* (a league from La Belle Alliance), he at least ought to have occupied the wood of Paris.

In the different phases of the battle one can follow the development of the Emperor's plan such as he had explained it in the morning to Prince Jérôme—preparation by the artillery; attack of d'Erlon and Reille's corps; charges of the cavalry; and the final assault by Lobau's corps and the Foot Guard. But the presence of the Prussians on his right made it necessary for the Emperor to employ, in order to hold them in check, the 6th Corps and the Young Guard and to hold the Old Guard too long in reserve. On the other hand, instead of operating against the English with method and *ensemble,* one acted by fits and starts, at first awkwardly, then at an unseasonable time, and, finally, desperately.

In order to judge with equity the commander-in-chief, who was the greatest of captains, it is necessary to bear in mind the manner in which his orders were understood and executed, when they were not obeyed. Marshal de Saxe has said in his *Reveries upon the Art of War:* "The disposition of the commander-in-chief should be correct and simple, as: *Such a corps will attack and stick an one will support.* The generals under him would need to be very ignorant in- deed, if they did not know how to execute this order and to manoeuvre as the circumstances required. Thus the commander-in-chief should not occupy and embarrass himself with the details. He will be able to see everything better and maintain a sounder judgment, and will be in a better position to profit by circumstances. He should not be everywhere and attempt to perform the duties of a *sergent de bataille*."

From the many faults committed at Waterloo, Charras, York von Wartenbourg, and Marshal Wolseley conclude that the Emperor, prostrated by sickness, lost all hope, remained inert and blind far from the field of battle, and left the combat without direction. Regarding the physical and moral condition of Napoleon on June 18th, the testimonies are contradictory. Colonel Baudus relates that the Emperor "was plunged into a sort of apathy." According to oral traditions mentioned by Marshal Canrobert and General du Barail, Napoleon slept during the battle of Waterloo. (He slept also at Jena and Wagram, and directed no less victoriously the combat.)

But Marshal Regnault de Saint Jean d'Angély, who made the Campaign of 1815 in the Imperial Staff, related that, far from sleeping, the Emperor was nervous and impatient, and lashed his boot incessantly with his riding-whip. (It is thus Coignet pictures Bonaparte at Marengo before the arrival of Desaix's division.) In his manuscript Journal, General Foy writes that he saw the Emperor walking to and fro, with his hands behind his back. I have read nowhere that the guide Decoster, so loquacious and lavish of details, has ever spoken of the prostration of Napoleon.

Walter Scott, who had questioned the inn-keeper some months after the battle, learned from him that the Emperor remained all the afternoon not far from La Belle Alliance, most of the time on horseback, and very attentive to all the phases of the battle. According to the words of Ney, spoken at Mézières, where he passed the day of the 19th of June, the Emperor had shown himself very brave. In addition to all this testimony, there are the facts, which testify more surely than all words. At eleven o'clock the Emperor dictated his disposition for the attack. At a quarter-past eleven he ordered the demonstration against Hougoumont.

At one he wrote to Grouchy. At half-past one he ordered Lobau to take position to arrest the Prussians, and enjoined Ney to begin the attack of Mont Saint-Jean. In the meantime he had caused Hougoumont to be bombarded by a battery of howitzers. At three he launched a brigade of *cuirassiers* against the cavalry of Lord Uxbridge, which had attacked the great battery. At half-past three he ordered Ney to take possession of La Haye Sainte. At half-past four he caused the Guard to advance near La Belle Alliance. At five he sent the Young Guard to the assistance of Lobau. At half- past five he ordered Kellermann to second the charges of Milhaud. At six he renewed the order to take La Haye Sainte.

Soon after he detached two battalions of the Old Guard to drive the Prussians from Plancenoit. At seven he led his Guard into the bottoms of La Haye Sainte for the final assault. On the way he harangued the soldiers of Durutte, who were beginning to give way, and sent them back into the fire, and directed all his officers to traverse the line of battle and announce the arrival of Marshal Grouchy. In the evening he formed in squares in the valley the second *echelon* of the Guard, hastened to Rossomme, still resisted there with the grenadiers of Petit, and fired the last volley of grape at the English cavalry.

Never did Napoleon exercise more effectively the command, and never was his action more direct. But, obliged precisely to play that *rôle* of *"sergent de bataille"* which is condemned by Maurice de Saxe, he employed himself entirely in repairing the mistakes, the forgetfulness, and the faults of his lieutenants. And, seeing all his combinations miscarrying, all the attacks proving unsuccessful, his generals wasting his finest troops, his last army melting away in their hands, and the enemy laying down the law to him, he lost resolution with confidence, hesitated, confined himself to providing for the most imminent perils, awaited the hour, allowed it to pass, and dared not risk all in time to save all.

ALSO FROM LEONAUR
AVAILABLE IN SOFTCOVER OR HARDCOVER WITH DUST JACKET

CAPTAIN OF THE 95th (Rifles) by *Jonathan Leach*—An officer of Wellington's Sharpshooters during the Peninsular, South of France and Waterloo Campaigns of the Napoleonic Wars.

BUGLER AND OFFICER OF THE RIFLES by *William Green & Harry Smith* With the 95th (Rifles) during the Peninsular & Waterloo Campaigns of the Napoleonic Wars

BAYONETS, BUGLES AND BONNETS by *James 'Thomas' Todd*—Experiences of hard soldiering with the 71st Foot - the Highland Light Infantry - through many battles of the Napoleonic wars including the Peninsular & Waterloo Campaigns

THE ADVENTURES OF A LIGHT DRAGOON by *George Farmer & G.R. Gleig*—A cavalryman during the Peninsular & Waterloo Campaigns, in captivity & at the siege of Bhurtpore, India

THE COMPLEAT RIFLEMAN HARRIS by *Benjamin Harris as told to & transcribed by Captain Henry Curling*—The adventures of a soldier of the 95th (Rifles) during the Peninsular Campaign of the Napoleonic Wars

WITH WELLINGTON'S LIGHT CAVALRY by *William Tomkinson*—The Experiences of an officer of the 16th Light Dragoons in the Peninsular and Waterloo campaigns of the Napoleonic Wars.

SURTEES OF THE RIFLES by *William Surtees*—A Soldier of the 95th (Rifles) in the Peninsular campaign of the Napoleonic Wars.

ENSIGN BELL IN THE PENINSULAR WAR by *George Bell*—The Experiences of a young British Soldier of the 34th Regiment 'The Cumberland Gentlemen' in the Napoleonic wars.

WITH THE LIGHT DIVISION by *John H. Cooke*—The Experiences of an Officer of the 43rd Light Infantry in the Peninsula and South of France During the Napoleonic Wars

NAPOLEON'S IMPERIAL GUARD: FROM MARENGO TO WATERLOO by *J. T. Headley*—This is the story of Napoleon's Imperial Guard from the bearskin caps of the grenadiers to the flamboyance of their mounted chasseurs, their principal characters and the men who commanded them.

BATTLES & SIEGES OF THE PENINSULAR WAR by *W. H. Fitchett*—Corunna, Busaco, Albuera, Ciudad Rodrigo, Badajos, Salamanca, San Sebastian & Others

AVAILABLE ONLINE AT **www.leonaur.com**
AND OTHER GOOD BOOK STORES

ALSO FROM LEONAUR

AVAILABLE IN SOFTCOVER OR HARDCOVER WITH DUST JACKET

WELLINGTON AND THE PYRENEES CAMPAIGN VOLUME I: FROM VITORIA TO THE BIDASSOA by *F. C. Beatson*—The final phase of the campaign in the Iberian Peninsula.

WELLINGTON AND THE INVASION OF FRANCE VOLUME II: THE BIDASSOA TO THE BATTLE OF THE NIVELLE by *F. C. Beatson*—The second of Beatson's series on the fall of Revolutionary France published by Leonaur, the reader is once again taken into the centre of Wellington's strategic and tactical genius.

WELLINGTON AND THE FALL OF FRANCE VOLUME III: THE GAVES AND THE BATTLE OF ORTHEZ by *F. C. Beatson*—This final chapter of F. C. Beatson's brilliant trilogy shows the 'captain of the age' at his most inspired and makes all three books essential additions to any Peninsular War library.

NAVAL BATTLES OF THE NAPOLEONIC WARS by *W. H. Fitchett*—Cape St. Vincent, the Nile, Cadiz, Copenhagen, Trafalgar & Others

SERGEANT GUILLEMARD: THE MAN WHO SHOT NELSON? by *Robert Guillemard*—A Soldier of the Infantry of the French Army of Napoleon on Campaign Throughout Europe

WITH THE GUARDS ACROSS THE PYRENEES by *Robert Batty*—The Experiences of a British Officer of Wellington's Army During the Battles for the Fall of Napoleonic France, 1813.

A STAFF OFFICER IN THE PENINSULA by *E. W. Buckham*—An Officer of the British Staff Corps Cavalry During the Peninsula Campaign of the Napoleonic Wars

THE LEIPZIG CAMPAIGN: 1813—NAPOLEON AND THE "BATTLE OF THE NATIONS" by *F. N. Maude*—Colonel Maude's analysis of Napoleon's campaign of 1813.

BUGEAUD: A PACK WITH A BATON by *Thomas Robert Bugeaud*—The Early Campaigns of a Soldier of Napoleon's Army Who Would Become a Marshal of France.

TWO LEONAUR ORIGINALS

SERGEANT NICOL by *Daniel Nicol*—The Experiences of a Gordon Highlander During the Napoleonic Wars in Egypt, the Peninsula and France.

WATERLOO RECOLLECTIONS by *Frederick Llewellyn*—Rare First Hand Accounts, Letters, Reports and Retellings from the Campaign of 1815.

AVAILABLE ONLINE AT **www.leonaur.com**
AND OTHER GOOD BOOK STORES

ALSO FROM LEONAUR
AVAILABLE IN SOFTCOVER OR HARDCOVER WITH DUST JACKET

THE JENA CAMPAIGN: 1806 *by F. N. Maude*—The Twin Battles of Jena & Auerstadt Between Napoleon's French and the Prussian Army.

PRIVATE O'NEIL *by Charles O'Neil*—The recollections of an Irish Rogue of H. M. 28th Regt.—The Slashers— during the Peninsula & Waterloo campaigns of the Napoleonic wars.

ROYAL HIGHLANDER *by James Anton*—A soldier of H.M 42nd (Royal) Highlanders during the Peninsular, South of France & Waterloo Campaigns of the Napoleonic Wars.

CAPTAIN BLAZE *by Elzéar Blaze*—Elzéar Blaze recounts his life and experiences in Napoleon's army in a well written, articulate and companionable style.

LEJEUNE VOLUME 1 *by Louis-François Lejeune*—The Napoleonic Wars through the Experiences of an Officer on Berthier's Staff.

LEJEUNE VOLUME 2 *by Louis-François Lejeune*—The Napoleonic Wars through the Experiences of an Officer on Berthier's Staff.

FUSILIER COOPER *by John S. Cooper*—Experiences in the 7th (Royal) Fusiliers During the Peninsular Campaign of the Napoleonic Wars and the American Campaign to New Orleans.

CAPTAIN COIGNET *by Jean-Roch Coignet*—A Soldier of Napoleon's Imperial Guard from the Italian Campaign to Russia and Waterloo.

FIGHTING NAPOLEON'S EMPIRE *by Joseph Anderson*—The Campaigns of a British Infantryman in Italy, Egypt, the Peninsular & the West Indies During the Napoleonic Wars.

CHASSEUR BARRES *by Jean-Baptiste Barres*—The experiences of a French Infantryman of the Imperial Guard at Austerlitz, Jena, Eylau, Friedland, in the Peninsular, Lutzen, Bautzen, Zinnwald and Hanau during the Napoleonic Wars.

MARINES TO 95TH (RIFLES) *by Thomas Fernyhough*—The military experiences of Robert Fernyhough during the Napoleonic Wars.

HUSSAR ROCCA *by Albert Jean Michel de Rocca*—A French cavalry officer's experiences of the Napoleonic Wars and his views on the Peninsular Campaigns against the Spanish, British And Guerilla Armies.

SERGEANT BOURGOGNE *by Adrien Bourgogne*—With Napoleon's Imperial Guard in the Russian Campaign and on the Retreat from Moscow 1812 - 13.

AVAILABLE ONLINE AT **www.leonaur.com**
AND OTHER GOOD BOOK STORES

www.ingramcontent.com/pod-product-compliance
Lightning Source LLC
Chambersburg PA
CBHW031617160426
43196CB00006B/174